NO MORE LAYERS

Praise for No More Layers

"In order to live a life of true success, you need to uncover who you really are and live from that place of your real self, not your personality self. That is when you'll find ease, joy, and peace. Once you read this life-changing book and discover how to shed the old layers that don't serve you, true success will be yours."

— **Debra Poneman, bestselling author and founder of Yes to Success and Ageless Seminars**

"*No More Layers* offers a beautiful, well-lit and accessible pathway to discovering our true nature. Martine Cohen's journey is extremely relatable and her revelations are universal. A must-read for anyone looking for deep and lasting fulfillment."

— **Marci Shimoff, #1 *New York Times* bestselling author of *Happy for No Reason***

"A thought-provoking examination of the true nature of the Self. This is a great book for anyone who is ready to emerge from beneath their 'layers' and embody who they came here to be."

— Dr. Sue Morter, bestselling author of *The Energy Codes*

"Martine Cohen's *No More Layers* is a deeply personal exploration of what it means to be human. The book reads like the best kind of adventure story, and I encourage you to go on that adventure of transformation for yourself."

—Gay Hendricks, PhD, *New York Times* bestselling
author of *The Big Leap*

NO MORE LAYERS

Discover Your Inner Power and
Reclaim True Freedom
from the Inside Out

MARTINE COHEN

WORLDCHANGERS
MEDIA

Paperback ISBN: 978-1-955811-79-8
E-book ISBN: 978-1-955811-80-4
LCCN: 2024910318

First paperback edition: September 2024
Author photo: Barrie Fisher / www.bfisherphoto.com
Cover artwork: Mila / www.milabookcovers.com
Layout and typesetting: Bryna Haynes
Editors: Marie Schnoor, Paul Baillie-Lane

Published by WorldChangers Media
PO Box 83, Foster, RI 02825
www.WorldChangers.Media

*To Benjamin and Jessica, my two miracles
who inspire me every day to be the best version of myself*

Contents

Part III: Alignment

NO MORE LAYERS

Introduction

"Free from unconscious thoughts, protective layers, and limiting beliefs, we can each accomplish what we have been put here on earth to do."

In the aftermath of a traumatic car accident that left me with a serious concussion, my awareness of who I was changed dramatically. Before the accident that led me on this journey, I believed that I had to be one thing or the other: intellectual or intuitive, grounded or spiritual, professional or playful. But as I delved deeper into myself, I began to witness my own layers for the very first time. Layers, as will be discussed in more depth throughout this book, are what I call those limiting beliefs, fears, brain constructs, and identities that we become confined to, controlled by, and ultimately believe defines who we are.

During my recovery, I discovered and went through my own *No More Layers* journey. I grew to understand that it was never an "either or" proposition, and that none of us need be anything else except who we are, what we choose, and what is truly right for us. The balance of deep and approachable, playful and profound, intellectual and intuitive, is a space I now happily live in, and one that is accessible to all of you.

In the years since my own transformational journey, I would come to realize that my journey was not meant to just serve me. There was a higher purpose, and ultimately one that led me on to yet another journey, that of helping others. I came to know and trust that what I experienced could, and would, help people.

I have seen it in the private sessions I have with clients, as they gain the courage to delve within, make breakthroughs, and heal past traumas. I have witnessed it in my small group and speaking engagements, as people open up, shift their mindset, and awaken their awareness to consciously choose their path in life. I see it in my own children, as they move into their next phase of life as self-aware human beings who have the strength to remain grounded and the tools to remain deeply authentic. I have been led to this work to help as many people as possible step into their power and live a freer, more fulfilling life. I am deeply honored to show you the way.

How this Book Came to Be

Truth be told, I never set out to write a book. In fact, I never considered that I would write a book until my clients started urging me to do so. They saw that a book could help others benefit from similar shifts and insights to those they were experiencing in our sessions. I hesitated to sit down to work on it for a long time, and then one day something inside of me shifted. It was a visceral feeling that called me to take the challenge and begin writing. I could see the transformational shifts my clients were experiencing, and I knew they were right. It was time. A written version of this work could reach many more people and serve as a guide along the journey, one that they could experience, refer to, and share with others. From that moment on, the ideas within this book began to take shape.

I started by setting my intention for my writing. I knew that I wanted to share a unique and enriching personal journey that would encourage and invite exploration, awareness, and growth. It was important for me to create a book that could meet you, the reader, right where you are, and be what you need most in that moment. Most of all, I wanted to create a safe space for awareness and insight, without it becoming overwhelming, though the subject matter itself goes deep. It wasn't a simple process, but I was deeply committed to it, and so I embarked on this labor of love.

And then something fascinating happened. While I had created an outline, it seemed like the book had a mind of its own. While I had intended to write this book in a way that would create an experience for my readers, what I didn't realize was that it would become an entire experience for me as well. I sat in a quiet space, readied myself, got out of my own way, and the information started flowing in. I wasn't thinking and writing in the way I had imagined it would happen. I was accessing universal wisdom and downloading the contents for a particular chapter, sometimes faster than I could type or dictate. Inspiration would strike whenever it would strike. At times I would be exhausted writing at 1:00 a.m. and yet my creative juices were flowing. I knew it was a process I needed to respect. On two separate occasions, the content itself led to the addition of new chapters, ones I had never envisaged would be part of this book. Writing this book has been one of the most authentic experiences I have ever lived. Putting all of myself aside, being of service to something greater than myself, and fully trusting the process before me has been enlightening, inspiring, sacred, and beautifully humbling. I feel blessed to be able to bring it all to you.

How This Book is Structured

I've written this book as a transformative journey for you and a transmission of a deeper reality. As you go through it, you will begin to discover the innate wisdom, resilience, and untapped potential that is uniquely, divinely yours to claim. This book is meant to guide you through the vast terrain of your own thoughts, emotions, and layers, to the seat of your personal power: your true self and essence. It's here to offer you an experience and is structured much in the way a journey would be. The chapters walk you one into the next, serving as stepping stones along your path. They are meant to allow you the opportunity to experience your own personal transformation. As you read through them, my heartfelt hope is that they will help walk you down your own extraordinary path of self-discovery.

As you embark, I ask that you trust yourself to venture inward and follow the flow. I know it's not an easy ask. We are much more comfortable with familiar ground, as it satisfies our need for control. But I'm asking you to be in the moment, trust the creative process, relinquish a little of that need for control, and replace it with openness and curiosity. Allow yourself to venture into the realm of awareness that will open up for you, as the richness of the experience is in the journey itself.

I have intentionally written this book so as to allow you the space to experience this journey in your own way. *No More Layers* is more of an experience and a shift than a structured step-by-step methodology. Nevertheless, my intention is to do my best to meet you where you are. Just as there are different learners, there are also different readers. For those of you who would prefer to have some additional concrete pointers along this road, I chose to include a chapter that breaks down the *No More Layers* process into three foundational pillars, which you can always refer back to as you continue to advance in this work. The Three Pillars are helpful in getting you ready to shift your mindset, explore your layers, and make empowered choices. If it is your preference, I invite you to read Chapter Fifteen at any time along the way, but if you can hold off and follow the flow of the journey this book leads you on, I would encourage you to do so.

You will also notice that there are epigraphs at the start of each chapter, and also within various sections of the chapters in Part II. All quotes are pulled from my own teachings and writings, which is why you won't see author attributions. They are meant to direct and focus your attention to the material at hand, and also to give you "bite-sized" content to post on your social media if you choose to share your own journey through your layers. (Just be sure to add the hashtag #nomorelayers to any posts you make!)

How to Experience This Book

This book is not intended to be devoured in one sitting. As you read through the chapters and explore who you are in relationship to yourself and to others, you will encounter inspiring stories, transformative concepts, and practical exercises. Give yourself the time to sit with each chapter, take the opportunity to journal, question, and be with each chapter's prompts. Feel free to go back and re-read things whenever it might be helpful, as you further explore and integrate the concepts. Whatever comes up for you in this process, honor and validate it. Remain open to all the opportunities and possibilities that lie ahead as you immerse yourself in the experience of getting to know yourself better from the inside out. Stay brave, intentional, and curious.

As you step into the great adventure of life, my hope is that this book will help you tap into the adventurer in you, gain the awareness of your own layers, the curiosity to explore them, the courage to release them, and the deep understanding of who you truly are. Once you're aligned with your true self, and you know what that feels like, you'll be able to return there and live from an empowered place within you, experiencing the deep joy and contentment that comes with the awareness and authenticity of choosing how you experience everything that comes before you.

Lastly, I want you to know that this book will not tell you who to be, how to be or what to do. Nor does it offer a step-by-step plan you must follow. Instead, it's an invitation for you to embark on your very own journey of discovery and to experience your own paradigm shift. One that will bring you into the awareness of who you truly are, and where your inner power resides, beyond all your layers. I offer to be your guide through this journey, providing you with insights and tools along the way as you begin to live your life with *No More Layers*.

With so much love,

Martine

Part I

ADVENTURE

CHAPTER ONE

My Origin Story

*"We are born worthy, capable, authentically ourselves, and spiritual.
We just need to discover all of the resources that are within us."*

When I was seven years old, I nearly drowned. This was my first encounter with a near-death experience, and my first brush with the power of prayer and visualization, which is something I would only later come to realize is innate in each of us.

My family and I were on vacation in Atlantic City. I didn't know how to swim, and yet somehow, I found myself in a swimming pool with a newfound friend. It probably wasn't the smartest thing to do, but I was trying to be careful. Before I knew it, however, I had gone deeper into the pool and lost my footing. I started to drown.

I could feel myself starting to sink, and I didn't know what to do. Funnily enough, as I think back, I wasn't yelling or screaming. I just went deep inside myself and started to pray. To this day, I cannot tell you intellectually what made me do that. It was instinctive. Something else inside me rose up and took charge at that moment. With my entire being, I visualized myself being saved. What was really strange about this situation was that I had never been taught about prayer or visualization, and yet I pictured the way in which I would be saved exactly as it happened. I visualized an older boy—a teenager, I suppose—carrying me out of the water and putting me to the side of the pool.

The next thing I remember is being placed on the side of the pool ... by just that teenager. He looked like the one I had pictured, and he had just saved my life. I was shaken up and didn't quite understand what had happened, but I wasn't struggling for breath anymore and was ever so grateful to be alive. I was shocked for sure, but what struck me the most was that—in defiance of all logic—I had actually been saved in the exact way I had visualized.

It was my first encounter with something where I could potentially have died; I had felt myself slowly slipping away. And yet, I had been saved. Although I didn't quite understand the significance at that age, it was my first conscious encounter with spirituality and what some might call a near-death experience. While I certainly was not able to process it fully at the time, it is an experience that has stayed with me to this day. As it turns out, the power of visualization and prayer had been within me all along. Though we may not know how to access it, we all have it. In my case, I was able to call upon it when the situation became a life or death one, as if a higher wisdom within me took over and knew exactly what to do. I believe the critical nature of the situation allowed me to access something I didn't know existed.

As a young child growing up, I was very attuned to the spiritual energy of the people around me. I felt it inside of me. No one I knew around me spoke of self-exploration. Rather it seemed adults would often say and do the opposite of what they meant, and I could sense when they weren't being authentic. I felt that they were afraid to show their true selves, and this, in turn, made me afraid to show my true self. Perhaps the adults knew something I didn't; perhaps it wasn't safe to explore the unfamiliar terrain of the inner self and spirituality; perhaps we are meant to go through life disconnected from these unknown parts. Everyone else had their eyes closed, too.

But my grandfather was different. He was very spiritual, and as I reached my early teens, we would have wonderful conversations about souls, our connection to a higher power, and energetic channels. While fascinating and deeply enriching, I had yet to really connect the dots. I never associated our discussions with what had happened when I was seven years old, and with the way in which I was saved. I had put it behind me and would only reflect on it again years later.

I continued working hard, putting my best foot forward, trying to fulfill others' expectations of me as well as those I had of myself. I never considered myself to be ambitious, but I probably was. I was hungry for life experiences. I love to learn, feel a sense of accomplishment, gain knowledge, and give of myself. I have a teaching diploma, studied law, graduated with two degrees, began my career in a national firm, and became licensed in two different legal jurisdictions. And yet, at the time, there was always this voice inside of me, one I didn't quite understand and couldn't define. It would nudge me every so often, as if to awaken me to something more, and yet I didn't know what to do with it. It didn't seem like others around me had that voice—or if they did, it wasn't something they ever talked about. And so, most of the time, I tried to quiet the voice, hoping it would go away. But it never did.

There was a struggle within me: do I follow the adventurous, spiritual side of me, or do I follow the path of my logical brain? My soul had a thirst for deep life and human experience. After all, isn't the soul having a wide array of human experiences in a body the purpose of life? I believe that it is—and for those of you already going through spiritual growth, you know that the soul never settles down, though rest assured its energy can be reframed and channeled.

The journey of growth does not flow smoothly. I avoided fully acknowledging the possibility of my spiritual gifts because I didn't know where they would lead. How could I reconcile being a lawyer with my spirituality, with that flame that burned so strongly inside of me? Today, some of my friends jokingly refer to me as "the spiritual lawyer." It makes me smile, and it reminds me of a time when I thought I couldn't be both. I'm so grateful to have discovered that I can simply be who I am, with all of my different facets. But back then, before I reached the balance I now feel, my rational brain was very strong and the fear of my spirituality, of the intangible, would kick in whenever I felt like there had to be something more. Whenever I felt that pull, I tried to control it, hoping it would slow down. No matter how hard I tried to stop the flow, it kept coming back. My brain was trying to keep me safe and grounded, while my higher self, my soul, wanted to soar and experience it all. I knew one day I'd have to address it head-on, but for a long time, I simply kept juggling between the two.

If you're a seeker of clarity, spirituality, and understanding, then you know what it's like to feel part of you pulled in one direction, while your logical, sensible, safety-first brain pulls you in another. You may even have experienced the cycle of trying and failing, struggling and pushing, reaching and achieving, and then finding out that it didn't make you as content or satisfied as you thought it would. You can see what you're chasing just on the horizon, but no matter how hard you grasp for it, it remains out of reach. Through it all, there are parts of your inner self that remain inaccessible to you, despite any personal development, self-actualization, or mindfulness you may practice.

Intuitively you may sense that there is an easier way, but, as was true for me, you just don't know how to access it.

Long before the accident that radically changed my life, I had an awareness that there must be more flow in life, but I didn't know how to reach it. In many ways, it was like walking into a room with less-than-optimal vision. What I hadn't realized at the time was that every decision I made was, in part, predicated on a need to create perceived certainty and safety. Somewhere in my deeper knowing, it was clear that this need for protection was interfering with ultimate growth and authenticity. But I still got up each morning to keep doing the same thing, always trying to push aside my inner reality. I had the keys to gain access to authenticity, flow, and the freedom that is gained from acknowledging my truest, deepest self, but I was too afraid to open the door to the wealth of resources within me.

Doorway into the Self

What is that door? What are these barriers that stand between each of us and the flow we can sense but cannot reach?

These are your layers.

Layers are what lie between the external, constructed identity you constantly strive to live up to, and your true, internal self. Layers are the subconscious, internal rules we have defined for ourselves so that we can keep ourselves safe. Keeping safe, however, also keeps us static and prevents us from growing.

Layers are formed from the messages we received in childhood, the lessons we unconsciously clung to in order to survive in a new and, for some, confusing or chaotic world. Maybe the layer you learned as a young child was "Girls don't act so bossy," or "If I cry and try to reach for comfort, I'm making my parents angry because I'm so needy." Maybe your layer from adolescence was "If I'm beautiful, I'll get positive attention," or perhaps it was "Getting the best grades is the only way I can prove my worth."

From each of these lessons, a layer is gleaned. Those layers solidify over time and limit you, until you become aware of them and begin to peel them away. And until you do this, your layers will continue to prevent you from seeing who you truly are, and from knowing yourself. Until this process happens, all the discomfort—this sense of formless despair and disconnection from your true self and inner innate power—will continue to persist, too.

All of us have layers.

Before becoming aware of my layers, before knowing I could change my own story, and before life literally hit me on the head and made me finally pay attention, I believed that *I was my brain and my brain was me.* Just like an athlete who defines themselves by their wins or measures their success by their stats, I defined myself by my brain. Looking back, I truly believed I *was* my brain; and I never questioned it. Although I'd received what I now know was an invitation to the awareness of my own inner being, until I started to open the doors to my own layers, I didn't know then what this was all about, or how to approach it. At the time, not only did I work as a lawyer, but I *was* a lawyer. That's what I understood myself to be. I had no idea how much more there was to discover within me.

The layers we use to protect and insulate ourselves from the world are the same things that stand in the way of our authenticity. Let me say that again because it's absolutely crucial to understand this before you can move forward: that feeling you have, the feeling of yearning, of wanting something more, but being unable to define what it is, let alone how to reach it, comes from your deepest self. It's who you are when you strip away all of the layers you or those around you have built. You're not sure what your higher self is seeking, or you may even be unsure why you need so desperately to find it, but you can no longer ignore that feeling, no matter what you do, how high you reach, or what you achieve. This is a sign that you're ready to start opening the doors to uncover your layers and gain access to your true, authentic, self-designed life.

The Search for Authentic Purpose

Working as an attorney, strategies consultant, mentor, and guiding my clients through the process of identifying and removing their own layers, I find that many of the people who work with me are at the top of their game in a wide array of fields. Professionally, they have achieved their goals and earned their wealth or well-deserved accolades, and yet deep inside they have a sense of hollowness. A sense of, "Is this what success is supposed to feel like? There must be something more."

Many, if not all, of my clients reach out to me when they're grappling with a seemingly impossible situation. No matter what it is—career, relationships, family, or some other external thing—they haven't found a way around what was blocking them, and the frustration, discontent, and distress continue to steadily grow. Although many of them find me after trying various tools, from the brain-based to the esoteric, they can't access the peace, balance, and real fulfillment they're searching for. They keep yearning for more, for different. All of them have one key thing in common: the belief that this external obstacle or situation is the true cause of their discomfort and that if it were to shift, be resolved, everything else would fall into place and their deeper yearning would finally be quelled. I'm here to tell you that it won't.

There is so much more; a deeper, more authentic truth waiting to be discovered and honored within you, and there are many more layers you are yet to uncover. I know this not only because of the people I have worked with and the profound shifts I have seen them make, but also because this process—the removing of layers—happened to me in an earth-shattering and life-altering way.

Before that moment, every time my higher self spoke to me, though I did hear it, I wasn't sufficiently paying attention. I tuned it out by working harder, doing more, protecting myself, and striving to be better. Still, it kept persisting. I could feel a pull within me. When I couldn't hear it whispering, it shouted. And when I didn't hear the shouting, it hit me over the head, literally. While I had been content for so very long with who I thought I was, that was all about to change. I would soon be shaken to my core and stripped of every layer that kept the true me hidden.

Unbeknownst to me, I was about to embark on a whole new journey, leaving nothing more to interfere with my path to accessing a wholly purpose-driven life of pure potentiality.

CHAPTER TWO

The Concussion

"It is often within traumatic events—when we experience
a literal or metaphorical brush with death—that a
drastic life shift has the potential to take place."

I was driving down the street on my way to run an errand and about to merge onto the highway when my whole world changed in a horrifying crunch of glass and metal.

A speeding car collided with mine, crashing into the driver's side. I had no chance to avoid it or swerve away. I lost consciousness.

As I came back to awareness, I could hear myself thanking God that I had survived. I could hear myself in conversation, but it wasn't me, or at least it didn't feel like it. It was as if I was hovering over the scene, having been inserted into the tail end of a conversation I was witnessing. Paramedics were talking to me, asking me questions. Trying my best to respond, I spoke as loudly as I could, and they barely heard me. They kept asking me, again and again, what I could feel, where the pain was, all kinds of questions. I mustered all of my might, but still, only whispers came out. They moved me carefully out of my crumpled van and put me in an ambulance.

Laying on the stretcher, my thoughts immediately went to my

children. I don't know how I managed—it felt like the brain equivalent of a mother's sudden burst of strength, lifting a car off of their child in a moment of extreme duress—but I somehow got my phone and sent a text. My children were at school and would need to be picked up. "I don't want them to worry or be scared, they just need to be picked up." To this day, I'm not sure if that was a thought or a mother's instinct. Despite what had just happened, I deeply knew I was a mother. My instincts had kicked in, despite everything else no longer functioning properly.

The EMTs checked me for injuries. They rushed me to the hospital—I couldn't tell you which one. All I knew was that when the tests were performed, the doctors said I had no reflexes at all on my left side, and my left eye had a significantly diminished range of movement. Everything hurt, and yet in a way I couldn't even fully feel the pain. I just felt blurry. Not visually blurry, but mentally. My brain was clouded in a tumble of confusion.

It was a severe concussion.

The pain I experienced during this time was more than physical, it was profound, almost existential. The way the head hurts when the brain is concussed is not the way any other part of the body hurts. It's not like an ache or a sprain or a broken bone, but rather as if all of your nerve endings are inflamed. It's functional pain, and since our brain is never dormant and always working, the pain is constant. Only the intensity fluctuated. Every stimulus was painful. I could hardly tolerate lights or sounds, and I couldn't communicate well. It felt as if there was a dark, opaque veil between me and everything else in the world.

I can remember the first week, staring at my son as he talked to me about hockey. I worked so hard to follow what he'd been saying, and while I understood each word individually, by the end of the sentence, the meaning of it all had vanished. Understanding language was like trying to hold water and having it run between my fingers, spilling out onto the ground. My brain wasn't working for me, and I could no longer filter the world as I had before the accident, as who I thought I was, as Martine.

In the weeks that followed, which felt like very long months, a diagnosis of post-concussive syndrome meant that my recovery was taking much longer than expected. I was told I would know within a year what damage would be permanent and what would heal, but until then, it was all up in the air. "Wait, what?" I panicked. "I have to wait a whole year?!" The news from my neurologist absolutely terrified me. "It's a wait-and-see situation," he said. It turns out that there's not much that can be done for the brain in these cases.

At this point in my journey, the most frightening thing wasn't actually the concussion, the pain, the confusion, or even the sensitivity to light and sound. It was the sinking feeling that there wasn't anything I could do, no list of tasks to perform, nothing extra of myself to give, no clarity on how to "solve" this. As someone who had been in control all of my life (or so I'd believed), this terrified me down to the very core of my being. It was unchartered territory.

My Injured Brain

The brain is profoundly finicky, sensitive, and unpredictable. There's no straightforward pathway to healing an injured brain, and, in my case, there were no non-invasive or surgical options. "Make sure to gradually use your brain," the neurologist told me helpfully, "but not too much. Don't overwork yourself. We'll have to see what functionality comes back."

I felt like a circus performer on a tightrope. What did that even mean? I wondered. Was I ever going to get better? Would I regress, and would the damage be permanent? Is this just the way it was going to be from now on?

My identity, the sense of who I thought I was, was slipping away, and, with that, the prospect of living disconnected from myself for the rest of my life was the most terrifying of all. Had I just lost everything?

My brain didn't have the information, let alone the capacity to help itself. It felt petrifying. My biggest nightmare was having regrets, or in other words, finding out I had not done something that could have helped me. Being at that crossroads and not knowing where to go, I couldn't bear to reach that one-year mark and hear my doctor say, "You have residual damage." If there was something I could have done and didn't, I couldn't have borne that.

Our thoughts are ours to evaluate and choose. While my brain was concussed and I couldn't formulate many thoughts at that point, I had a recurring one. One that felt more like a fact than a thought. I don't know who I am anymore. What will become of me? What I didn't fully realize at the time was that we have the power to choose which thoughts to keep and which to discard. And thoughts, while triggered by facts, are only one of many interpretations of a fact.

For those who don't know me, I'm a bath girl, bubbles and all. For as long as I can remember, it's always been one of my preferred ways to recharge and check in with myself. One night, as if by rote, I remembered baths, so I drew myself one. Immersing myself in the warm, soothing water should have been familiar and comforting, and yet it wasn't. I had never felt this afraid in my entire life. That being said, I also didn't get out of the bath. I stayed, and let my fear fill me. I didn't push it away, deny it, or fight it. I just let it be right there with me that night in my bath.

My concussed, dysfunctional brain wasn't in any position to fight this fear. It could not "protect" me through its usual methods of distraction and denial, as any eager or overactive brain normally would. It couldn't offer resistance to the feeling of fear, block it, or suppress it. In that moment, the fear was so intense and my brain so concussed that it couldn't offer any thoughts to counter or diminish the fear. It just allowed it to be. I felt the fear and got to experience it full-on, with no filter, no accompanying thoughts, and therefore no interpretations.

For me, this was the beginning of everything else that followed. It allowed space for a path I had never fully embarked on until that moment. It was the silver lining. In hindsight, it was the blessing of a dysfunctional brain. With the numbness, the automation taken away, in that space of loss, I was left with nothing more, and nothing less, than my self. I witnessed myself in the darkness, being at what felt like rock bottom, experiencing the tenuous and uncertain recovery ahead of me. Staying with myself while still lying in the cooling bathwater, an awareness came over me. It wasn't groundbreaking, it was more a line of questioning that began with this magical opening:

Without my brain, who am I?

How was it that my brain wasn't very functional and yet I was able to observe myself and have awareness of myself? It was almost as if this was happening from beyond a body and brain perspective. And if this wasn't my brain, then who or what was processing these feelings and witnessing them? And who or what was doing all of this questioning? These questions gave me a strange sense of hope, and a surge of energy flowed through me. It was new, and yet strangely familiar.

Could it be that I was reconnecting from within? That there was more to me even without a functional brain?

These questions brought me face-to-face with a newfound sense of clarity and curiosity. In that moment of understanding, I saw that I had been living my life through a lens—viewing the world through the unquestioned belief that I was primarily my brain and my brain was me. For the first time, I sensed that was not the truth.

This revelation was shocking to me. I was so sure that any limiting beliefs I had were addressed many years before my accident. I had previously believed that any discomfort or stress experienced in life was because I wasn't trying hard enough or giving enough of myself. I just needed to aim higher, go further, and my brain would work that out for me as it always had. But suddenly everything had changed, and there was no longer anything my brain could do for me.

I had passed through a truly devastating, life-changing experience, and yet I was still here. As a result of my concussion, not being able to focus on the outside world, I was forced to look within more deeply. It was then that I began to discover how many more inaccurate beliefs I still possessed.

In time, I came to understand and name those beliefs: those were my layers. At first, I could only witness them, but eventually, I could learn to evaluate them, test them against the truth of my soul, and eventually learn to remove them if they no longer fit me. All of this would come later, as I healed. But this was the first moment of true awareness that there was something deeper within me, something I'd always been defined and affected by but had never truly seen.

The World of Layers

I use the term "layers" for these beliefs and opinions because that's what they are: layers that stand in the way of accessing your true self. Layers are often formed at some point in our early lives based on the subconscious response to the messages we receive and internalize. Once upon a time, my layers had been put in place in order to protect me, show me a direction, or help me to follow a certain pattern to keep me on a specific path, but clearly, they were no longer serving me. In fact, like training wheels that have been kept on far too long, these layers were getting in the way by hindering my growth, learning, and confidence.

I never would have stopped to consider them, much less witness them, if the accident had not stopped me in my tracks and made me question everything I had once believed to be true and held so dear about who I really was. But now I could see them, acknowledge them, and feel that they were separating me from my higher self, all under the guise of being helpful.

It's important to understand that layers are neither good nor bad, they just are. Many of my clients—who are accustomed to approaching their lives in a very analytical, linear, progress-focused way—regularly have a difficult time with this concept. My clients are often very successful in their fields, responsible for making many key decisions, and they hold themselves to a very high standard. Any perceived flaw, imperfection, or weakness is something to be avoided at all cost, not explored, let alone embraced.

Like many of us in the professional world, my clients are juggling many things at once, and are looking to get on with it, fix what's "wrong," and start feeling better. But while you can aim to change the outside world, if you don't begin with a search within, real change cannot take place, nor can it be sustained. The process of searching within entails accepting your layers just as they are. Not bad, or damaged, or flawed. Just layers.

Layers are simply an indication that your past self was trying to survive. They are protective mechanisms, formed as a result of many external stimuli, from parents to culture to society, but the core reason behind all of them is the same: your brain perceives a threat as a reality, and it forms a layer to try and keep you safe from that threat. The layer becomes the bookmark tucked in place in the story of your life: an easy-to-reference decision-making tool that bypasses your higher self in favor of a reference point where similar situations can simply be handled the same way. At no point in the process are we ever consulted. We just react, but we don't act. We don't choose.

Every layer we have is a signal from our past selves and an opportunity to do something different, but we moved past it and accepted it as if it were an integral part of the book. How strange would it be to consult the reference book of *you* and take the bookmark as guidance for how to live your life? Would we not want to be in control of our own lives, rather than surrender our decision-making power to some layer that was created years or even decades ago, and may no longer apply to our lives? When we are offered a moment to observe our layers rather than rush through life without stopping to consider why we do the things we do, profound insights await us. When we stop to look at the book of our own lives, taking time to consider what's actually written on our pages, and what's merely been tucked in on a scrap of paper, the contrast becomes obvious. But we can't change it unless we stop to look at it first.

Remember the conversation I had witnessed as I was regaining consciousness? The one where I could hear myself thanking God that I had survived? To this day, I believe that witnessing this conversation was a gift from above. It truly saved me from what could have been much deeper emotional and spiritual angst. It afforded me a deep inner knowing from the get-go that there was a positive and greater purpose behind all of this. It's what initially carried and sustained me. It ultimately led me to the path of inquiry, facing my fears, discovering my layers, and finally finding myself. I became the observer, a role I didn't even know existed. This observer role allowed me to begin questioning almost freely. What was really happening? Who was doing the observing, and how was I aware of it? Even though I felt the darkness, with no idea what its ultimate purpose could be, I finally knew there was one. In time, I would come to discover it, step by step, layer by layer.

The Questions in the Darkness

It seems we only begin to question when we're uncomfortable, and we're only uncomfortable when something shakes us up so much that there is nothing else to do but question.

This is why rock-bottom, catastrophic, and earth-shaking experiences so often have such a profound impact. While many people do experience a certain amount of life-changing clarity as a result of catastrophic incidents, we should not need to experience a traumatic event to gain insight, let alone literally be hit on the head, as I was.

It is, however, often within traumatic events—when we experience a literal or metaphorical brush with death—that a drastic life shift has the potential to take place. In these moments, the things we have done intentionally and subconsciously to distract, redirect, or numb ourselves are stripped away, and we cannot ignore them any longer. These experiences are profound, and usually intellectually and scientifically unexplainable. You reach a point where you are facing yourself at your clearest, most intimate being—the real you underneath all of the layers. And when you get those first peeks into the real you, you start realizing that the choices you thought were set for you aren't as limiting or constraining as you had once thought them to be. You start finding ways to change what you used to think was unchangeable, and a shift of some fundamental aspect of your being takes place. This is you uncovering and removing your layers. And as this unfolds, you begin to have a deep understanding of yourself.

The first step to becoming reacquainted with the real, authentic you and living a life of joy, peace, and purpose is becoming aware that you even have layers. We all do. Once you get to know your layers and realize the extent to which they have been affecting you without your knowledge or even permission, you can choose whether to keep them in place or remove them.

The impulse for many of my driven, high-achieving, successful clients is to optimize. They want to "fix" things and get back on track. But without first becoming aware of their layers, they can change whatever they like about their external environment and still not come close to addressing the source of their discomfort. The true "fixing" comes from the inside out, and it begins with the exploration and questioning of our layers.

The deeper the layer, the more we believe that it must be an absolutely integral part of who we are. Just like a bookmark tucked into place and, over time, assumed to be an integral part of the book, a layer kept in place continually reinforces the belief that we need the protection it was created to provide, whether that continues to be true or not. Rather than acknowledging the layer for what it is, removing the bookmark and writing a new story about our experience (thereby consciously choosing a new outcome), we keep returning to that same limiting bookmark, relying on it. We become that bookmark. We become that layer.

But what if the bookmark was never placed there to begin with? What then would you believe makes you *you*? Would it be something else, something more? The moment you begin to ask these questions is also the moment you begin to realize that the layer could never have been you to begin with. And if that layer is not you, then what is? It's a complex question to ask and to answer, but it is the question each of us must examine if we truly want to connect from within. We owe ourselves that answer. Without it, we will go through our lives never fully knowing who we are.

You deserve to know about your layers because you're the one who has been living with them. Granted the way you show up in the world also affects other people, but it all starts from within you through a process of getting to know what your layers are, what might have caused them to be put in place, and whether that protection is still required or essential.

The Path Forward

In the following chapters, I hope to lead you to understand more about layers. Together we will explore creative tools and techniques to help identify your layers and truly hear their messages. I will guide you through the creation of your very own inner boardroom, a safe and inviting space within which you can explore your inner landscape and layers, gain insights and awareness, and exercise your freedom to choose how to address them.

Once you remove your layers, and finally have a clear view into who you truly are, it becomes so much easier to choose a path that is authentic, meaningful, fulfilling, and purposeful. The way you show up to life will change too. Free from the protective thoughts, beliefs, default mechanisms, and shields you once thought you needed, you can accomplish what you have been put here on earth to do.

This shift in awareness will change your life and relationships, no concussion (or other crisis) required! Once you know who you are, you will never want to be anyone else.

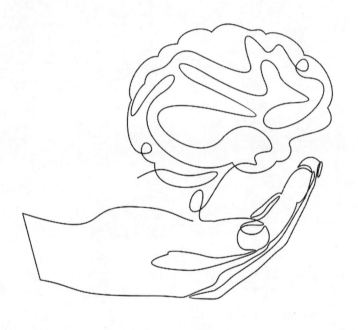

CHAPTER THREE

The Journey into My Brain

"As you discover your layers, you will uncover new ways to grow and heal. Trust the process and you will, without question, create an enhanced life experience."

I f I am not my brain, then who am I?

The question echoed through me as I continued to physically recover from my concussion. Yet despite my progress, my world did not return to the way it had been before. I wasn't the same, and I grappled with fears I didn't even know I had. Without my brain to rely on, I felt exposed and vulnerable, holding on to my brain for dear life, trying to cling to what I had believed for so long was my foundation, my constant, my self.

Despite the fear and discomfort that arose at the start of this journey, I knew I could not deny it. I knew I had to address these layers. The ones that separated me from my true self. I needed to deal with them in a thoughtful and intentional way if I was ever going to heal. I had to take responsibility and ownership of my own life. At the end of the day, there was no one else who could do that for me. It was up to me, but was I up for the challenge? Was I ready to go within and explore? Was my realization enough for me to be ready?

I didn't know, and in that moment, it didn't matter. I felt I owed it to myself. To honor who I truly am, I had to go exploring and see what I would find.

As a very visual person, it is no surprise that while I sensed my layers, the energy of them also drew me a picture: a landscape of sorts. It was as if I had walked into an overgrown woodland, parting the tall grasses as I went, trying to find my way, mindful of my footing. There, within myself, I discovered layer upon layer, built up within me, guiding me and shaping me, directing the course of my life and the beliefs I had held about myself, all without my knowledge or conscious permission. I had fears, limiting beliefs, and all sorts of thoughts I had never even questioned before. When did this start, and why hadn't I ever noticed? Were they true? Did I actually agree with them?

To answer any of these questions, I would have to take a deeper dive into all these layers—and so I did. Layer by layer, I faced my deepest fears, the ones that had been around for so long. One at a time, I began to remove them—along with the helplessness and sense of feeling lost—and what I found beneath them all was an intense and all-encompassing fear. It wasn't easy to face, but it was the first step toward breaking it down.

I practiced staying with my feelings, boldly facing them, resisting the natural tendency to define, qualify, judge, or deny them in any way. I remained there, deep inside my fear, and observed my thoughts and feelings. I observed their intensity flowing through me. As challenging as it was, I didn't fight them or try to change them. I literally did *nothing*.

For those of you who have experienced it, you know that doing nothing is easier said than done. Nothing is often the hardest thing to do; it takes the most effort, but it also yields the most profound results. It is the basis of mindfulness and witnessing. It allows things to flow through you so they can be released. In time, the veil of darkness lifted, and the space they had occupied made room for *me*. For my *self* to re-emerge.

The accident had taken away something I'd once believed was essential, integral, me—but I had passed through that, and I was still there on the other side, searching, seeking. The worst had happened, but I continued on. If I was still here, still questioning, seeking, and observing, then there must be something else, something more, something beyond my brain.

Who am I? I wondered. Beyond my brain, beyond what I had known myself to be, who was I, really? I'm not sure I had ever asked myself that question before, but here it was.

That day in the bath—the moment I had courageously decided to take a closer look at my fear and bore witness to my layers for the first time—became like the eye of the storm for me, the calm amidst the chaos. I remember it so clearly, that moment of realization, of understanding. That was the epiphany: if I'm still something without my brain, that means I am *not* my brain and my brain is *not* me.

At that moment, I finally knew I would eventually be okay and would move forward. It had finally clicked. My brain was this amazing tool, but it wasn't me. It was never designed to be. While I had lost its full use, there was still a me, my true self that had remained. With that realization washing over me, my body breathed a sigh of relief unlike any other I had ever experienced before. I felt like me again.

Still concussed with a long road ahead of me, for the first time I was starting to reconnect with myself. I could feel my self, my essence, my purpose. The darkness started to lift, and I was able to slowly gain some clarity, as if an internal fog was being lifted. While the physical aspects of healing came later, I would continue working from the inside out.

Reflecting back on this moment, I'm grateful for it. While it felt like so much of me had been stripped away, it afforded me a clearer picture of what was really going on. I was able to discover my layers, and, beyond all of them, I knew I could find the true me: my soul. With this awareness came shock: how had I surrendered this much control, this much agency, even in my own identity and sense of self? All that I had been doing in my life, identifying with, all of the points of discomfort and limitation, were based on these layers, not on my authentic self. Was that even possible? My true self, the one behind all of the layers, tried to get me to listen, but I had never quite heard it fully.

While it seemed I had lost so much, I had actually reclaimed something that was even more important: my true self. I had survived what I thought would end me—thankfully not a physical death, but the death of a constructed identity. There was more to discover, a new way I could grow and heal, and once I saw that, I was no longer afraid of what might be there on the other side. And once I named my fear and withstood it, it began to dissolve. I followed the path laid before me and discovered that my fear had been created by my brain, not me or my soul, but this magnificent intricate organ which was intent on protecting me at all costs.

Healing My Brain

I took the following few months to heal my brain. Initially, I attempted practical approaches, like using software to enhance cognitive skills, but these efforts proved premature. I had to slow down and respect the rehabilitative process, and in order to do that, I needed to not only allow myself to feel my own fear but also to let go of it and begin to trust in this new process.

It felt like I'd been thrust into unchartered territory and had everything to lose. I connected from within, prayed and meditated, and the same answer came to me every time: "Don't fear. This is happening for a reason—just go with it."

Deep down, I knew what this meant: I needed to trust in the flow of the universe, and in its goodness.

Discovering who I was beyond my brain, fears, and layers led me to tap into the core of who I truly was. Although my brain's capacity was still diminished, the rest of me wasn't: my capacity to sense, my existence, and my essence were intact. Somehow my intuition guided me to explore my injured brain itself, in a similar way to how I'd been exploring my layers.

As I delved within, I began to energetically sense my brain: its fears, its limitations, and where it'd been injured. I cannot explain what happened next other than to say that I started tinkering with my synapses. I felt my way through, identifying the damaged synapses in my brain, and, using energy and visualizations, started to work on each one. I repeatedly placed my attention and full energy on each synapse, trying to mend and heal it. Some of the synapses I was able to help heal, while others were too damaged, and I needed to bypass them and create new ones. It was truly a labor of deep love, premised on a deep trust, one that took all of my energy, inner focus, and will. It was an endeavor I never knew I could undertake. One that was intangible and esoteric, and yet I could feel its effects from the inside out. I was healing my brain, without having full use of my brain.

As my doctor did what she could to help me, I continued to fill in the blanks through this newfound energy work. All of it was coming from somewhere else, a feeling of internal knowing that had taken over, similar to the one that had guided me to pray when I was seven and almost drowned. It was sacred work that showed me how expansive and limitless we truly are.

At one point I felt a shift. As if some blockage had been lifted, a kind of flow restored. I could feel some connection had been healed and would only come to know its significance a few weeks later, at my next doctor's appointment. I boldly explained to my doctor as best as I could what I'd been doing in my free time and how I'd tried to help myself. When the doctor proceeded to examine my reflexes, she was astounded that those on my left side had suddenly returned. She couldn't understand how it was medically possible, except for the reasons I'd explained to her. She was in awe, and frankly, so was I. In awe of the tools gifted to us at birth, and humbled to have discovered they could be used in this way.

We do hear about people healing themselves from all sorts of illnesses and injuries, but it's quite hard to imagine the process, let alone the result. Through this journey, I discovered that we are much more capable than we could ever imagine. All of us have this capacity within us; the essence of who we truly are resides beyond our logic, thoughts, emotions, and fears. Whatever we imagine ourselves to be, the truth is that we are so much more.

Nurturing My Self-Discovery

This period of self-discovery taught me a lot. It taught me about self-nurturing, and about having patience for life's most delicate processes. It taught me to become acutely attuned to my body and inner voice. But most importantly, it showed me that no matter the situation, we always have the power and choice to do something about it.

This newfound awareness was the invitation I needed. Even though I thought that I'd been open to it, and at times had waited patiently, listening and ready to receive, I could not stand on the outside, waiting for something to reveal itself to me. I needed to start walking the path and intentionally grow my inner awareness.

Throughout the healing process, my spirituality and ability to sense energy helped me see that we all have spiritual channels within us, and an inner spiritual connectedness. I had found a new path. As I detected the presence of any energetic imbalances, I worked through the layers and the fears, going back inside myself to take a look at my brain. I couldn't believe it. I had never done that before. I knew I had to see if I could get to the blockage, the energetic wall, that dense cloud that was holding back my brain from healing itself. I found it! I learned to work through it. No matter the circumstances, I finally knew I could and would still be me. I would find a way.

I learned more about myself and the flow of life in this one challenging year than in all my other years combined. I learned that all we need is within ourselves. It always has been. We just have to remove the layers, whatever they are, no matter how long they've been there. After all, we're the ones who inadvertently put those layers there, one at a time. And we can remove each of them when we look past the fear and clear our own path.

Our Brain's Duality

Our brains are incredibly adaptable, with the ability to grow, heal, and change in profound ways. It is what ultimately allowed me to heal my own brain. And yet, it's a profound irony that our brains are also hard-wired—on a chemical, neurological level—to resist change. When you consider the history of our development as humans, this contradiction makes sense: we thrive because we are adaptable, can learn, grow, and evolve, and yet we survive because our brains are highly efficient at detecting threats, both real and imagined. We evolved to make quick and efficient judgments about our surroundings, and to also categorize things into safe and unsafe.

Sometimes this threat detection is helpful. Our instincts take over when we see a car coming at us too quickly. Chemicals are released, our muscles tense, and we are primed to react in order to avert disaster. It works for us now in the same way it did for our ancestors when they confronted a bear in the woods or a prey animal in the desert. It is the primal fight-or-flight mode, and it gets triggered without conscious awareness. Our brains are excellent at this kind of automation, and it happens instinctively.

So, what does all of this have to do with awareness of our layers?

The answer is simple: most of us may not be living in a world where we're likely to encounter bears in the forest or poison berries on a bush, but our brains are still wired for it. The world around us has changed, but the mechanisms our brain uses to keep us safe really haven't changed at all.

The net effect is that any change is still perceived by the brain as a threat, and to the brain a threat represents the possibility of real danger, which could lead to death. Just as our brain is excellent at making life-saving judgments and categorizing things with snapshot efficiency, it also rejects anything that could threaten our safety—or rather, what it deems could threaten our safety. It exists to keep us safe.

Remember, at no point in this whole process have we, our conscious selves, been invited to the discussion about what constitutes a threat and what doesn't. This attempt at keeping us safe shows up like an overprotective parent, hovering so close to us as we toddle through the beginning of our lives, trying to learn about the world. It shows up like fear: don't run so fast, don't make that mistake, don't ask questions, don't make waves, don't stand out, don't step out of your comfort zone, always step out of your comfort zone, don't take up too much space, don't take up too little space. Instead of learning and growing from natural, non-fatal mistakes, our brain finds new and creative ways to protect us by making us believe that we're "choosing" what's best for us.

The brain loves the status quo. For the brain, change is unsafe. Any change. Even a positive one such as starting a new healthy habit can trigger resistance. We all know how hard it is to change our eating habits or start an exercise program. "Don't run so often" can turn into "Don't run at all," which can turn into "Don't even get up and go anywhere, you're so much safer right here." While this example is exaggerated, the brain will go to great lengths and adopt faulty reasoning to keep us "safe."

The more this happens, the more we start believing it. We eventually become reliant. The more we rely on this automation, the more it reinforces the message to our brain that this automation must be crucial, since we are, after all, generating it and relying upon it. It becomes this somewhat absurd circular thinking that further feeds the belief that we desperately need our brain to be in charge, as it must know better. It knows how to keep us safe. Our brain creates the fear that makes us reliant upon it. Eventually those fears and beliefs become layers.

It is important to acknowledge that layers themselves are neither good nor bad. They are part of a protective mechanism and often formed for perfectly straightforward reasons, though without conscious thought and awareness, and therefore without the proper input from our higher selves. Without you knowing, your brain took in all kinds of information from the world around you—from your very first childhood experiences to foundational moments in your teenage years, young adulthood, and beyond—and decided on your behalf what rules you'd need to follow in order to be protected.

All of this has been happening behind the scenes, without our conscious knowledge or agreement. We accept it to be the truth, usually without question or further thought. But consider this for a moment: what if it wasn't the truth at all? If you blindly or unknowingly continue to make the same decisions, over and over, based on distorted views of yourself and the world, you'll continue to experience the same feelings of disconnection, disempowerment, and lack of clarity, no matter how much you achieve in life.

Permission to Question

"Who am I, really?"

"Is this all there is?"

"What if there's something more?"

Questioning how you have defined yourself all these years can really shake things up. But there is a reason why difficult times often allow us to question in the first place: the resistance we so often have is stripped away in times of crisis, and we're able—at times for the very first time—to ask those questions. Until these moments, many of us don't even know that we can question who we are, what we believe, and how we unconsciously approach the world. We don't realize we have permission to ask questions, and we take it as a *fait accompli* because it's been decided for us, yet effectively without us.

In reality, we do have permission to question these supposed truths about ourselves. In fact, it's our right and duty to question. So often, however, there is so much going on around us that we're too distracted to look within us, until we're pushed or forced to do so. We are surrounded by a constant, ever-changing array of stimuli that overload our senses. We're tugged in different directions, told what it is we should want, buy, and have in our homes and on our bodies. We're made to believe that every object we own says something about who we are, or who we want others to think we are. We are constantly bombarded with thoughts and ideas, resulting in a constant state of overwhelm which the brain perceives as unsafe. The constant flow and influx of stimuli causes our brain to go into overdrive and start panicking, as if it were facing true life-or-death danger. This is not the life we were wired to be living.

So, when you uncover your layers for the first time, be kind, know that while they may feel like a hindrance, they're ultimately a result of this misguided attempt at protection. Your brain was trying to keep you safe. Your brain will always try to keep you safe. It will offer its help, even unsolicited—it is hardwired that way.

From this moment forward, give yourself the right to question and become curious about *you*. What do you believe to be true about yourself? What would it be like if that weren't true at all?

What you believe about yourself is much more adaptable than you think, and you can ask these questions at any time and in any moment.

Awakening from the Inside Out

Although the physical healing process after my concussion was slow, once I was on the other side of the physical recovery, I caught myself engaging more authentically with every encounter. It felt more real, genuine, and strangely peaceful. People seemed to gravitate toward me—friends, family, and people in my circle of acquaintances—asking me for guidance and wisdom about issues they were facing. It had always been my nature to be good with people, and happy to help in any way I could, but after my recovery something had changed. I could see beyond the surface and sense what people needed to do, or the perspective they needed to see. Somehow, I could provide clarity. I found myself connecting dots in whole new ways. Something had opened up within me that allowed me to delve right into the core of a given situation.

At first, I was apprehensive to say what I sensed because there was no intellectual, logical basis for it. A human mind is about external proof, about knowing, based on pattern and the stability of solid ground, and I did not know if my intuitive sense could be trusted. Was I imagining it? How could I "know" things that I did not "humanly" know? The doubts were a reflection of my brain at work, jumping right back in and trying to protect me, setting its own limitations.

I'm not sure why I had always thought that my spirituality was at odds with my intellect, reason, and logic. Yet, despite pushing my spirituality aside throughout the years, my intuition never left me, and throughout this healing process, my human learned to better trust my higher self. I had never thought of it as a question of trust. This process of discovery and newfound insight that became so helpful to me and others was fascinating. I knew I'd been saved for a reason, and I knew I had to pay it forward.

The Journey Inward

If you're reading this and grappling with any fears, sense of limitation, or perhaps discontent—any of those uncomfortable feelings inside that keep searching for something, anything, so that you will feel better, safer, and happier—you will not find it by changing what's on the outside of you. This is the reason why other external methods you may have tried, or even found short-term success with, haven't been sustainable. The most effective change and work begins from the inside out.

Embarking on this journey takes courage and radical honesty. It's often difficult to have the kind of honesty with ourselves that we really need. When you finally see a layer, truly see it, that changes everything. In that moment, there's no resistance and no fear. You see it, and it's as if a light goes on.

This process often touches on areas in our lives that hold deep and profound significance and meaning to us. For me, it was the question of how much I relied on my intellect to define myself and how it specifically prevented me from my purpose. When that was taken away, and I was forced to confront some uncomfortable truths and self-beliefs, I got to know myself in a radically new light.

Even though all of this was sparked by the trauma of a concussion and the subsequent recovery process, this experience was, in a strange way, an incredible gift. It allowed me to look at myself not from the center of my own layers, but from miles above. I finally knew who I was, having experienced the essence of me. What I didn't know, however, was how much grip my brain had had on me. I loved my precious brain and had believed what it told me. I believed it was my voice of reason and it had become an integral part of my identity, my primary identity. I was mistaken in that belief, though I didn't realize at the time: that being spiritual and logical actually wasn't a duality at all. I later discovered that unity of brain and soul takes us where we're meant to go in life. It is this unity that unlocks flow and leads us to our true selves, without struggle or strain, without self-denial or being in constant protective mode.

Truth be told, after everything I have been through, I *still* love my brain. It's an amazing human tool. But it's just that. A great asset. Today I see its limitations, with care and compassion. When we direct our brain properly, it is the best assistant in life we will ever have, but it's not supposed to be in charge. While a brain may be detail-oriented in executing orders and routines, it can't give us our essence.

My goal with this book is to guide you to your essence. To help you discover who you are, and to become more deeply aware so that you can truly know yourself and act from a place of inner choice.

Once you know what's inside of you, you can choose to keep it or change it in any way you see fit. You can work on any perceived shortcomings, address false beliefs, and in the process you will inevitably begin to see unlimited possibilities and different paths to take. In doing so, the way you see and relate to yourself, to others, and to the world will shift. You will experience your essence, the *you* that is authentic, joyful, free, and empowered.

Ready?

Let's get started.

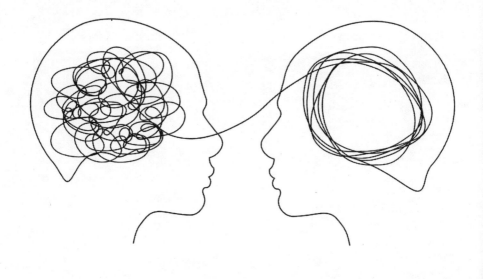

Part II

AWARENESS

CHAPTER FOUR

Me, Myself, and I

"We deserve to know ourselves fully, from the inside out, the same
way we would get to know a partner, a child, or a best friend."

B efore my concussion, I believed I had done all of the inner work necessary to truly know myself. I was confident and even proud of my brain. But after the accident, I was forced to accept that my brain was no longer going to work for me in the way it always had. I soon came to realize I was about to embark on a whole new adventure, one that had been calling out to me. There were layers within me I'd never examined, much less even noticed or questioned.

The healing that had occurred came from within, and it looked very different from what I had expected, which had always been to be able to rationalize and reason my way back to the way things had been. There had to be a logical answer, something quantifiable, an external solution. But there wasn't. The doctors and specialists had told me that all they could do was wait and see and allow things to take their course. This passive waiting was almost unbearable.

I had to do something else. But what else could I do?

For me, there was no other choice but to act. There wasn't anything

I could change about the external situation; I had to make a commitment to heal myself. Once I set aside the logical, rational, analytical part of my brain, the only place left for me to go was within, to the spiritual side. As I began the journey to find my true self, the layers I discovered caught me completely off guard.

All this time, so many things I internalized through the years and believed to be true had defined me. Yet it was those same beliefs, those layers, which had guided me to where I was now. As much as those had felt set in stone, fixed and utterly immutable, that wasn't the case at all. They could change. And, in fact, as soon as I discovered them, I was surprised at how much I wanted to change them.

Finally, I was starting to feel in control. It took a concussion for me to realize that my relationship with myself and my own spirituality was just that: a relationship. It wasn't a goal to achieve, or a point to reach. Just like any relationship, it involves give and take, negotiation, rough times and good times. But it wasn't some static place, some destination I had been waiting to arrive at. The dynamic with myself was far more of a relationship than I could have ever imagined.

As children, we know this truth intuitively, even if we can't explain it. This state of being, one where the soul and the physical self are working in unison, is how we come into existence. We go with our gut and our intuition. We are born with zero filters, no layers at all between the soul and the physical self, but in order to survive in a world we can't control, we quickly learn to be outwardly focused, and so these layers grow within us. Again, layers are meant to protect us, but the layers that were formed to protect us as children cannot do so for us now. The key to all of this is going within. Just as having a concussion is not the only way to unlock this power, there's no prerequisite to go on a retreat or seclude yourself somewhere in the mountains in order to find yourself. Finding oneself is not an end point. It's the beginning of our discovery.

The Most Important Relationship

"Although we strive to have good relationships with the people we care about, we neglect the first and most vital relationship: the one we have with ourselves."

Pause for a moment and imagine yourself amidst an interconnected web of all the people in your life, some close to you and some farther away. Between each connection stretches a thread of energy which represents your relationship with that individual. These relationships flourish or fade away depending on the energy you put into them, and at the heart of all of them are three key elements: trust, awareness, and communication.

The same is true for the relationship we have with ourselves. But are we ready for it? In fact, not only is it true but it's also even more important than the relationships we have externally. We can end a friendship that's toxic or no longer serving us, we can break up with a partner who doesn't respect us anymore, and we can distance ourselves from a family member with whom we don't see eye-to-eye, but we can never leave ourselves.

The relationship with the self either thrives or withers based on these same three elements: trust, awareness, and communication. And because of the layers we carry, we often go throughout our lives, and our inner lives, without trusting ourselves, without any awareness of our internal selves, and without having healthy communication. In order to heal, and to find joy and authentic soul purpose, these three elements need to be as strong within us as they are in each of our healthy external relationships.

Do You Trust Yourself?

The first and most important element is trust. Trust is at the heart of every relationship, but so often we do not trust ourselves at all, and we don't even realize it. If you're a lover of sweets and desserts, you may have said something similar to this before: "I just don't trust myself around chocolate!" You might say this in a joking tone, but with every word you speak, you're preparing your unconscious mind to receive instructions for what is true, and what you can expect from the world, and from yourself.

If we look more closely at a statement like this, it denotes much about how we view ourselves on a deeper level. Think of that familiar saying: "There's truth behind every joke." At best, we are telling ourselves we are unsure if we can resist the third piece of chocolate. At worst, we're actually reinforcing the idea that we are, quite literally, untrustworthy around chocolate. Over time, your brain will make you believe this idea is the truth, as the brain will always look to prove itself right.

By treating ourselves in this way, we begin to erode our trust in ourselves. When we repeatedly reinforce the idea that we're not trust-worthy to care for our own needs, we remove choice, agency, and ownership over our choices. We surrender to our layers, and we don't question them. They become a part of us, and we believe them. It makes us feel helpless, like a child being sternly told by a parent, "I don't trust you not to make a mess with these markers, so you can't draw with them at all." What would such a message teach a child to believe about them-selves? Would they grow to be resilient and know what to do when messes in life do occur? Would you?

Having trust in yourself means that you are committed to listen-ing to what your body needs from you. It happens when you choose to prioritize your body's needs on a consistent basis and truly take care of yourself. Instead of remaining helpless in the face of chocolate cake, you can indulge and yet also draw the line when your physical body has had enough.

Layers show up as barriers which separate each of us from our soul self. In order to protect ourselves, we formed layers, and it is those layers we now use to define what we think and feel about ourselves. If the message of untrustworthiness has been built up over time into one of those layers, removing it means you will be able to trust yourself again, and trust the messages your body and soul are bringing to you.

Are You Aware of Yourself?

Trust is foundational to every relationship. Once you begin to develop trust, you become more aware of everything going on within you. You become aware of your own needs, of what makes you react to certain things, of the layers you have within you. Awareness is what helps shift people from being reactive and controlled by their layers to being proactive and led by the soul self. Awareness means you can choose.

Imagine walking down a hallway in your house and stubbing your toe every single time. Without awareness, you might become angry at the house and yourself, and feel helpless or disempowered. You might think, "Everything is against me! I'm helpless, and I'm in pain!" But with awareness, you will be more mindful, you will pay attention, avoid that table in the hallway, go by a different hallway, or simply move that table to a more convenient location so as to avoid stubbed toes and pain. While this is a basic, simplistic example, you can choose to walk a different path when you gain new awareness, and that path will be one of less resistance and more flow.

We teach children to use all of their senses as they move throughout the world, so that they can have the awareness that will keep them safe. Using their eyes to look both ways, their ears to hear for oncoming traffic, their balance to keep from falling, their noses to smell fire, their touch to feel if a doorknob is warm. From each of these types of sensory input, understanding about the world is gained and a choice can be made. Without the awareness of looking for a crosswalk sign and a lack of cars, the only decision that can be made is: "Should I step out into the street?" But with that awareness, children learn what's safe, and they can choose the right time to walk.

Awareness, particularly self-awareness, is a lifelong process. Many of us walk through life utterly unaware of what's going on within ourselves.

The funny thing is, we often think we're very aware and know ourselves well. And yet, because we are not aware of our layers, we continue to repeat the same mistakes and the same actions, not knowing why.

One of the things that is so special about working with private clients is this journey to awareness. Often, clients have to come to a certain level of trust within themselves before they can begin to ask the difficult questions underlying their issue. Experiencing fear or resistance is an indication that there's something to examine. Later in this chapter, I will share an awareness exercise that can bring some key insight to even the darkest corners.

While trust is the foundation, awareness allows you to choose. Once you build trust within yourself, and once you are truly aware of your inner workings, the way you communicate with yourself is what defines your entire relationship to self.

How Do You Communicate with Yourself?

Communication is not necessarily always with words, it's an exchange. Your body, emotions, hunger, and so forth don't talk to you in words. But every feeling has a definition, and everything from gift-giving to betrayal is translated into a thought, which means into some form of communication. We are constantly in communication with ourselves.

A few years ago, I led a day-long workshop all about internal communication. As part of the day's opening session, I asked the group to consider what their first conversation of the day had been. Some had spoken to their spouses or partners first thing in the morning, and one had called her mother for a quick chat to see how she was doing. Another had spoken to her child. All of them were surprised when I said that each and every one of them had been in conversation even before these moments.

"Before you opened your mouth and uttered a single word to another human being," I told them, "you had a conversation. It's the inner conversation, the way you speak to yourself, the one that is most often overlooked." I went on to explain to the group that it is the first thought of the day that's often the quietest, but which resonates the loudest and often sets the tone for the rest of your day.

What you think of yourself and what you say to yourself matters. It's much easier to be aware and present when we have conversations out loud with other people, but internally, we often don't have the clarity to discern when we are speaking with ourselves. But that inner conversation is just as powerful, impactful, and meaningful as what is spoken aloud. What do you say to yourself when you roll over in bed and come to consciousness? Are you kind to yourself, or are you mean, maybe even cruel? Do you trust in your abilities, respect who you are, or do you knock yourself? Do you take time to consider what you are saying, and how you are saying it, when you have that inner conversation? We say things to ourselves and about ourselves that we'd never tolerate from another person.

I asked the group to consider what was the first thing they had said to themselves that morning. Had they bombarded themselves with negativity and criticism, nitpicking at every one of their perceived flaws and inadequacies? If someone was standing next to you saying all of those things to you, would you feel positively about that person, or would you grow to hate them for their constant attacks? Do you often second-guess yourself? Criticize your every choice? Micromanage yourself?

Chances are, we are so much harsher and more hostile toward ourselves than we ever realize. It's just harder to notice because this internal conversation is going on within us all the time and has been since the moment we were born.

One of the women in the group raised her hand to share how this had landed for her. She said, "To be honest with you, I didn't want to come today. It's nothing personal, I just had so much to do, and so many other things I was worrying about. I also woke up late again, so I barely had time to get ready and then I had to rush out the door. I hate when that happens. I can't seem to get it together. But as I'm sharing out loud and hearing what you're showing us, I realize that I've been saying things to myself all morning, not just about this workshop but about everything."

As she continued to share what had been on her mind, it was clear that she had not even realized that every single day started off with hostility and confrontation, even when there was no other human being around. Yet it tired her out just the same as if she had started every single day arguing with another person. Why do we do this to ourselves? It's all about our awareness or lack thereof.

This kind of mean-spirited, critical internal communication happens so often, and we're simply not aware of it. The moment we take the time to trust ourselves and look within, we become aware that it's happening, and it's often shocking how little respect we have for ourselves, how little nurturing we put into our relationship with our self.

The concept of self-respect is centered around what we allow ourselves to think about ourselves. It's not about the actual thoughts our brain generates, it's about those we subscribe to and choose to hang onto. It goes to the core of our self-esteem, our self-worth.

The woman in my workshop was able to see herself more clearly as we delved deeper, and what she found was that she actually did not have the best relationship with herself. Hers was predicated on believing she was not trustworthy and could not set herself up for a successful day. Because she did not respect her needs, she often experienced internal chaos and dissatisfaction with herself. She almost came to expect it. The discussion helped her discover that not only did she actually have a relationship with herself but also that she'd been neglecting it. It was an eye-opener for her and many others at the workshop that day. "I need to be more aware of what I say to myself and how I think about myself," one of the other participants felt comfortable enough to share. "I need to make sure I have some time for myself and do things in a less frazzled way." The others agreed. They had become aware of a whole internal dynamic that had been at play inside of them, and over which they never realized they could have a say.

Primary Layers

"Your conscious self might not know or understand how this primary layer was formed, but your protective self does remember, and uses that layer and self-belief to shape the way you move through the world."

With this new awareness of our internal world, many of us begin to see patterns emerge, common threads that weave their way throughout many of the layers of our lives. At the onset, we may not be aware of why these similarities exist, but as we begin our journey inward, they help paint a fuller picture of how we think and feel the way we do, and why we approach the world, ourselves, and others in the ways that we do.

I call these common themes "core layers," or "primary layers of protection." In the case of this particular workshop participant, it became clear to her that her primary layer was around trust. Over and over again, at the core of the issue was the fact that she didn't believe she was trustworthy, which meant she didn't believe herself worthy enough of her own trust.

Trust in oneself or others is one of the earliest layers that can form within us. Take the workshop participant, for example. If as a young child she was criticized rather than given the opportunity and guidance to learn how to do things for herself and at her own pace, she will begin believing that the people in her life do not trust in her abilities. She will internalize that message and, once accepted as fact, her subconscious will keep confirming its truthfulness by unknowingly setting her up for disappointment and failure. This may show up throughout her life as chronic disorganization, chaos, tardiness, lack of closeness in relationships, not trusting her own inner voice and truth, always looking to others for the answer, and yet she repeatedly senses that none of these ever lead her on to the right path. "I don't know how to do this, so what's the point in trying." "Somehow, I'm always disappointing myself and never able to reach my goals, no matter how hard I try." What seemingly starts off as a benign message, left unchecked over time, becomes an internal layer. In her case it became a truth that she unequivocally believed about herself, a core idea that "I am fundamentally not trustworthy." Imagine how different her life could be if this layer was examined, resolved, and removed.

Another early layer is one surrounding shame—both the shame of not being enough and of being too much can be very destructive. Take the example of a small child who eagerly starts school but struggles, and whose efforts are not reflected in their marks. Or the child who is repeatedly made to feel that they are too slow or, despite trying their best, told they aren't paying attention otherwise they would have understood what's being taught. Over time, the child may develop an identity around their intellectual capacity and worthiness, and ultimately will believe they're not smart enough, able enough, or good enough.

Children who carry shame make themselves smaller and smaller, often believing they don't have the capacity to learn, improve, or accomplish anything they may want to achieve. That layer and identity will reach far beyond the classroom and ultimately develop into generalized feelings of inadequacy and shame. It creates the belief that we are not enough and our needs are too much, that we should pretend we understand because it's unacceptable not to, and ultimately that we feel shamed for struggling this way in the first place. Over time, and as we grow into adulthood, that layer of shame sits there, getting more and more entrenched and embedded within us, until we believe that it *is* us. We believe we're inadequate, stupid, and eventually that we're deserving of shame.

Very young children don't have wants, only needs, and if a need is not met, they will develop a layer around it. In fact, all of us will. We will often blame ourselves or others for those unmet needs. We can feel shame for having needs, feel unworthy of having those needs met, or even develop a layer around trusting ourselves to meet those needs. When our basic needs—care, compassion, empathy, human contact, food, shelter, a sense of safety—are not met, we may also settle for wants and try to meet those instead.

It can be very challenging to discern needs from wants, and for many people, the line between them is blurred at best. Even the most high-achieving, professional, well-respected people I see often mistake their wants for their needs. But the reason behind this confusion is very simple: a want comes to mask a lack of something, something we need and didn't get, because a want is more within our control. As people we need love, stability, and safety. If these were never shown to us as children, we may instead turn to and want things, a sense of power, and control so we can prevent our inner selves from ever feeling abandoned. Power and control may be something we can create in our outer environment—perhaps by pushing ourselves to gain a lucrative promotion, devoting ourselves to work or surrounding ourselves with expensive material things and believing they are necessities. We focus on what we think will make us feel powerful and gain the control we crave—but no matter what we do in our outer environment, our deeper needs will never be satisfied.

This is why, for example, burnout happens: we push ourselves to fill wants that will sadly never meet our needs. A want may not necessarily be correlated to a need, but it usually comes into play to numb, mask, or help lessen the void created by a need not being met. And at the core of these needs, we can find our primary layers of protection. Often, it may be difficult to see what our primary layer is because there seems to be no clear pattern to the struggles we have within ourselves, with others, or in the world around us. There can often be a lot of distraction and noise that can prevent us from seeing this primary layer clearly. We have to explore our surface level layers before we can get a glimpse of the deeper ones. However, if we know we have a tendency or a pattern to default to one state, that's a good indication that we have a primary layer of protection within us, and maybe we should take the time to explore that further.

Shame—along with trust, worthiness, perfection, agency, identity, entitlement, and others—can all be primary layers. We will discuss each in more depth in Chapter Eleven. Because these deepest layers within each of us were formed at our youngest and most vulnerable moments, even witnessing these primary layers can often be intense. We may cry, be indignant, feel pain, or even disappointment in ourselves when we witness a primary layer being triggered. It might startle, surprise, or upset us.

I often say that layers are stored stories. When you think back on your own childhood, there may be stories that arise, times in your early life when something didn't seem to click into place. Your conscious self may not even know or be able to pinpoint where and how a primary layer formed, but your inner world absolutely remembers and uses that layer, that self-belief, to shape the way you move through the world today.

Primary layers are formed within us the same way every other layer is: because we're born with no buffer between us and the world, we need to learn the specific rules and frameworks for how to be a human being. Children learn about the world, and about themselves, in two ways: observation and action. If there is some profound experience or observation that takes place in early childhood, a child will automatically form a layer around it. This can be one jarring experience where a child experiences a lack of safety, stability, or proper care in some way, but it can often be formed through repeated action. Repeat this again and again, and the layer is reinforced so strongly that it feels as if it's not just a part of us, it is us.

Early layers are formed the way very young children think and perceive the world: binary, black-or-white, good-or-bad, yes-or-no. But as we grow and mature, the layers we form can be more nuanced. These nuanced layers are often built upon the foundation of our primary layer.

It's important to remember that layers are neutral. All layers, primary or otherwise, were formed within us at times when we sub-consciously believed we needed the protection from a world that either seemed too vast for us, could hurt us, or one that we misunderstood. We observed or experienced things, and when those things happened to us over and over, they formed a layer that told us "This is just how the world works. This is what you should expect. These are the rules." By gaining awareness of these layers, however, we create just enough space between us and any given layer, and that allows us to consider if they are really true or useful to us. With that awareness comes discernment and choice.

With all of these primary layers (and there are many more, which we will continue to uncover throughout the book), the key point here is that there should be absolutely no judgment toward the young self who was just trying to survive in a challenging world.

Wherever you are, whatever is coming up for you, treat yourself gently, and don't berate, judge, or condemn yourself for the layers you may uncover. The past informs our present, yes, but it doesn't define our future. Layers may be firmly fixed within us, but the moment we shine the light of awareness on to them, we understand them—and ourselves—so much better.

We are not meant to sit back and passively surrender to these layers as if we are in a room while others talk about us like we're not even there. We are meant to be proactive. We must learn to become aware that our layers exist, and we must learn to trust that we're not broken or damaged (anymore), with or without our layers. Trust that you're not going to dis-appear if you remove a layer. Remember your layer was placed there to protect you at a time you needed it, but you are not your layer. Trust that you're going to be more than fine, even better, without it. You'll be freed from it! Just like a cast that is temporary, so too are your layers.

With this understanding, you can finally begin to choose what serves your higher self, honoring and thanking your layers for bringing you this far, keeping you safe in the only way they knew how. Because of them, you're alive. Because of your layers, you now have the choice to free yourself and move forward.

Exercise — Awareness Practice

You owe it to yourself to become aware of the conversations happening within you. You have probably heard the term "inner monologue," but I invite you to think of it as a dialogue, a series of conversations. You might find it helpful to think of each of the different parts that comprise who you are as a group of acquaintances whose conversation you have just overheard. Simply listen, without judgment, and consider what it is you hear.

When you wake in the morning, what is the first thing you say to yourself? Is it kind or critical? Do you feel weary and defeated before the day has even begun, eager for the first cup of coffee to get you going, or optimistic for the day ahead?

During the day, tune your awareness inward and observe what information you receive. Note whatever comes up, whether it is a fully formed thought or simply a feeling, something from your emotional body or physical body. It doesn't have to be a profound message, and in fact, most likely it won't be. Remember, simple messages of pain, pleasure, joy, sadness, and fear are what make up the majority of our inner chatter.

You may find it helpful to acknowledge these thoughts out loud, if appropriate. Or you can write them down. The key purpose of this practice is not to guide or change your inner conversation, but rather to simply gain awareness. What do you hear yourself thinking or saying? How does it land for you?

Exercise — Inner Conversation Practice

After you have practiced this awareness exercise, you can begin to go deeper. As you track your thoughts, take some time to reflect on them.

- What was my initial response to receiving this information?

- What does that bring up for me as I consider my response?

- Do my internal thoughts and conversations revolve around recurring messages?

- If I could choose, what would I instead say to myself in this moment?

As you begin to deepen your awareness of your inner conversations, you may also find yourself holding that awareness in all spaces of your life. Here are some moments where you might want to check in on your inner conversation:

- When you wake up in the morning.

- As you get dressed and ready for your day.

- When you are speaking to a friend, family member, colleague, or neighbor.

- When you are preparing a meal or sitting down to eat.

- When you are laying down for bed and preparing for sleep.

What do you hear? How do you respond to your thoughts in the moment, and would you change that answer if you felt you had the power to?

CHAPTER FIVE

Your Inner Boardroom

"With open, bold, and honest boardroom inquiry, you can finally reach your layers and choose to dissolve them."

As I began to go deeper inside myself, further exploring my layers, it became apparent that there was much more going on than I had ever expected. I soon came to realize that there was an essential relationship that I had not truly paid attention to, much less nurtured: the relationship I had with myself. Healing my brain, then working through my layers, I found that this inner relationship was the key to further self-discovery. I had a relationship with myself, and as is intrinsic to every relationship, there had to be a form of communication.

Now, as we know, not every type of communication is verbal, but the communication is always there. In our relationship to others, verbal communication as well as tone of voice and body language form part of our overall communication experience. When we speak of having a relationship with ourselves, that relationship is even more encompassing as it engages every part of who we are. Every emotion, every sensation, every part of us is in constant conversation. The question is, how much of it do we hear? How much of it do we listen to? The deeper I went, the more I realized that there was a lot of communication happening. As I tuned into my internal communication and began to openly and boldly listen, I could become a part of the conversation at a conscious level. Once you hear, you can begin the process of choosing what you're going to do with it. Do you even agree? What, if anything, do you have to say in return?

Conscious Communication

"If every relationship is based on communication, then it is within the flow of our communication that we will find the true nature of the relationship we have with ourselves."

To begin to explore this relationship, let's first start with the most obvious: the vehicle we are born into. Our physical body speaks to us through the language of physical sensations, ones that we can categorize as either pain or gain. We experience physical pain when we push our bodies beyond their limit and into damage or danger. We experience physical gain as that empowered feeling we get after a satisfying run, good workout, or a great swim. It allows us to feel our strength, and it's our body's way of letting us know that we are on the right track. This experience is communicated to us as a sensation of physical power and a feeling of empowerment. In contrast, physical pain lets us know that we've injured ourselves, or are about to cause damage. When something in our body is overused, used incorrectly, out of alignment, or not being tended to, it requires our attention. Physical pain serves as a message that some care is needed, a message that we should listen to or potentially risk even worse damage. Both physical pain and gain are forms of communication, ones we are often left to process subconsciously, unless we take the time to tune into what our bodies are saying to us.

Our emotional body communicates with us as well, but while our physical body communicates to us through the language of physical sensations, our emotional body speaks to us in the language of feelings and emotions. Whether physical or emotional, the experience of pain comes to us from many sources. Sometimes pain is generated by a thought, a reaction to something external, or an unmet need inside of us. Sometimes, it's just from a stubbed toe. The experience of both kinds of pain can be felt in the body, though we don't often identify it as such when it's emotional. We can feel emotions in our gut, our heart, or our solar plexus. Each sensation, whether physical or emotional, is translated by our brains into a thought. While things may get lost in the process of such a translation, we rarely question its accuracy and usually go with it, whether it's comfortable for us or not. When we receive these translations, we process them and attach different meanings, personal connections, and judgments to them. Our body senses and feels, and our brain tells us what it means and how we should feel about it. So where is our conscious awareness in the midst of this endless conversation?

Our consciousness works in words. The world was created with words. Words are powerful and are the language of conscious communication. Our brain takes our subconscious sensations and brings them into our consciousness by way of translating them into silent words, which we call thoughts. Those thoughts are a bunch of brain-generated interpretations of these sensations, which are formed and shaped by the way our brains are wired and the programming that we have installed. They are also informed by the stimuli we process, and the energy around us. The more we sense and feel at the subconscious level, the more thoughts flood our conscious mind, and once we become aware of them, the more we can choose which to keep and which to discard.

When these thoughts pop into our heads, it's important to understand that they don't just arrive fully formed, as a direct message. Before we are aware of a thought that has been delivered to us, it's already been subjected to subconscious interpretation, analysis, and even debate. While that thought is being processed, a negotiation takes place, and our mind may begin questioning or countering that thought.

This process, which unfolds far below our awareness level, can escalate a seemingly innocuous thought to a dilemma, doubt, or full-blown internal conflict. Before we are even aware of it or had any conscious input, the thought arrives, and we're meant to deal with the interpretation of it, a message that perhaps has been distorted, filtered, or misinterpreted based on this internal conversation. We are made aware of the conclusion and most often will take it at face value.

The thoughts we have, while generated by our brain, are not our thoughts until we choose to make them ours. It is as if our minds are mailboxes, and the thoughts are a stack of letters which have been delivered to us. Do we accept, open, and live our lives according to that mail? What if it's junk mail?

There are so many messages sent to us in bulk that could affect us, but they are sent with not much thought or consideration. Do we review the addresses and discover that, perhaps, the letter we've been given doesn't really belong to us at all? Do we sift through the letters and choose what aligns? If we opened our neighbor's credit card bill, for example, we might be swept up into a frenzy of overdue fees that are not even ours and are based on information that doesn't pertain to us at all.

It is much more obvious and easier to triage misdirected mail, but when it comes to our thoughts, it's not so simple. This is because the thoughts that our brain generates are often mistaken for our thoughts, ones we quickly believe and hold as truth. A thought arrives and we respond without distance or awareness: "It must be so since the thought I have is telling me it is." Without awareness, we get caught up in believing that we and our thoughts are one and the same.

Thoughts, however, are generated constantly by our brain. Whichever ones we latch on to are the ones our brain will keep generating for us. This discernment gives us the ability to choose which thoughts we own, and which ones we can say, "No, thank you, I don't agree with that particular thought. I don't subscribe to this way of thinking. It doesn't reflect who I am, who I want to be, and what I choose to believe." While we are often capable of responding in this way to someone else's thoughts and opinions, imagine applying that same ability and discernment to yourself. Imagine the freedom and alignment it brings once you develop the awareness to question and respond to any thought your brain generates, as if it were someone else's. This is what I wish for you.

In the previous chapter, we explored how the relationship we each have with ourselves is the closest and most important relationship we will ever have. In order to nurture this relationship, we must first be aware of what's going on within us. Thoughts are constantly being generated, countered, reinforced, and delivered by our brains to our conscious selves. This happens every day and all day long. We experience near-constant mind chatter, and without the awareness to develop and grow our inner relationship, we often struggle to find clarity or even quiet the chatter down.

It's difficult to lower the volume, let alone mute that mind chatter. If you find you can pause—even if it's only for a moment—and allow yourself to be still, you can simply bear witness to it. You'll get much insight on what your thoughts are telling you about your perception of yourself, and the type of dynamic and inner relationship you have. Once you know, you get to direct your inner dialogue and consciously create the relationship you want with yourself moving forward.

The Handbook for Human Living

*"You will ultimately find and keep what
you seek by journeying inward."*

When we are born, we come as a package. We are the fusion between a soul and a body, and intrinsic to that fusion is a relationship between those two entities. The soul and the body are supposed to work in unison, and at the very beginning, they do. At birth, this union is a blank canvas. It's the inception of a relationship that's brand new, pure, and—as yet—not interfered with.

As a young child your ego is not yet formed. Your personality is underdeveloped, and who you are is uninfluenced, pure, and natural—and then the journey of life commences. As we begin to experience and learn to process external stimuli, people start telling us how to see the world. They tell you who you are, and what you can and cannot do. You find out about your surroundings and how to live through other people, and because you have no filter, you start believing that this is actually your own belief system, your own set of values, and it becomes part of your identity. It may or may not be aligned with who you truly are, but you're not aware at that point.

We're not delivered with a customized handbook for how our specific personality and our soul are going to work together to accomplish our goal on earth. There is no assigned mentor, guide, or teacher that comes to let you know that you have a relationship with yourself. No one tells you, "Hi, there! Your mission, whether you choose to accept it or not, is to find out who you truly are, what your personality is, and to transcend it, discover your soul purpose and mission, and execute it. Oh, and in the process, you'll be encountering and connecting with others doing the exact same thing."

Instead, we are invited to embark on a journey of self-discovery, curiosity, awe, adventure, empowerment, and return to self, but we have to do that with all these external messages flying at us from every direction. We absorb these messages, and if they conflict with our true essence, they become misalignments. Over time, these misalignments start creating layers. Layers that either protect you from what you're being told about yourself and are asked or made to believe, or layers formed because you actually have to conform to something and must contort yourself in order to do so. They are installed without your awareness or permission as a safety measure when some kind of psychological threat is detected. Unfortunately, we have no say in when and where these layers are created, but we still have to live with the result of them—that is, until we start to question and address them, instead of merely dealing with their symptoms.

Some of us may go our whole lives with the constant, nagging ache of discomfort, never realizing or understanding its true source. We numb those feelings in all kinds of ways, but none of our coping mechanisms really get to the heart of it, and so nothing changes. It's akin to changing the wallpaper in a house where the foundation itself is crumbling.

At some point, though, we not only want to change but need to change. We become aware that something foundational needs to shift. As individuals, that moment of awareness is different for each of us. I've worked with people across a wide spectrum of ages, and the common factor for when this shift in awareness happens isn't so much defined by age as it is by the stability in our lives. This sounds almost paradoxical; how can stability reveal layers? Let me explain.

Our brains take time to fully develop, and it isn't until around our mid-twenties that they're fully formed. The last portion of our brain that develops fully is the same area that covers long-term planning, consequences, executive functioning, and risk assessment: the prefrontal cortex. Before we have our full capacity for those skills, we're more likely to run into situations where we take action without being able to fully conceptualize the results. In other words, we're at risk of being more impulsive before our prefrontal cortex is fully formed. Impulse means potential for more risk, and risk means danger.

When you reach adulthood and begin to move toward all the goals which, for you, represent stability—defining your career path, working to become financially stable and save for the future, starting a family, finding a partner, striking out into the world—you'll likely apply yourself diligently to the task. For a few years, you're in the grind, striving toward these goals. During that time, you may not stop to consider your layers at all, because you already have a lot to think about, manage, and plan for. But once your foray into the adult world is stable and established, a strange thing happens: you begin to subconsciously feel that you don't need your layers anymore.

Just like a cast supports a broken bone as it heals, it becomes a hindrance and an obstacle once the bone has healed. This is true for layers as well. As soon as you no longer need them, your layers will start to speak to you. They start finding ways to get your attention, to let you know, "Hey, I'm still here! You might want to take a look and reassess. Do you still need me? I think I'm in your way. Might you be ready to let me go?"

Your layers do this as soon as you no longer need them. Once a layer has served its true purpose and you no longer need a layer—when you're strong enough to live without it—it'll start becoming more and more obvious that you don't need it. In a way that's truly amazing. It will come up to remind you and invite you to release it. "You don't need me anymore. I've become a hindrance to you, but I just can't leave on my own. You've placed me here, therefore only you can face me and let me go."

The people I work with usually don't know that whatever problem they are experiencing is because of a layer. In fact, they almost never know it. What they want, instead, is a solution. They want to feel better, to fix something, to feel whole. And that's our soul calling out to us: our whole job is to be more of ourselves, and once we're capable of doing that, there is an innate yearning to be free. We don't get to choose when our layers come up for us, because if we did, we'd never choose it at all. Our brain would keep us from wanting to remove a layer, while our essence would yearn for it. Doing anything else other than removing an unhelpful layer is just replacing one fiction for another fiction.

Our layers speak to us, and we can hear them if we listen. They communicate in the language of feelings and emotions like pain, shame, greed, discomfort, disempowerment, loss of control, or even FOMO (fear of missing out). And when layers speak to us, we start feeling that uneasiness, akin to some kind of internal tug of war; we can feel something is off, but we don't quite know what it is.

Jen's Story — The Body Speaks to Us

One of my clients, Jen, was an incredibly driven woman who always held herself to a very high standard. She expected that she would be able to keep up with her activities and excel at her demanding job. She had risen to head the accounting department of a medium-sized company and worked long hours. When she came to me, she was at her wits' end dealing with recurring knee pain. After visiting numerous doctors and professionals, doing scans and tests, nothing physical could be found that was causing this pain. With no other avenues to explore, she brought the issue to me.

"I just want to get back to my life," Jen said, impatient and frustrated with herself, and with her body. "I don't have time for this. I want to find whatever the emotional cause of this is and get over it already!"

Jen was understandably annoyed about this mysterious pain. But even more than that, Jen was angry. It bothered her deeply that this pain had no medical explanation, and it kept stopping her literally in her tracks. Her knee pain would come back every few months, and it would be so severe that it would impede her quality of life, hobbies, walking routine, everything.

Deep down, Jen knew she didn't want to have to listen to her body. And so, in her quest to find answers for this physical pain, Jen had been attributing it to other things. Like many of us do, she was ignoring the signs that her body had been sending her. She often tried to deny her emotions, and instead pushed herself harder. In reality, Jen was running on the path toward exhaustion, and her body was trying to find every which way to let her know. The pain was a warning; her body needed her to slow down.

The more she ignored this emotional message, the more the pain intensified. Knee pain often denotes a fear or inability to move forward. In her case, she was pushing herself too much all the time, and she didn't hear when her body spoke to her. Just like Jen, so many of us either pretend our emotions aren't there, or we try to bury them, to numb our emotional distress and pretend everything is fine. Or we may feel it, but we simply don't understand the message behind the pain. Without this deeper searching, Jen had been frustrated by the pain she was experiencing. As we worked together, it became apparent that there was a layer in effect, one that she needed to address before she could move forward.

Our Soul-Body Connection

"Our personality and our soul are meant to learn to work together to accomplish our goals here on earth."

Jen's story is not unique. Science has shown that emotional health and physical health are closely connected and can impact each other. Chronic stress can, over time, lead to all kinds of medical issues, from ulcers to high blood pressure and cardiac problems. Because of this soul-body connection, there's no way to avoid it; one will always affect the other, but it can be challenging to pinpoint exactly what the true cause is.

Now, it's important to note that this book is not intended to diagnose, treat, cure, or prevent any disease, and it's an important part of your overall health and wellness plan to consult with medical professionals who can apply their expert wisdom to your mental or physical health concerns. But because we're born as this union of soul and body, using the *No More Layers* approach to go deeply within ourselves and explore the whole body gives us another aspect of wisdom that can work in parallel to medical advice and treatments. Physical pain often has physical reasons behind it, but that doesn't mean it can't also have emotional or spiritual reasons for it as well. While the approach to each is different, they are more often than not intertwined.

Even though I had set out to heal my physical brain injury, the journey I ended up going on was one that went beyond physical healing.

What I came to understand was that despite being confident that I knew myself, and knew my brain, there were actually parts of myself that I didn't even realize I had been neglecting.

We deserve to know ourselves fully, from the inside out, the same way we would get to know a partner, a child, or a best friend. But the sad fact is that many of us go our entire lives not knowing ourselves at all, and that's because it's harder to look within than it is to see outside of ourselves. It's often easier to understand and accept what makes a partner or friend tick. We understand what a child's basic needs are and we can tend to them. We seek to understand traumas or layers that a friend or family member might have, so we can be there for them. However, we often overlook our own needs, especially in the business of our daily lives. Nurturing our relationship with the self becomes something we have to consciously remind ourselves to choose to do.

When you give somebody what they need, not only does that person grow and thrive but your relationship with them also grows. And when you give your physical body what it needs—sleep, food, oxygen, water, movement, the basics—then your relationship with your body flows better. You're attuned to your body's needs, so your body will give you its best and do what you ask of it. It will not resist you because you have shown it you can be trusted to provide for it. You don't unnecessarily push it to exhaustion or put your wants before its basic needs. "You can trust me to take care of you and give you what you need. I'm listening, and your needs come before my wants."

Just as we are a union of a soul and a physical body, we also have an emotional body, and it has needs, too. Not only are we responsible for finding out what our emotional, mental, and spiritual needs are, but we're also responsible for trying to meet them on a regular basis. And when we don't meet them, that internal tug of war happens.

When our internal needs are not met, we can experience all kinds of repercussions, such as:

- A feeling of internal dissonance, where we don't feel like the different pieces of our self fit together the way we know they should.

- A sense of inner conflict, where we are at war with ourselves, and where our needs and wants pull at us in opposite directions.

- A lack of clarity.

- A repeated pattern of self-sabotage.

We become disappointed by ourselves and in ourselves. Over time, we stop trusting ourselves, and our inner relationship is damaged right down to its core. But we can rebuild this trust. In fact, it's our responsibility to do so, to know ourselves, fully and completely. In order to do this, we must open ourselves up to conversation, listening and responding to what all of the parts of ourselves are really saying. This relationship cannot be hurried. It cannot be rushed. As much as Jen wished she could power her way through it, the kind of deep relationship we build with ourselves in order to truly listen and trust ourselves cannot be rushed.

I listened to Jen as she expressed the frustration and anger with her pain, and I invited her to go deeper into her layers. Among other things, Jen asked her inner self, "What do I need to nurture? What's calling out for my attention that I've been neglecting? What am I overdoing that I don't need to be doing anymore? What am I not giving myself?" Through this exploration, Jen learned what those hidden needs were, and that her needs would continue to persist as long as she kept on ignoring, denying or burying them. Jen needed to slow down so her body wouldn't have to keep playing catch-up. She didn't need to push herself so hard all the time, because it was no longer serving her. It was, in fact, harming her.

As Jen turned her attention inward, she was able to discover all kinds of internal conversations that had been constantly happening. Soon, as we worked together further, she began to identify areas she wanted to improve, all through the process of questioning, listening, and holding space so that she could, at last, receive these vitally important messages. Jen was shocked to discover these things within herself. She knew that without ever seeking, questioning, and exploring, she—like all of us—would simply stay in the place of discomfort. When the layers that no longer serve us remain unquestioned, unexplored, and unexamined, we simply don't have the awareness of what it is we really want. And so we never truly get to choose what we want, and we feel disempowered. We remain distanced from ourselves, and yet the messages we desperately need to receive don't just go away. They will go somewhere, and when they show up for us, we might not even know the origin, let alone how to fix it.

Like Jen, we might experience anything from deep emotional discontent, disconnection, and discomfort to real physical symptoms. Whatever layer is there will continue to show up for us until we listen and work through whatever is at its core. When we seek to raise what's at play at a subconscious level to a conscious level, layers are no longer hidden, and they can no longer fully be in control of us. They become known and, in turn, we can dissolve them.

Sam's Story — Worthiness and Self-Sabotage

Different types of pain mean different things. In Jen's case, it was physical pain which spoke to her of a deeper, emotional layer she needed to clear in order to heal and move forward. For my client Sam, the pain he was experiencing was emotional, and even more difficult to pinpoint than an aching knee.

Sam, a driven and capable financial controller who was well-respected, had always aspired to become the CFO of the company he worked for, and now the position had opened up after six years of striving. Until then, he had run the accounting department, eyeing the CFO position all the while. He applied for the position and got called for an interview. The first interview went well and he was asked back for a second interview.

Elated at this possible opportunity, Sam felt happy, and yet the following few days played out very unexpectedly. As if a switch had flipped in his brain, Sam found himself going on autopilot. He stayed out late with friends. The next night he went to bed even later, binge watching a TV series. At work the next day, Sam made a serious mistake in one of the major accounts. He found himself falling into behaviors that seemed hopelessly incongruent with his hopes and plans.

What was going on?

Sam reached out in a panic and came to me the morning before his second interview. He was distraught and disgusted at himself for his actions, and now he understood that they could interfere with him realizing his dream. Not only was Sam angry about his actions but he was also angry for feeling angry, which only intensified the layer that had come up for him. His anger about the situation, about his behavior, and about his own anger had clouded his judgment, affected his opinion of himself, and was leading him to draw inaccurate conclusions about himself, deeply affecting his self-worth.

"Was I being unrealistic to think I could ever be CFO?" he wondered. "Why am I self-sabotaging like this? I thought this was something I wanted, so what's wrong with me? I can't believe I'm doing this. I'm unreliable. I can't trust myself. I probably shouldn't have even applied."

We are so quick to berate ourselves. We easily think the very worst of ourselves, lose trust in ourselves, knock ourselves down, and be harsher with ourselves than we ever would be with other people. As adults, do we believe we must be perfect? Always get it right, no matter what? Is life not a path of learning, discovery, and growth?

Instead, what if we could pause, ignite our curiosity, and ask ourselves, "Is this truly me? Is this what I would choose to do, who I believe I am, when I'm in alignment?" In order to answer this question, we must acquaint ourselves with our layers, especially when these layers are vying for our attention. There's a way for us to learn and understand the language of our layers.

If you aren't quite sure what alignment feels like, you are not alone. Imagine that gut feeling when you just know you are doing the right thing for yourself. The one that isn't mind-based or intellectually driven and feels better than logic. It is your inner knowing, your core sense, and it puts you at peace rather than creates doubt or inner conflict. It requires no explanation or justification. All of you just knows. It is the moment in which you are aligned.

Sam was self-aware enough to catch himself and say, "Hey, wait a minute, what am I doing staying out late with my friends? I've been working toward this for years. I've had this goal for so long and now I have an opportunity, so why am I behaving in a way that makes no sense to me?" When Sam came to me, he desperately needed to know what was fighting him so hard and preventing him from moving forward to accomplish his goal.

In order to delve deeper into these layers, I invited Sam to do a visualization exercise to further explore these questions and the mis-alignment he was now facing.

First, I asked Sam to close his eyes and imagine a boardroom. Because he'd spent the last ten years in the corporate world, that was easy to imagine. I encouraged him to craft not just a boardroom but *his* boardroom.

- What does the space look like?
- What color are the walls?
- What size and shape is the table?
- Are there windows, lights, decorations on the walls?

As I guided Sam through this process, he began to create the look and feel of his boardroom exactly as he wished. He chose yellow walls and soft lighting above an oval table made of polished wood. This was his space, and now that he'd customized it precisely to his own needs, he felt safe enough to enter and call a board meeting with his inner committee.

"Your inner committee," I explained to him, "is every single part of yourself that's ever been a part of your decision-making process. You get to call these meetings, and you get to direct whatever happens here because you're the only one in charge. At different times, different inner committee members will show up, because not everyone is a player in every situation. You can always call a boardroom meeting for whatever situation or layer comes up for you."

Sam's inner committee members began to trickle into the boardroom: resistance, fear, patience, ambition, and self-sabotage were amongst the voices that showed up. Standing there in his boardroom, with many members of his inner committee assembled, he was ready to listen. Sam knew he wanted this job, but applying for it seemed to have triggered some kind of layer that was threatening to block his success. He laid his decades-long goal on the table to look at. It was clear to him that he wanted it, but unclear what else was going on.

"Okay," Sam asked, open and curious, "what's behind my self-sabotaging behaviors about this job?" As we worked together, his inner committee had many profound answers and insights to show him.

The Answers Within the Questions

"In every question lies the path to the answer, like an arrow
pointing in the direction of where the treasure lies."

Questioning is at the heart of *No More Layers*. Through questioning, we can push aside judgments and fear to gain insight. Questioning stands in direct contrast to instinct—and, as we know about the brain, it's instinct that causes us to make snap decisions in response to real or perceived threats. Instinct has allowed us to survive as a species; we wouldn't have made it very far if we paused and asked: "Why is that giant black bear coming my way?" Or if we pondered: "I wonder whether the speeding car has enough breaking distance to avoid hitting me?" Instead, our survival instinct kicks in, because the impact of a speeding car could kill us and a black bear could maul us. Layers give us snap judgments in much the same way, keeping us in fight-or-flight mode. But when we get curious, we can slow down and assess a "threat" for what it really is: simply a challenge to a layer. This curiosity and slowing down makes questioning possible, and with those questions we can gain insight into ourselves and our layers.

Questions are also flexible and expansive, while layers and instinct are rigid and binary. Have you ever noticed that you get different answers depending on the way you pose a question, or the words you use? This flexibility offers a different understanding, not only of what's being sought but also of the question itself. The better you become at questioning, the better you'll become at uncovering the layers that lie below your consciousness. Questioning in the boardroom is an essential part of the process. Inherent in every question is the potential for the answer. Imagine it like an arrow pointing you in the direction to where the treasure lies: you reach your layer, discover it, dig it up, and begin to dissolve it.

Knowing how to ask the questions that reveal our layers is where that process begins. Not answering a question directly is actually a form of distraction and an indication that there's an underlying layer, one you're unknowingly resistant to uncover. For Sam, he began to go deeper, questioning and uncovering as he went.

Was he secretly underqualified for the role? Sam asked himself—his inner committee—this question, and it didn't elicit any discomfort. He clearly believed and felt he was qualified.

Was there something wrong with the job? Again, Sam felt perfectly comfortable, and he continued with deeper questioning.

Was there a need he was ignoring that could be competing with his want?

Was it a limiting belief preventing him from his path to success?

Had he lost confidence in himself somehow? No, but the answer to that question led him to something much deeper. To his shock, he realized that judgment, criticism, and shame were all around his boardroom table.

"Shame?" Sam wondered aloud. "Why do I feel shame? Why is shame here at this meeting?"

All this time, Sam had been berating himself like a parent upset with a child. It turned out, the things he was saying about himself were not that different from what his parents had said to him as a child. The spoken and unspoken rules he had been raised with about the dangers of reaching too high, wanting too much. Sam explained that he had grown up in a home where his parents let their own fears control them, and believed ambition and success were unnecessary, too risky or plain wrong, and meant that you were greedy and ungrateful for what you had. These were the values he had internalized, and what it had done to him was to create internal messaging that strongly discouraged initiative, making him feel wrong for wanting more now as an adult.

While he had not consciously been thinking of his parents or his childhood, the messages Sam had absorbed as a child still actively resided deep within him as an adult. He was deeply conflicted and didn't even know it. On the surface, he knew he wanted this job, believed he was qualified for it, and knew he could succeed at the interview and prove his worth. Deep down, however, there was a layer that he didn't even know was there, causing him to feel he was wrong and trying to stop him at all costs.

Sounds confusing, right? How can we be at odds with ourselves? Why is it we work against ourselves in what we want? In any internal conversation, there is an exchange of ideas and information within us all day long, but unlike a conversation between two separate individuals, in every internal conversation we are both the speaker and the listener, the giver and the receiver. If we could take a peek inside of ourselves and listen in, what conversation might we overhear? For Sam, taking an honest look deep into his own subconscious revealed a conversation that brought him back to those childhood messages which had become layers.

Sam became aware, through his boardroom and inner committee questioning, that he had a layer around success, a layer that told him it was shameful, too risky, undesirable, and wrong. He had substituted his parents' belief system for his own, never giving his own truth a voice, but as soon as he uncovered this layer, he could choose what to do with it. He chose to let it go, let it dissolve. He didn't truly believe ambition was wrong, bad, or shameful. He was proud to have taken the leap to apply for the CFO position. As the layer lifted, he realized more and more how much he was aligned with his choice and how much he had needed to finally spread his wings and take a risk toward advancement.

That day in the boardroom, Sam showed immense openness and courage. He didn't silence, ignore, or deny any of the voices that showed up for him. He boldly questioned and bravely listened to each board member, and through that questioning process he realized he had never truly allowed himself to be himself. He had ambition, initiative, and courage, and all that had been stifled—without his knowledge and most definitely without his permission—by none other than a deeply rooted layer that he wasn't even aware had been there.

After releasing that layer, he felt relieved, happier, and free. He was no longer angry at himself, and the courage he proved to himself that day in his inner boardroom trickled into the company boardroom during his interview.

A Light in the Darkness of Self

*"Wherever you shed light, no matter how small, the
darkness dissipates in that particular space."*

Each of us has an inner committee. Your inner committee consists of all of the various pieces of your inner self that make you one whole being, one whole person. The members of your committee include your physical body, your emotions, your soul, your fears, your joy, your hunger, every single aspect of you that you can think of, and several others that you might not have thought of yet. It is every voice that speaks to you in this internal conversation.

This process isn't about judgment, it's about acknowledgment, exploration, awareness, and choice. When Sam gave himself the mental space and perspective to check in, he was able to create distance between himself and his layers. It's within that space that the power and possibility to choose happens.

This is what happens when a layer gets uncovered, brought to awareness, and dissolved. It creates an internal shift, fosters a deeper trust, and positively impacts our relationship with ourselves. Once Sam faced his layer and heard it, he was no longer pulled in opposite directions. No part within him even attempted to rebel, self-sabotage, or stop him. Allowing our body, whether physical or emotional, to speak to us, hearing all of it out and having the conversations around the inner boardroom table, instantly empowers us to be able to dissolve our internal dissonance and resistance to bring about deep and profound awareness.

Awareness is powerful. It's the forestep to choice, and choice leads to alignment. Once we find the source of our layers, we get to actively choose whether or not we want them anymore. We get to be fully in control of ourselves, seated where we should be: at the head of the boardroom. We get to call upon our inner committee any time we need guidance and insight, creating space between our self and our layers. We become aware of where our layers end and we begin.

Your inner boardroom is where consciousness sits, and that's where your power to consciously choose lives. When you choose, you create. You get to create your own life experience. If there's any key point I wish for you to take from this chapter, it is to trust yourself. To trust yourself enough to take a pause, bring awareness into yourself, and to check in with yourself through your boardroom when things don't feel quite right. It might be the language of a layer poking around for your attention, a discomfort, an emotion coming up; whatever it is, it's worth exploring. You are worth exploring.

In the previous chapter, I challenged each of you to engage in an awareness and listening exercise with yourself. Now, I invite you to go deeper, and begin to open up to other aspects of your inner self: your own inner committee. In order to have a conversation with this inner committee, you need a space.

Exercise — Shaping Your Inner Sanctum

If it was somehow possible for you to put this book down for a moment, close your eyes, and still follow me through this next paragraph, I would ask you to do just that. Instead, I'll ask you to take a deep breath and clear your mind. As you are reading these words, visualize them in your mind. Imagine that you have a boardroom. Yes, your very own inner boardroom, the one you'll be inviting your subconscious into for many, many meetings.

Take a moment to create the look and feel of this boardroom however you like. For some of you, the boardroom might be a fun experience, and it might be warm and pleasant. It could be vibrant orange or a cozy caramel color, or a bright yellow, whatever color it is you're drawn too. Yes, you can absolutely have a yellow boardroom! This is your imagination, your inner boardroom, and it's personal to you. You get to choose it all because this is your inner personal space.

Here are some questions to get your imagination going. Feel free to journal, draw, paint, or sketch your boardroom:

- What does the room look like? What color are the walls? What type of flooring is there? Are there windows?

- What kind of lighting would you like? Would you like a soft light? Would you prefer it to be bright and vibrant?

- How is your boardroom decorated? Are there photos hung on the wall, artwork, trophies and awards, credentials or diplomas?

- What about the table? Will it be a long rectangular table, or maybe oval or round, where everybody is basically equal?

- What's the atmosphere around the table? Is it tense, loving, welcoming, cold, inviting, hostile, or confused?

- Is the lighting overhead bright and clear, or are some parts of the room—and perhaps some committee members—in shadow?

- Who shows up to your boardroom? What do they look like, and how do they address you?

Think of this as a personal boardroom meeting, where you're the CEO in charge of your introspective exploration, and follow these steps remembering that each meeting you call will be different, and that's perfectly fine.

Imagine you're in a boardroom where all important decisions are made. Invite all the different parts of yourself to come to this meeting and pay close attention to who and what shows up. At times your layers will show up as the input of emotions, fears, and judgments, and at other times, voices from the past, so to speak. Your critical layer, for example, may be the embodiment you carry forward of a parent who had a certain impact on you in your childhood.

You can always use this strategy and visualization to call a boardroom meeting with whatever situation or layer comes up for you. You're committing to making space for this questioning process, which is an essential process of self-discovery. From there, you are safe to question and to receive answers from all these parts of yourself, the members of your inner committee, your boardroom members. The better you become at questioning, the better you'll be at uncovering the layers that lie below your consciousness, dissolving their grip, and allowing more of your true self to shine through. Stay open to receiving them all.

Below is a mindset exercise to help prepare you for your inner boardroom meeting. Remember these guidelines as you take your seat at the head of the table. For now, practice taking the lead so you can get more comfortable. A more in-depth inner flow practice follows the end of the next chapter, which will help you navigate and prepare you further.

Exercise — Your Boardroom Meeting: Taking the Lead

Take the Lead

As the CEO of this inner boardroom, you have the authority to direct the agenda. Remember, you're in control. Each "meeting" might have different members present, based on their relevance to the situation or the challenge/discomfort you want to explore.

Engage in Dialogue

Start a conversation within yourself. Allow each part of you to express its thoughts and perspectives. Take notes on what each contributes to the discussion. Embrace the diversity of voices and viewpoints that arise. Stay open to what's being communicated.

Reflect and Integrate

Truly listen to all the parts of yourself. Reflect on the insights gained from each member. How would their input have directed your decisions in the past? How might they influence you now? It is up to you to choose.

Remain in Non-Judgment and True Listening

As you begin to step into your own boardroom and engage with this practice, don't be surprised if it's challenging at first. Please don't judge yourself if you struggle with it. I think you can probably guess why that would not be advisable; any judgment would only serve to create yet another layer, which is one you don't need and certainly don't want!

***

Remember, this is a process. There's no end goal or destination to this work. It's a journey and the mastery lies in the experience and awareness gained. If you simply attempted it, even for a moment, acknowledge yourself for it. Congratulations on your first foray into your inner world. The more you step into your boardroom, the more you'll be able to take your place at the head of the table and eventually truly choose your own life experience.

CHAPTER SIX

You Are Not Your Enemy

"Now that you know more about your own inner committee, and about the power of trust, awareness, and communication, you can begin to shift the relationship you have with yourself and experience more flow in life."

Now that you have more knowledge and are gaining more awareness, how do you begin to shift the relationship you have with yourself so that you're able to experience more flow in your life? The answer can be found in the exploration of your layers, through allowing yourself to see them, to view them without criticism, self-judgment, or rejection, and through either accepting them as the support system you're choosing to keep, or by consciously releasing them and opening yourself up further to the realness of your higher self.

As I began my inner exploration, I realized the internal conflict that had been within me all along. Spiritual or logical. Brain-based or intuition. I truly believed I had to choose, that I could only be one or the other. But once I began exploring, questioning, and opening myself up to discovery, my "either/or" rationale no longer made any sense.

Why was I restricting myself? Why couldn't I be all of who I was? The more I delved deeper, and the more I discovered my own layers, the more I understood that there was no distinction. I had followed my passion of a legal career, and yet, as I came to realize, my spiritual self had still remained a huge part of me. All this time, before the concussion, I thought I had to choose. I had been witnessing this internal tug of war, believing I had to compartmentalize and give precedence to one over the other. I thought those two sides that were in me and part of me couldn't co-exist.

The more I questioned this within myself, the more there was to question. And the more awareness I gained, the more I accepted what my higher self had always been calling me to embrace. I could be spiritual and connected within the deepest recesses of my self while retaining my logic and analytical curiosity, which had brought me so much richness and intellectual fun. In fact, as I realized over time, one enhanced the other.

Let me ask you this: Is there a part of you that you aren't paying attention to? Perhaps even denying within yourself? What might it be like for you if you didn't have to choose one or the other?

Acceptance vs. Judgment

"Through awareness, curiosity, and a non-judgmental approach,
layers can be examined simply for what they are."

As I went through my own discovery, I was initially shocked at how much I had been unaware of. I felt exposed and uneasy, and I didn't have this book to prepare me or anything else to help frame it for me. Still, I kept questioning, remaining open to what answers I received. I discovered that when we start asking these types of questions, we challenge ourselves— and we challenge our layers. Remember, layers aren't good or bad. All we are meant to do with them is look at them, come face-to-face with them, and observe them so they can be understood. It is important to know our layers and understand them, otherwise we'll constantly be judging them, and ourselves. Questioning paves the way to a better understanding of ourselves, and ultimately, to more freedom from our layers. Therefore, there is no reason to fear layers, hate them, or judge them. All you need to do is be curious, open, and ask questions.

So why are we not kinder to ourselves? Why are we not being grateful for how our layers showed up to sustain and support us through events and situations when we believed we needed them most?

Discovering our layers brings us back to that point in time, that experience when we were younger, less empowered, felt more vulnerable and dependent. In childhood, we're told what to do, how to think, and what's good and what's bad. These ideas come from both people who are responsible for us, and the environment around us. Whether knowingly or unknowingly, other people's ideas and beliefs are transmitted to us and absorbed by us. More often than not, like Sam (in Chapter Five), we carry those thoughts and core beliefs into adulthood. Even as grown adults, we still judge ourselves for supposed shortcomings that aren't based in present-time reality at all. It is why encountering these layers stirs up all kinds of uncomfortable thoughts and feelings, ones we prefer to avoid at all costs, even if it means judging ourselves for having them in the first place.

Our layers were originally formed as a misguided but ultimately well-meaning attempt at protecting us, keeping us safe, and ensuring our survival. Yet most of us will not offer any gratitude to our younger self for trying to keep us safe. Can you imagine yourself saying: "Oh, you allowed me to get here, you stabilized me, and you protected me in the only way you knew how. Thank you for creating this layer. I can take it from here."

Instead, we often tend to have an almost visceral negative reaction when we first discover layers within ourselves. If you pay attention, you may catch yourself thinking:

- This layer, blockage, limitation, or pain point should not be here.

- Why do I feel so uncomfortable? So vulnerable?
- Is something wrong with me?
- How do I make all of this go away?

Yet while we most often don't love the layers we uncover within ourselves, we often also resist letting them go. We still hold tight and resist releasing them out of fear—fear of what exploring them will be like, feel like, and whether we can withstand it. We are still trying to protect ourselves, even if it's from ourselves. It seems counterintuitive. Why hold on to these layers when so many of them were formed by a younger, less developed childhood mindset?

Think of it like this: Did you ever have a favorite t-shirt when you were young? The one you wished you could wear every day? Imagine holding on to it, and truly being upset that it no longer fits you today. Most of us can agree that trying to fit into that particular child-size t-shirt now as an adult is silly. The same is true for layers. They were meant for a certain time, event or situation, there to serve you at a time that perhaps now you have outgrown. Layers that were formed in early childhood and served us well then can only become constricting as we grow, just like that favorite t-shirt perfectly sized to fit a five-year-old child will no longer fit you as an adult.

What if instead of trying to fit ourselves into our outdated layers we could bring all of those beliefs to the forefront, consciously reevaluate them, and get to choose whether or not they hold true for us now? What if you were the one to set your own core beliefs and define yourself?

Here's a brief and easy challenge. Take a two-minute stop and lean into a layer. Step outside of the fear if you can, stay with the layer, and keep reminding yourself that this is only a holdover from an earlier time. As you explore whatever feelings come up for you, release whatever judgments arise.

Through awareness, curiosity, and a non-judgmental approach, layers can simply be examined for what they are. Then, you can choose what to do with a layer. You might decide that it actually doesn't align with your own values and beliefs, that it no longer serves you, or no longer helps you on your way to your true self. It is the awareness that leads to the choice, and it is the choosing, more than anything else, that leads you to a place of alignment, one in which your choices empower you to become the version of yourself you long to be and know you can be.

It is a protective position our brain takes to have us believe that disrupting "the way it's always been done" will lead to chaos. If things are working well enough, we don't want to mess it up with change, unless something drastic comes along and almost does it for us. This is why, for me, experiencing a concussion was more than enough to shake me up, unsettle me from the ways I had always thought and believed to be true, and begin to question whether there was another way. Our strong negative reaction to our layers is caused by this fear. We built the layer, and yet we think that if we get rid of it, or poke it, or even look at it, we will lose all sense of self.

Once you venture inside, however, you gain a deeper knowing that the opposite holds true. You will no longer be at odds with yourself or have incessant unhelpful mind chatter. When you go inside, you can rid yourself of limiting beliefs, mental constructs that you may not even agree with, and you will finally begin the journey to finding your true self.

Learning to Trust

"The areas of chronic unmet needs within us, where trust has been broken, are the places where each of us has the most work to do."

The foundation of every single relationship is trust. Without trust in others, we cannot surrender to a relationship or allow ourselves to enter the flow of joy, pleasure, and delight—the kind that only comes from the discovery of another person. We'll be making a deeper dive into the person-to-person dynamic in later chapters, but for now, let's focus on the most essential kind of trust: the one we nurture and develop with ourselves.

Even though the relationship we have with ourselves ought to be the one we hold as the most important relationship—and it is the foundation for all external relationships we'll ever have—many of us simply don't trust ourselves. Without trust in ourselves, our inner relationship can never be strong enough to sustain us. And when this happens, things fall apart.

Why does this happen? If having trust in yourself and building a relationship with yourself is so foundational, why is it that so many people struggle with it? Where does lack of trust in ourselves come from? To truly answer that, we need to go back to the beginning.

All of us are born with basic needs, and as helpless as we are at birth, we rely completely on those around us to meet those needs. As we grow, we become more and more self-sufficient, taking in all of the information we are shown or told, using it to create our worldview and our view of ourselves. Layers are formed when external experiences are internalized as core beliefs, and often, one of the biggest ways we form layers is around our basic needs that were never truly met.

When our basic needs, either physical or emotional, go unmet for too long, they don't fade away, get better, or stop being a need. They persist, and they often get deeper and more profound. When our needs remain unmet, we learn that we cannot trust others or even ourselves to fulfill our needs. We put layers in place because our first instincts are to survive, to be protected, and to feel safe. Layers create a scaffolding of sorts that holds us together in this time of distress. Over time, once a layer is formed, the need falls below our conscious awareness, and our survival brain takes over. In effect, we're saying to ourselves, "This reality and this feeling of the unmet need is untenable. It needs to be buried so I can stop feeling unsafe."

It may seem strange to realize that we are doing this to ourselves, but that's precisely what's happening. Because of these unmet needs, we form layers; because of the layers, we reinforce the idea that we cannot meet our needs and thus we cannot trust ourselves. Once we lose that trust in ourselves, we no longer listen to our needs and, if and when a need does make an appearance in our conscious mind, we will do everything we can to numb, limit, judge, quash or bury it ... but whatever we do, with that layer still in place, it will be much harder to trust ourselves and access that authentic place within us we yearn for.

Once that layer becomes ingrained in us, it begins to define us: who we are, what we think we need, and what we expect from the world around us. We're always subject to the loudest voice, the bossiest one, the meanest one, and we believe what it tells us wholeheartedly. The intrusive committee members of caution, criticism, and limitation take us over and prevent us from tapping into creativity, conciliation, courage, and curiosity. It's as if we're standing outside of the boardroom, getting yelled at like a mistreated junior staff member. And the worst part is, we can never leave, because it's us doing the yelling and us being yelled at.

To have a good relationship with yourself, you have to consciously shift how you think, feel, and treat yourself. After discovering your inner committee and starting to become aware of the internal conversations that are constantly happening within you and at you, you've likely identified areas where you wish your relationship with yourself could improve. How to make that change is entirely up to you. What do you want to nurture? And can you trust yourself to provide the nurturing that you need and deserve?

Whatever your struggle—body image, self-esteem, career, your partner, your children, your boundaries—every single one of those external things is, ultimately, a result of the yearning for an unmet need deep within yourself. These external issues become a distraction from the internal relationship you have with yourself—whatever it may be. The truth is, for a lot of us, just the idea of going inside can be frightening. Remember our brain is highly uncomfortable with the unknown, and venturing within, down to our subconscious layers, is definitely a world of unknowns.

The areas of chronic unmet needs within us, the places where trust has been shaken or broken, are the places where we have the most work to do. We are to take the first step within, accept the messages coming from our internal committee, be open to them, not judge them or hide from them. Explore them and understand what caused that trust to be broken. Only then can we begin to heal.

Joseph's Story — Trusting Enough to Go Within

Joseph came to me a few years ago. He was an older gentleman, who had heard me speak and had reached out for a session. He was sad, unhappy, and looking for a solution.

As we began talking, it became evident that his life had been anything but easy. He had been through a war, had always seen his parents fight, and had experienced many hardships. More than that, he himself had always chosen the path of struggle.

"I don't know how to make life easier for myself," he told me. "I just know I don't feel happy."

As I listened to him share his past and his struggles, I realized a lot of his unhappiness and sadness was focused outwardly. "What does make you happy?" I asked.

He couldn't answer this question. In fact, not only was he surprised but he also became visibly uneasy. My question seemed to have caught him off guard. As we kept speaking, he began realizing how much he had never questioned himself about how he felt. He had resisted going inward, for fear that it would make him feel even worse. Somehow, at some point in his life, he had come to believe he would only find darkness and even deeper difficult feelings, ones he feared he could get lost in. It's not uncommon for us to fear exploring a layer. We are afraid to explore, believing that it will bring on more of the same feelings: A "tip of the iceberg" type of thinking. If it feels bad at surface level, it must be worse underneath.

We continued talking and Joseph disclosed that he loved nature. As it turns out, he is also a visual type of learner. That gave me parameters to be able to reach him. I guided him through a visual of nature, during which I helped him reconnect to a more positive side of himself, one that was not wrought with pain. I helped him expand his imagination to a safer place within. It helped him realize there was also goodness inside of him, not just heaviness and darkness.

The meditation became a stepping stone to more sessions about layers. In future sessions we were able to start touching upon certain things from childhood. People don't always realize they have trauma. For the most part, they usually know if they have gone through a clearly definable traumatic event, but there can also be emotional or mental trauma that they are unaware of that still resides within them. Often it may not even be something we would intellectually consider traumatic today as an adult, but something that may have caused a layer to form, because we processed it as traumatic at the time it occurred.

Joseph had not trusted himself to have an internal landscape he could face. He had never trusted he could go inside, explore the sadness and unhappiness, work through it and release it. His lack of trust in himself had led to an almost intentional lack of awareness, because his fear of going inside had always felt greater. It isn't always an aspect of self-trust we think about, but often this limiting belief prevents us from reconnecting with our true self.

Emotional Needs

"The fulfillment of emotional needs is as essential and vital as addressing hunger and thirst, but often much harder to achieve."

Many of my clients start off their growth journey needing to work on accepting that they have emotional needs, respecting them, and then setting boundaries so others respect them as well. The struggle that I see time and time again is the perception we seem to have that any emotional need is a sign of weakness and something we need to just get over and move on from. Chances are this is the message we received at some point in our lives, and as adults we now continue that same message ourselves, often on autopilot.

When an emotional layer is in place within us, it may tell us that we are not deserving of love and affection, that we will always be second-best, that we aren't desirable, attractive, or interesting enough to have the partner we wish we could have. Where do these ideas even come from, and why do we accept any of them as true? We won't know the answer to any of these questions unless we check in with ourselves. But, in a sense, each of us has the ability—and I would say the responsibility—to check in, call a quick meeting, and scan ourselves. "Where am I at today? Is anything coming up? What does my body need? How can I meet those needs?" To begin even asking these questions rebuilds trust. We can start to show ourselves that we really can listen, provide for ourselves, and meet our own needs. And it all starts with going inward.

We are that conscious part of ourselves. To look within and ask those questions takes courage. Once you are brave enough to look within, doors open offering tremendous gifts and clarity. Once you are ready to tend to your inner committee, the power no longer belongs to the layers sitting at the table. That power, your power, is returned back to you. Remember, just as we are not our brains, we are not our bodies, either. We are not our emotions, nor our hunger or thirst. We are the observer that asks those questions, the part that both rises above our needs and cares for them, looking within ourselves and assessing what has been met and what remains unmet.

Stuart's Story — Living with Regret

A few years ago, my client Stuart came to me saying, "My biggest wish is to buy a house for myself and my family. My biggest regret is that I haven't." He felt that he had failed his wife and twelve-year-old daughter for not being able to fulfill this one goal.

Stuart felt badly about himself, and it went beyond simply not being a homeowner. It went to the core of his need to provide. Somewhere in his mind, that need to be a provider had been translated to "own a home," and had become entrenched as a deeply subconscious layer for him. Despite everything else he had achieved and experienced, he felt increasingly like he had failed his family.

I asked Stuart, "What would happen if you changed your thought from, 'My biggest regret is not owning a house' to 'My biggest regret is that I haven't been working very long hours all these years'?"

Stuart had a puzzled look on his face.

"Humor me for a moment," I said. "Now add 'My biggest wish is to shift my mindset to that of a workaholic, so I can feel compelled to work longer hours and harder every day, and afford the house that I want for my family.'"

His face dropped, and I could almost see his mind start racing. "Oh, hold on a second. That doesn't feel right to me. I don't want to work crazy hours. I wouldn't be able to take my daughter to dance classes, spend leisure time in the country, or have dinner every night with my family. I would have no time or energy for them. I would see them so much less."

"Would you want to buy the house," I asked, "when it means you will have to work more hours to get it, take out some loans for the down payment, and take on a mortgage? What does that look like for you?"

"You know what?" Stuart replied. "That wouldn't make me feel good or happy. I would never be home for them. I don't know why I never saw it like that before."

Stuart had discovered a limiting belief that owning his own home meant taking care of his family. Until he was able to call his inner committee and hear who was running the show, Stuart just kept going after this idea, chasing this want, believing it was a need.

The boardroom exercise had brought him clarity, and the clarity had brought him freedom. Through our session together, Stuart discovered that it wasn't the house he needed, it was the deeper need to provide. His love languages were quality time and acts of service, neither of which he would be able to express if he worked twelve to fourteen hours a day. He would have to be absent from his family, and he neither needed nor wanted that.

When Stuart considered this trade-off, he realized he was happy where he was. He was able to spend time with his daughter and had a close relationship with his wife. As soon as he held his boardroom meeting and became aware of his underlying layer, Stuart no longer wanted the house, and instead ended up finding new ways to become even more present in the lives of his daughter and wife. He chose to do what he needed, and what he needed became what he wanted.

Stuart returned a few weeks later and told me, "You know, I feel so much better. I live in the same place and I have the same lifestyle." He had begun painting a few rooms in warmer tones, which changed the vibe, got some plants for their living room, and planned on getting some new furniture and paintings. He allowed himself to love where he lived, and his whole perspective shifted.

"My enjoyment of life has improved, and yet nothing has changed," he said.

In reality, everything had changed—from the inside out, that is. Stuart was finally free of his belief that getting his family a bigger house was the only way to fill his need to provide. This belief had plagued him for years and made him miserable, all without his permission or even awareness. When he did call a meeting in his boardroom, he discovered that he neither needed nor wanted the house. What he truly needed was the opportunity and time to be present for his family, and once that need was met, the want was no longer relevant.

This is the kind of clarity that can arise when we take pause, call our own boardroom meeting, and check in with our inner committee. Until we can create the space to engage with our own inner world with curiosity and openness, we may never know that the things we believe are needs in our lives are really just wants. Understanding the distinction between the two, and the connection needs and wants have with our layers, can help make the difference between a life lived in eternal striving mode and one lived with peace, contentment, and self-awareness.

Needs vs. Wants

"Unmet wants will come and go, but unmet needs will continue to be unmet until they are fulfilled."

When you don't express your voice fully to yourself—just like when you ignore, silence, or neglect the needs of a child, spouse, or friend, causing a rift in the relationship due to a lack of trust—your inner self will rebel, and it will grow to resent you. It forms a layer, and later on it comes out in a different form of communication. Often, when people don't listen to or meet their own needs and don't give attention to whatever is going on inside of them, a part of them will eventually speak up. It may come in the form of critical thoughts, emotional pain, or even physical discomfort.

In Chapter Four, we began talking about the difference between needs and wants, and how they can affect us. We began to understand that prolonged unmet needs never go away, but they turn into wants that may or may not be related and give us a false feeling of power over our lives. And we know by now that no matter what we do and how much we strive to meet our wants, this will never really resolve our needs at all. With all that in mind, let's delve a little deeper and look at what's going on behind the scenes.

Rationally, we do know that wants and needs are not the same thing. Hunger is a need, and so is thirst; we need calories and energy to keep functioning, and we need water to stay alive. A craving for a slice of chocolate cake or a Diet Coke (yes, I used to be hooked on Diet Coke), however, is not a need. We may want that flavor, but what our bodies need in that moment is fuel for energy and hydration.

While the example of hunger is simplistic, we can imagine the same pattern in other areas of our lives, where wants and needs are not as obvious. How can we tell the difference? When we say or believe that we either need or want something, what we need to explore is whether we equally need or want to go through the process to get us there. Whether it is the thing itself we are drawn to, or merely the idea of it. We may want to be something, but do we also want to take the actions and invest the time and energy necessary to become that something? How does the idea of walking that path and taking those steps settle in our physical bodies? Does it make us feel anxious and resistant, or excited and curious? Do we need it, or do we merely want it—and if we discover we want it rather than need it, then what do we actually need?

When Stuart realized that he did not want to choose the lifestyle of long hours and overtime that would be necessary to make the kind of money for a house, he could see more clearly what it was he did want: to be present for his family. Ironically, the process that would have been required for him to get that house is specifically what would have prevented him from ever being present in his family's life in the way he needed. If he had done it and bought the house, it never would have been satisfying. How could it? It wasn't what he truly needed.

Awareness gives us the ability to consciously separate our needs from wants, and makes it easier to meet the needs. This is a process that is deeply personal to everyone. But there is one common factor to this process of discernment: Unmet wants will fade, but unmet needs will continue to be unmet until they are fulfilled. And the pain caused by an unmet need has to go somewhere. In the case of unmet physical needs, there are real and dangerous physical consequences. If we don't eat, we starve. In the case of unmet emotional needs, there are consequences as well, and they can be just as profound and damaging. When we are not "fed" with the emotional nourishment we need, we starve in a different way.

When we lack awareness and self-ownership, the decisions get made anyway. It's as if our inner committee had an early board meeting that we were not even invited to. Everything gets decided without our conscious input, and we are just told of the outcome. Imagine a craving, negative thought, or fear suddenly pops into your head, seemingly out of nowhere. Each one of these is the result of a meeting, where some want or need ended up taking precedence, one you may not even agree with or believe in. Since all this takes place below your awareness level, you end up being stuck with the concluding thought or emotion, taking it at face value and going about your day often feeling pained and disempowered, even defeated at times. Imagine how much simpler it could be if you had the awareness and could consciously choose the thought to have or emotion to feel. Imagine how much freer you might feel knowing that you have the choice to remove a layer if it's no longer serving you.

You can be. In fact, it is your right to be.

Our needs are what we inherently are born with, and what we come into this world with. On the other hand, our wants are created by us as we gain awareness of the world around us, what we see others have, and what we believe would make us happy. Without this awareness and discernment, however, we often bypass our needs so we can run after our wants, not only because they seem more exciting (and they're external to us) but also because we are aware of them, since we consciously created them through desire. Meanwhile, needs are intrinsic to us. They are part of our DNA, as is our capacity to meet them. Recognizing that we are given the sacred responsibility to meet them is the first step to everything else.

When you consciously create whatever meets your needs, then your wants are simply just that: wants. They're no longer created by your layers as a way to mask your needs or replace them in the hopes that if you can meet that want, the need would be quelled. You can trust yourself to choose your wants, and you can trust yourself to choose how, if, and when to go about accomplishing them.

You are attached to yourself for life, and your personality, your soul, your body, all of the inner aspects of you are meant to work together to accomplish your great goal here on earth. It is both a duty and a privilege to be able to go inside, reclaim power over your layers, and be able to drive your own choices. You are meant to put your tremendous power toward what you truly need, not just what you want in this moment to numb, distract, or deny a deeper yearning. By developing a relationship with your inner committee and working through your own boardroom exercises, you can begin to make conscious choices. From there, you can continue to discover your true self, reacquaint yourself with your own needs, and learn how to live aligned.

What Higher Self-Care Really Looks Like

"There will always be things that others cannot do for us, no matter how hard they try or how much we wish they could. Those are ultimately our best self-care opportunities."

So, what kind of relationship do you want to have with yourself? If you could shape it (and you can) then what would it look like? If your truest, deepest needs were met, how much would that change every other aspect of your life?

In the last chapter, I encouraged you to begin to engage in conversation with your own inner committee and start to dip your toe in the water. As you go deeper and as that trust is rebuilt within you, you will start to see more aspects of your life where needs and wants may have gotten confused for each other. Even if you have tried in the past to meet a need and take care of yourself, you may have gained awareness that, in reality, it wasn't a need at all.

There is a lot that is said about self-care, and while the sentiment is often good, the actual specifics often address surface-level care, such as an organic face cream or a new hair product. Real self-care is the practice of caring for the self in a way that meets your core needs—physical, mental, emotional, and spiritual—and prepares you to receive what the outside world has to offer. It is crucial to learn to identify what those needs are for you, how they show up, and what's required of you to meet them. Are you a person that needs more sleep, more quiet, more mental stimulation, or a different balance? What makes you feel free, fulfilled? Can you get to know yourself well enough to know what you need to feel whole and how to provide for yourself? The outside world cannot do it for you.

This is a lifelong process and, as you get better at it, every single relationship you have with another living being becomes enriched because you are more fully yourself. When you're responsible for meeting your own needs, you hold yourself accountable for them, prioritize them in a way you never considered before, and use the awareness and trust you have built to be more aligned with what you actually want to be doing in life. You're in flow, with eyes and hearts wide open, engaging in the great, creative adventure of life, rather than swimming frantically against the current.

You might instinctively say, "Well, it's just not possible to have every single need met. That's unrealistic." But I am here to tell you that not only is it possible but it's essential—and it's in your hands. We must take care of our own needs because it's impossible for anyone else to do so. There is a reason why airplane instructions tell people to secure their own oxygen masks before others'. How can you help others when your own immediate needs are not met? Women, and especially those in a mothering or caregiving role, are constantly told by society to put their own needs aside and prioritize the needs of others. And it's true that sometimes this is necessary. For example, the pressing need of our hunger or thirst must give way to the more urgent need of saving a child from immediate danger. But long-term self-denial is no virtue. We need to eat, sleep, tend to our wellbeing, and create balance. Constantly ignoring our needs will not serve us, and it will not serve those who depend on us, either.

This self-denial over a long period of time drains us, and it leads us to expect others to fulfill our needs, which they can't. Others cannot eat or sleep for us, or take in oxygen, nutrition, and hydration on our behalf. We must do all of this ourselves. The same is true for our deepest emotional needs, and yet we often tend to expect others to fulfill them for us, but it's just not possible. The interactions we have with others are wonderful added bonuses to the soul experience, but there will always be things that others cannot do for us, no matter how hard they try or how much we wish they could.

While it is vital to put our own needs first, why does it feel difficult? When you read these words, do you feel a gut-punch reaction, a resistance to it? Why is it we feel incapable of meeting our own needs? Why do we expect or believe others can meet our needs for us better than we can?

This expectation for others to take care of things for us that they cannot help with, in turn, leads to disappointment, resentment, a sense of emptiness, distress, and ultimately disempowerment. We each have a duty to ourselves to get to know our needs and tend to them. This means checking in, being aware, and being radically honest about what we truly, deeply need.

Preparing for the Great Adventure

*"When the foundation of your relationship is built on
deep inner trust, you can venture out into the world, and
be prepared for anything that comes your way."*

Every single external struggle, whether it's related to relationships, career, family, children, partner, or boundaries, is ultimately a result of the yearning we have for an unmet need deep within ourselves. And it all comes back to our layers.

These external issues become a distraction from the relationship we have with ourselves—if we even know we have one at all. Despite it being the most important and fundamental relationship we will ever have, we do everything in the world to distract ourselves from examining it.

There are two main ways we do this: we either detach and try to distance ourselves from the feelings of our unmet needs, or we numb ourselves by taking on so much that there simply isn't time to stop and consider our needs at all. We often set ourselves up for disappointment by expecting others to do things for us that we are unwilling or feel incapable of doing. It's not something we do on purpose, though. We just don't realize that we're expecting others to meet our needs when it's simply not possible for them to do so.

This isn't to say that others don't add richness and meaning to our lives, or that we can't trust or rely on anyone, or that we can't form close bonds with the ones we love and engage in an interdependence that adds joy to our human experience. Far from it. But if you start with the premise that you have internal needs that only you can meet, what would change in your life? If you went into every relationship knowing this, what kind of relationships would you nurture, and which ones would you separate yourself from? This is a genuine question. Now that you have done all this inner work, you're in a better position to show up for life and for others very differently from how you did before. When the foundation of your own internal relationship is built on deep self-trust, you can venture out into the world and be prepared for anything that comes your way.

So often we cling to the layers, routines, and old beliefs because so much of the world is seemingly uncertain, unknowable, dangerous, and threatening. We don't know what the future will bring, but we look to have some kind of control over it, even if it's just the illusion of control. Layers give us that illusion, but that's all they often are: an illusion. They do not provide real control or any certainty, and they most likely are not serving us now.

Imagine for a moment that you're preparing to take a hiking trip somewhere you have never been before. What would it take to truly be prepared for it? You would need proper gear, of course, and you would need to know the trail, and the weather, and the wildlife situation in that area. You would do everything to make sure you have what you need and set yourself up for success, so you're better equipped to handle whatever comes to you on the trail.

In the same way, taking care of yourself is neither selfish nor selfless, it is a responsibility you have to yourself. It is part of your relationship with yourself. It isn't about being self-centered, self-absorbed, or inconsiderate of others, it's about being self-sufficient. It's important you show up as you, fully and completely—as that is your greatest strength. With self-awareness, care, and trust in yourself, you can ready yourself to step out into the world, begin your great adventure, and go as far as you choose.

Exercise — Your Boardroom Meeting: Inner Flow Practice

As you work to rebuild trust within yourself and begin to see some of your layers, remember to create a judgment-free space, one free of any rigidity and black-and-white, good-or-bad thinking. Layers are inherently rigid, but they start dissolving once discovered, observed, and questioned. The counter to allowing your layers to control you is openness, access to yourself, and flow. This exercise will help you get into this state of inner flow more easily.

Preparing Your Space

Take some time to set aside a distraction-free space in whatever way that means for you. It might mean sitting in quiet contemplation, with or without calm music, peaceful soundscapes, or a scent that's calming to you. Or it could mean taking a peaceful walk in nature. Or if you're like me, a nice bubble bath. Whatever feels right and correct for you—you don't have to be an advanced yogi or expert at meditation. Just follow the guidance of your feelings as you turn your attention inward.

Initial Connection

- Take a few moments to settle into your chosen space.
- Take a few moments to settle into yourself.
- Trust your intuition.

Welcoming Your Inner Committee

- Call together your inner thoughts, feelings, and layers. Allow whatever comes up.
- Don't worry if there's resistance or skepticism. If it feels silly at first, you're probably doing it right. It's all part of the process.
- Embrace any thoughts, no matter how insignificant or uncomfortable they may seem.
- Create an open and accepting atmosphere for self-exploration. It's okay to acknowledge and continue to invite any feelings or emotions as they arise.

From this place of openness and honesty, as you observe a layer, instead of rejecting, judging, or closing yourself off to it, can you explore it a little deeper?

Acknowledge, Invite, Explore

- Become aware of every thought or feeling as it surfaces. Acknowledge each one of them.
- Allow yourself to fully experience any emotions that arise.
- Embrace the natural ebb and flow of your inner landscape.
- Gently invite deeper layers of thoughts and emotions.
- Avoid self-criticism or judgment; every thought is valid.
- Observe without attachment; simply witness the unfolding.

Use your breath as an anchor to stay present. Inhale calmness, exhale any tension or resistance. Maintain a sense of curiosity and acceptance throughout.

Mindful Engagement

- Engage with your inner committee with understanding and openness.
- Ask questions, seek clarity, and listen deeply.
- Spend as much time as it feels right to you, exploring your inner world.

Troubleshooting Internal Resistance

If you encounter any resistance at any time, a great way to circumvent it is to ask, "What if?" instead of rushing to judge. A mind that's playful, curious, and open is not stuck in fear and judgment.

- What if I could be comfortable with this feeling?
- What if I could shed this layer?

After each question, ask yourself what would then be different for you. As you explore these hypotheticals, you will likely find that your creative mind may become more comfortable with them. Indeed, since most layers form at a young age, they ought to be approached with compassion, not judgment. Having compassion for the child you were when that layer was formed means thanking yourself for providing safety when the outside world would not or could not do so for you. But the "protection" you needed when you were a child may no longer be necessary for you now that you are grown. You can examine these layers at any time, keep them, or discard them as you wish. You are the one in control.

Remember, this inner flow practice is a flexible and personal journey. Adapt it to your preferences and needs, and feel free to explore and expand upon the steps as you become more comfortable with the process.

Integration

To end this practice, return to your boardroom and thank the inner committee members that showed up for you—yes, all of them, especially the ones you wish never existed. They all have important messages to convey to you. Slowly transition your awareness back to the present moment. Feel the connection between your inner experience and the outer world. Breathe deeply, move your body, and take some time to journal out your experience and the insights you've received.

***

As you continue to become familiar with your boardroom and inner committee, you will grow more prepared to meet your layers as they arise. You may begin to notice patterns and themes. These will ultimately help you to identify your own primary layer.

CHAPTER SEVEN

Layers of Protection

"Having the courage to let go of a protective layer, even if only for a brief moment, starts the process of loosening its grip and, for that moment, you will have begun to walk the path back to your true self."

W e have spent three whole chapters talking about the importance of understanding, developing, and nurturing a relationship with ourselves. We have done so because the relationship with our self is the most profound and important relationship that each of us will ever have. You're learning to see your own layers, explore your internal landscape, identify protective mechanisms that no longer serve you, navigate those layers, and check in with yourself to live with more self-awareness and authenticity. Clearing layers and nurturing an authentic inner relationship is the way you will be able to live in alignment, to face what comes with a sense of openness and adventure, and to be truly aware of all that is you and within you. Ultimately, it is about giving yourself full permission to live as your true self.

Together, you and I have begun to explore and understand that— even if, like me, you love your brain—you're absolutely not your brain, and you're definitely not your layers. You have begun doing the awareness work to regain a seat at the head of the table within your own inner boardroom, and you're practicing working on listening to and honoring the requests that your inner committee members bring to your attention. Hopefully, you have begun to work through some layers and patterns in your past that no longer serve you. These are all wonderful and essential first steps in the process of *No More Layers*.

Through the process of exploring your own layers and considering (without judgment) what arises as you look within yourself, it is likely that you will begin to see a pattern emerge. There probably is a recurring theme underlying your layers and woven into your life. Whatever that core theme may be, it can tell you quite a lot about what you believe to be true about yourself, about others, and about life itself.

We have already explored just a bit about the concept of these core layers, or primary layers of protection. Now, it's time to go a little deeper to find out what our new discoveries could teach us about ourselves, before we continue on to those external interactions and our relationships with others.

My Primary Layer of Protection

For as long as I could remember, I had struggled with the belief that I had to strive to be perfect. What I had understood from my environment was that anything less than perfect was unacceptable, inadequate, and simply not good enough. As a result, I formed a layer early on around perfection, and as I accumulated more layers along the way, most, if not all of them, were based on that foundational layer.

Despite the discomfort it caused and the challenge it presented, I continued on that path. My upbringing and choice of careers certainly contributed to that belief, but in some way, I think continuing to strive for perfection felt familiar and safe. I knew what to expect when I looked at the world and myself through that lens. I would just keep trying to be better. What I didn't realize at the time was that, in doing so, I was never giving myself a break or allowing myself to pause. Because of this core layer, I never saw that " good enough" was actually good enough. In fact, success brought me pressure because I mistakenly believed that I could always do better and, therefore, should do better. This, in turn, reinforced the initial core layer. Perfection—or near-perfection—was an impossible standard and, in reality, one that can never be met. I was intuitively aware of this, but my core layer would often take over, and for a long time it felt like continuing on the path of perfection was my only option.

The truth is that the pursuit of perfection is futile, misguided, and actually undesirable. As we discover our own inner landscape, we learn and accept that we don't have to be perfect. In fact, it's impossible to be perfect. It is a path that can only lead to more layers because its very unattainability keeps us stuck and loops us into a constant cycle of restlessly seeking more. We strive for perfection, we inherently don't achieve it, and then we strive some more. We do this over and over and over, building and reinforcing layers within ourselves about ourselves, layers that tell us we are inadequate, not enough, flawed, or even worthless. Releasing this idea of perfection frees us up to discover more about who we really are and what we are truly capable of. The true path is never perfection. It is never the one that asks you to become someone or something else, based on some externalized ideal. The true path is the one that makes you more *you*. Isn't that a relief? When I finally realized and embraced this, I felt freer. Try it. Breathe it in for a moment. What if you didn't have to do everything perfectly? What if, instead, you could feel perfectly comfortable with doing things well, and you could allow yourself to just be "good enough"? Try it for a moment. Can you accept being good at some things and perhaps not so good at others? Imagine if your goal were simply to be more authentically you.

There's so much pressure on us to appear perfect, perform better, have more, do more, and be more than the next person. Perfect hair that takes hours to get just right. Makeup that makes you look as if you aren't wearing any and somehow just tumbled out of bed looking that way. Caring just enough but not too much, eating too much, eating too little, having a six pack for abs, being the last one at the office taking on the biggest projects, and the list goes on and on. "How can I be the best" is a thought that preoccupies us on a daily basis.

Before I understood this, I was stuck in a mindset that kept me striving for perfection, all the while believing I was feeling accomplished. Though misguided, it did force me into a direction, especially while working in a highly competitive legal environment. It was also what I saw around me and, at the time, it felt like the only way to go. This became my baseline. What I didn't realize was that the goal had become more important than making space for me and honoring my own needs. While I thought I was striving to empower myself, my brain was actually keeping me on a path that could only disempower me. I was working so hard to reach an unattainable goal.

Today, I gently laugh at those times. I admit I had not yet found my true authentic path. I can recall a time when I was fresh out of law school being in that striving mode. I was working as a junior at a national law firm, overworked like everyone else, constantly focused on improving my performance. While I thrived on the intellectual stimulation, as I think back it's very clear to me that I was under the rule of my layer of perfection. It was calling the shots.

In one instance, a senior partner had asked me to take on the drafting of a court of appeals memorandum. I had no previous knowledge of the case, it was in an area of law that was new to me, and I had never drafted anything for the court of appeals—and, as things always are when you're a junior, it was urgent. You get the picture. My plate was already full, and time can only be stretched so much. Was I lacking confidence? Could I do it? I can remember the feeling as I stood in the partner's office. The first thing that came to my mind was, "I wish the senior partner hadn't found me that day and hadn't asked me to take this on." The brain is funny that way. Sometimes when it's not ready to process, it stalls and hopes for a moment it could theoretically wish things away. It never works.

I was unsure what to do. What would it say about me if I couldn't do it? What would it say about me if, because of my lack of experience in this area, I made a critical mistake?

Here was a place where my soul and my brain were at odds. On the one hand, I believed this was a huge opportunity to stretch my comfort zone. On the other, I felt something in my gut telling me that this wasn't something I was ready for or had the expertise to take on. Because I was still under the layer of perfection, though, I ignored this gut instinct and took on the task, eager to prove myself.

Almost immediately thereafter, I realized I'd made a mistake. Not only had this request been way outside my comfort zone; it really was beyond my level of experience. As I sat down to work on it, I realized fairly quickly that I was utterly out of my element. I had to do what was in the best interest of the case. I mustered up my courage and returned to the senior partner the next day, telling her I couldn't do it. I knew how bad it would look, but I felt I had to own the moment and explain why I felt giving it back to her was the right thing to do. As you can imagine, she wasn't pleased. But what caught me by surprise was that her colleagues came to my defense. They felt I had acted diligently and responsibly, and my reasons for stepping away were valid. I was relieved but shaken up. Why had I put myself in this situation in the first place?

Sometimes the challenge is not to say yes, but actually to know when to say no. That was a big one for me. I would often say yes to things, and in hindsight realize that a no would have served me better. I felt the fear starting to creep up. Did this mean I couldn't trust myself to make good decisions? So many questions popped up, and yet so little clarity. I have always been the person who grabbed at every growth opportunity, stretched herself, and wanted to sink her teeth into growing more and more into the experiences of life. And now that person was experiencing an inner tug of war. Pulled by my drive to say yes on the one hand and listening to my gut and inner knowing on the other.

Realizing the tug of war and allowing for my heart to be heard was a victory for me that day. I learned there was more than one part of me, and I owed it to myself to hear it out.

Having the courage that day to let go of that layer of perfection, if but for a brief moment, started the process of loosening that layer's grip. For a moment, it gave me permission to honor myself, and I knew I had courageously done the right thing. Though it would take many more years to get there, I had begun walking the path back to my true self.

Brain Loops

I have shared before that the reason why our most primitive, protective brain fears and hates change is because change represents the unknown, and unknown for the brain means potential danger, and danger could ultimately lead to death. But what does that mean in practice? Paradoxically, for my brain it meant it was actually "safer" to continue to repeat this well-known, well-rehearsed pattern, one that it could run on autopilot. Anything other than that loop was like a big red danger sign, and my brain wanted, more than anything, to keep me safe and alive. After all, that is the brain's primary directive.

With my layer of perfection, striving for perfection made my brain feel safe. It kept me going in a specific direction, one where I always worked and tried harder, and though perfection could never be attained, striving delineated a clear linear path, one that allowed for very little deviation. I would never reach a place of perfection, just keep "striving for it." As a result, I had also never considered a different way of doing things and approaching life, one that could serve me better. It felt like I had a clear direction and a clear sense of self. In some convoluted way, one only the brain could have concocted, it was trying to keep me in its own loop of "safety", avoiding anything unknown, truly new, or different.

While this recurring theme did keep me focused, it also created unnecessary hardships. Even if I were ever to reach that goal of being perfect, just for a moment, I intuitively knew it wasn't sustainable. It was like chasing something that could never be. This perception of needing to be perfect caused me to live with the belief that I was never where I should be. It always felt like I should be better than I was, somewhere else, further ahead.

Does this sound familiar? Do you recognize this or any other underlying theme in your personal life? In your career? I invite you to take a moment and check in with your own body. How does it feel to be in overreach mode? Where in your body do you feel it most? Do you experience a sensation of uneasiness in your gut area, or does your throat get tight with unspoken words? Take a moment to sit with yourself and journal or visualize where this physically exists within you. What might it be trying to tell you?

A Mental Weight Lifted

For years I lived in overstretch, going to the limits of my capacity in order to meet the expectations of those around me, which, over time and unbeknownst to me, had become my own expectations of myself as well. It didn't always feel good, but I didn't know any other way. After I literally got hit over the head and began to unpack all of those unconscious expectations and beliefs, my whole approach to myself changed.

A few years earlier, I'd had a fascinating conversation with someone who was very much in tune with his own spirituality. This was at a time in my life when I still held those two parts of myself, spiritual and logical, as separate and incompatible. This person didn't know me, but he told me something I will never forget: "You hold yourself to such a high standard, and you're so hard on yourself to the point that your brain has managed to convince you that you're not being hard on yourself."

I did a double take. While intellectually I was trying to process what he had just said, intuitively it made perfect sense. I somehow just knew what he said was true. He had connected the dots for me.

It was a moment of revelation, a true "Aha!" moment. The relief it brought me was surprising and unexpected. It felt like a weight had been lifted off my shoulders. At that moment, I realized the "loops of safety" that brains were capable of creating. My brain had decided that being so hard on myself was the right thing to do, and it was intent with all its might to keep me in the loop of that belief. That day, something inside of me began to shift. Although it would take me years and a concussion to truly get there, I began to understand that there was a lot more at play in my internal landscape than I was aware of, but believing I needed to be perfect no longer gripped me in the way it had. At that moment, I felt a sense of freedom. I could ease up, let loose. It was as if simply being aware of this loop had finally provided me the freedom to choose to slow down and begin the road to discovering my own layers that ultimately brought me to where I am today.

We all have these loops, these cycles we get stuck in, are unaware of, and therefore never stop to question. It comes with being human, but it's meant to be overridden. There comes a time in each of our lives where we have to ask ourselves: is this what I want, or do I want something else in life? If you could choose (and you can), what would you choose?

The Courage to Look Within

"Once your layers around a core belief are dissolved, you will discover more of yourself underneath them. YOU, in all of your power, have always been there."

Our sense of self, and our entire self-worth, is measured against our layers. Identifying the common theme that's specific to you and your journey helps you by providing a clearer perspective of yourself and a more objective view of what really might be going on. Perhaps you resonate with my experience of striving for unattainable perfection, or perhaps the common underlying theme of your layers is different. Whatever it is for you, you have the power to pause for a moment, gain awareness, and question these patterns you may see with a curious and open mind. In the clients I work with, I have seen a few common core themes. One I have seen on numerous occasions revolves around being intelligent enough. It's surprisingly common and holds true even for high-achieving professionals who are at the top of their field, receive awards, and whose achievements you would imagine would make anyone feel smart and successful. Internally, however, these clients have a fear that they aren't smart enough, capable enough, or good enough.

George's Story — Being Good Enough

When George came to me, he was working in the management world as a consultant. He had always wanted a more permanent position but never seemed able to land one. He was experienced, well-regarded, and had a keen understanding of the vision of his clients and how to translate it into numbers, strategies, and efficiencies. After many years as a consultant and ten months into a contract with a new client, he was offered a full-time position as their Vice President of Operations. He came to see me, almost upset. "They offered me the position of VP of Operations," he said in a strange tone. "I can't do it." This was good. Whatever layer had been holding him back from accepting a permanent job, which he had wanted for the past several years, was about to surface. We had previously discussed different strategies for such an offer, and yet now that it had become a reality, something else entirely had taken over. "I know," he added. "Time to hold a boardroom meeting."

His members showed up as follows: excitement, a sense of pride, hesitation, and, as expected, lots and lots of fear. Fear's voice was very loud, the loudest in fact. We gently leaned into it together. As we uncovered the layers, he realized his biggest fear was to be "found out." You see, as a young student, George had been diagnosed with a learning disability early on in his academic life, and he had always felt his teachers treated him as less capable and certainly less intelligent. As he uncovered in our work together, he had chosen to be a consultant out of fear of having a boss to answer to. If you are trying to make sense of it, I completely understand. Layers are not rational. They do however stem from a deeply rooted fear. One that is usually set by a series of past experiences that served to reinforce them. George could not fathom having to relive that dreaded feeling from yet another person in authority. Though he was clearly capable, he had unknowingly allowed his limiting belief to direct the course of his professional career. He had ultimately disempowered himself, not realizing he had developed an expertise and had become, in his own right, a person of authority.

George's story is not unique. This can show up in other scenarios as well, whether in people believing they aren't fun enough, or well-spoken, or mathematically inclined, or athletic, or that whatever success they do achieve is just a lucky break. When a theme to a layer shows up again and again, it's an indication of something very deep that remained hidden and protected, and therefore will take some courage to approach.

As we know, courage can take many forms. There is the overt action-based physical courage of running into a burning building to rescue someone, the courage it takes to stand up against injustice, or even to step onto a stage. But it also takes deep courage to delve within ourselves. The mere idea of going within toward what is consciously unknown, to explore our layers, can elicit fear. Even before we empower ourselves to make different choices in our lives, simply bearing witness to those layers is an act of bravery. It means we're preparing to face our previous and existing vulnerabilities. When there is a common theme underlying many of our layers, that process can feel even more daunting, not because it actually is, but because that underlying theme can feel like one giant layer. In reality it isn't. It simply indicates an area where our subconscious believes we needed extra protection at that time.

As I went through my own journey, I understood that all of those layers had been put there to protect me, and that I had subconsciously constructed them at a time when I felt unsafe and believed I needed protection. Once your eyes become open to it, the awareness cannot be taken away. The work is never futile. Looking within and discovering that those layers had served their purpose and protected me to the point I now no longer needed them was the beginning of my path to inner freedom. The same will hold true for each of you, too.

And yes, it can be scary. After all, you are seeing the most vulnerable, tender parts of yourself, the parts that have long been categorized as shameful, unworthy, weak, stupid, bad, or wrong. It dredges up very old, deep hurt and wounds. The courage you are asked to muster is to stay open, curious, and inquisitive. In other words, delve inward and become aware. That's it. This process isn't about going out and doing things completely differently, walking across coals or tight ropes, faking it till you make it, or radically transforming your external behaviors. Instead, this process is about being adventurous enough to ask the deeper questions.

If we step out and make radical changes, the gravitational pull of self-doubt is so strong that we often get swept right back into our old patterns and layers. However, if we dare to press pause, to simply consider that things might be some other way than what we believe, or are used to, what would that be like? If we didn't have to be perfect, if that truly wasn't a requirement, what would change? If you really felt lovable and worthy of love, how would that feel? Could you accept the possibility that you really are intelligent, capable, and simply enough?

If you are like me, at times that process can feel like an adventure into the wild and unknown. Who knows what layers will be there? But when you tap into your courage, when you become curious and playful about the process of discovery, it becomes an awe-inspiring journey.

The Message in Our Pain Points

*"When a theme to a layer shows up again and again, it
indicates something very deep and is core to a limiting belief,
the truthfulness of which you ought to consider, especially if
that belief has led you to outcomes you never wanted."*

Having the courage to look within means having the curiosity to question and play, and then gaining the awareness of who you truly are.

So, who are you, really? I know it sounds like a strange question, but as you begin to tap into your innate freedom of choice and the power to choose what to do with your layers, what kind of life will you choose for yourself? How can you boldly venture within yourself, own who you are, if you don't know who you are? Seeking out new possibilities means opening up to a place of joy and adventure. But how do you allow for this new openness, this possibility, when a layer within you seems far too tender to touch?

When a common theme appears in your own layers, that means there is a reason why you once needed (or believed you needed) extra protection. For me, I found the theme of perfection underlying my layers, and it was this layer of perfection that stood in my way of choosing an aligned life. Perfection for me was a safety net. It protected me from harsh criticism, but it also didn't allow me to truly thrive. It was this tension, this struggle, that kept me locked in place, and fearful when I couldn't achieve the impossible.

Delving deeply within, facing past vulnerabilities, and coming out freer is a process where courage is absolutely required. Courage and perfection, however, cannot coexist. There can be no room for courage when one continuously strives for perfection. Perfection is a layer that is ultra-protective. It doesn't allow for exploration, learning, or expansive growth. We learn best from getting back up after falling down, success after failure, but if we make sure we never fail by never trying in the first place, where does that lead us? It is the pull to play it safe that ultimately makes us feel smaller than we are, until we inevitably start to feel disempowered. Playing small or not playing at all is the ultimate failure. Everything else is growth.

As humans, we are afraid of pain, be it physical, psychological, emotional, or even spiritual and existential. We recoil because pain goes against our instinct of self-preservation, signaling potential danger, and danger may ultimately mean some form of death. We are extraordinarily resistant to exploring these psychological pain points within ourselves because, if they are true, we don't want repeated confirmation of their truth, and if they aren't true, we fear not knowing who we are without them. Our pain becomes so great, takes up so much of our personal space, that it feels like it is all of who we are.

Pain is but a message, a sensory signal alerting us to what requires our attention and what may need to change. When we lack awareness, however, we cannot choose anything. When we fear the message of pain or discomfort, we tend to deny or numb it and never get a chance to tend to ourselves, and release that discomfort. Pain is meant to help create and direct our attention on to the path of awareness, so we're not merely stuck in a loop of chasing and/or avoiding.

Underneath our pain points is the source of so much hidden personal power. We are so much more than our pain and our fear. Just as scaffolding is put up to support the repairs of a building, and then taken down when those repairs are complete, when your layers of pain come away, there is still a *you* underneath them. It is actually then that the true you can emerge. You might not have experienced this part of yourself in a long, long time, but I promise you, *you* in all of your power have always been there.

We might believe we are our career, our brains, our looks, our status, or any number of things, but if any of those things are gone, do we disappear too? We don't. It may feel challenging, confronting, and upsetting to everything you believe to be true about yourself, but without those things, I assure you, you would still be the true you.

A change or a sudden demotion can engender much instability and internal turmoil if our identity is intricately tied to our job title or profession. In reality, however, what we truly are can never be lost, removed, or given away. Thus, we're also not our money or any material thing. We can become dependent on them to the point of forging an identity around them or even with them, but they are not who we are.

Elaine's Story — Gaining Clarity

Elaine had initially come to me with questions about her work–life balance, but very quickly we both discovered that her real issue was something very different. Elaine had worked diligently throughout her whole life and was justly proud of how far she had come. However, a change in company culture had recently brought about some interpersonal challenges that Elaine was finding incredibly difficult. Specifically, there was now a push to shift to a teamwork model, geared toward more collaboration and connection. She was asked to join a research team.

"I just work better when I'm by myself," Elaine told me during one session. "I don't like to wait for other people, and I don't see the point in pretending to need help when I have it all under control."

This attitude was very intriguing because, outwardly, Elaine had a very warm, kind, and personable attitude. She tried to act friendly, although she expressed to me that she felt much more comfortable in her own space. Being asked to collaborate with others, rely on them, and trust that they would follow through felt almost unsafe to her. She didn't know why and very much wished it could be different. Whatever this was in her mind felt insurmountable to her, and yet it was who she had always known herself to be. This was now causing friction at work.

When I asked Elaine about other areas of her life, the full picture began to emerge. As a child, her parents had been emotionally unavailable and seemingly unresponsive to her needs, and so she had learned from a very early age that she could only ever rely on herself. She'd never gained the tools to deal with her own uncomfortable emotions and had set them aside by immersing herself in the pursuit of excellence, a goal that felt safer, much more attainable, and one she believed she could accomplish on her own, without anyone else. She had a string of relationships in her past which followed a similar pattern: intense interest, strong boundaries, a need for independence, and, eventually, a decisive end. No matter what she did, it seemed, Elaine could never get close enough to someone. At some point, she would find herself pulling back, guarding herself against an imagined future hurt.

This, as it turned out, was the real pain point for her. Work was just another expression of it. Whether or not she collaborated at work wasn't the point. The point was that her core layer was telling her to push people away and cut them off before they became unreliable, let her down, or could hurt her. All of it went back to her youngest years. What she soon realized was that none of it had to be her reality today.

During the next few months, Elaine and I continued to work together to explore this core layer, asking questions in her boardroom as we got to the core of the expectation that was causing her to stay away in the first place. To her surprise, she realized that her brain almost always expected her to get hurt, so at every turn she would avoid teamwork, close relationships, or anything else that could be perceived as a risk. She came to realize that she was filtering the world as safe/unsafe. She had always known herself as fiercely independent and had never thought about it in any other way. It caught her by surprise. She was both a little shocked and very relieved.

"Does it mean this could be changed?" she asked.

"Absolutely," I told her.

Our life experience is all about choices. It is rarely, if ever, an all-or-nothing proposition. If you don't agree with the lens through which you experience life, that is definitely something you can change. By working through layers, fears, and limiting beliefs, you expand your mind, calm your brain, re-empower yourself, and make choices that are much more aligned with what you truly need and who you want to be. It's all about growing.

In our work together, we replaced Elaine's lens of safe/unsafe with the lens of discernment/choice. She learned that she could evaluate every situation and, rather than systematically avoid it, she could choose whom to work with, which friends to have, and what qualities in others she enjoyed. She learned to discern, choose, and ultimately discover what lay beyond that layer. She could finally see what had prevented her from more fully engaging with others all this time. Rather than repeat her past challenges, she chose a new path, one that led her to a different perspective and a more fulfilling and whole life experience. She was freer to do what felt good and right, rather than what felt confining and safe. As Elaine began to heal and dissolve her layers, she allowed herself to be more open to trust her own vulnerability in her interactions with others.

The Power of Awareness

"Awareness is enlightening, truly. It is like shedding a light into darkness. A little goes a long way."

At its core, the process of questioning and removing layers leads to deep, empowering awareness. The quest to find the answers helps uncover, discover, dissolve, and release those layers. This book is intended to help you acquire the tools and clarity to see these layers lying deep within yourself, begin to gain awareness of them, and eventually clear them.

While change can happen swiftly with a mindset shift—and in my sessions with clients it often does—working through layers is a process. In fact, I invite you to reread the previous chapters and repeat any of the exercises any time you need to refresh your perspective or check in with yourself as you feel out your own layers. Often layers are dissolved in stages, one sub-layer at a time. Further developing your ability to connect with, listen to, and guide your inner committee through this process will help lead you to a place of alignment and choice.

The primary layer you have within yourself tells you much about what you believed internally, but also what you expected of the world and from others. As you journey through this process, I encourage you to keep an adventurous, curious mindset. Keep your eyes open and ask every question without judgment, giving yourself permission to accept the answers that arise. Be compassionate and kind toward the little you, the one who took the initiative to create layers to keep you safe.

As you work your way through this internal journey and emerge out into the world to interact with others in this playground we call life, this new perspective about yourself will change the way you look at yourself, the world, and others.

Ultimately, this work we do within ourselves allows us to then venture out into the world and show up as a truer version of ourselves in our daily interactions with others. We are not meant to sit alone with ourselves in solitary enlightenment. We are meant to experience the world in all of its glory and radiance, to live and interact, not just exist. Living means richness and joy, fulfillment and satisfaction, challenge and growth, connection and relationships that nurture, support, and sustain us. Layers may protect us, but they also restrict us and keep us small. For many of us, we go along with our layers for quite some time in our lives, and it is only when we reach the place of external ease and apparent success that we stop to realize we aren't actually fully satisfied. We may feel confined or limited. Perhaps we feel as though there is something more, but we don't know what. While protective by nature, layers start constricting us over time and prevent expansion, growth, and real connection.

It is only by exploring our layers, diving deep down and finding what's beneath them, that we can remove the barriers that hide us from ourselves and begin to get to know ourselves, our real selves, often for the first time in our lives.

Exercise — Finding the Pattern

As you reflect on your own layers, you will likely find that there is some pattern, some common theme, that begins to show up for you in your life. If not, that's okay, but I would still encourage you to sit with some of these questions and consider whatever comes up for you with an open mind. Take a quiet moment today and try sitting with the following:

- Is there a common thread for you throughout the layers you have found?

- What is the most uncomfortable or difficult one to look at, let alone question?

- Are there any childhood memories that come up when you explore this question? Any past negative experiences or traumas?

- What would you change about yourself or your story if you could? Why?

Perhaps there is something you believe you cannot do, even though you're drawn to it. Perhaps you work long, crazy, stressful hours, running yourself into the ground to get that promotion or be made partner, or grow that business. If it's weighing on you, take a moment to question. Remember, questioning doesn't mean you must change anything. But it will lead you to know yourself better and discover who's in the driver's seat. Below are some additional questions to start you off:

- Are you aligned with whatever you are after or wanting to achieve?
- Could there be another path to achieve it, a path that's more empowering and less personally costly?
- Consider that new path and write it out. How does it feel to you? What would feel different for you on that new path?

Allow yourself to sit with these questions for a moment without judgment, shame, or condemnation. Simply bear witness to them, however they arise for you.

CHAPTER EIGHT

Our Relationship with Life

"Our beliefs about life tell us so much more about ourselves and our expectations than they ever could tell us about life itself."

None of us choose who we are born to, what kind of families we have, or where in the world we are raised. For most of our childhood, we don't have the agency to control our own life experiences, and we are told where to go, what to do, and given ideas as to what to believe about ourselves and life itself. We don't consciously choose any of it, and yet so much of it continues to affect us throughout our lives.

When asked, most people will say their closest relationship is the one they have with their spouse, their children, a best friend, their siblings, or their parents, but before we can consider any aspect of a relationship with any other human being, there is another dynamic I would like us to consider together. We are souls and we're using our physical body to interact with this world, and therefore every relationship we have with another person is itself a connection with another soul in another physical body. We cannot engage on a purely soul-to-soul basis with someone. We need a place to interact. Where, then, does all human interaction occur? It happens in what we call life. When we talk about life, what does that mean? What is life? While we all have opinions about it, how do we define it?

You may be surprised to know that life means something different to each of us. To some, life is synonymous with God. To others, life is what causes us to feel a certain way, a force we believe acts upon us or pushes us around. Life is created and offered to us, and it is the stage upon which all relationships take place. It is where we interact with all living beings, where we form, develop, and experience relationships.

While the interactions we have with others are by no means neutral, life itself is, at its source, neutral. Yet notice how most of us do not view life as neutral at all. In fact, we often have very strong opinions, thoughts, and feelings about life. We even go as far as to expect things from life: sometimes good things, sometimes bad. But expectations are tricky. When we expect something, it means we believe—consciously or subconsciously—that it is somehow owed to us, and that life has capacity and free will to provide it to us. This implies some sort of tie or relationship. However, life is not truly a living, breathing entity that gives or takes things from us, nor does it have free will. And if life itself is neutral, how is it we develop an expectations-based relationship with it?

The truth is, while we experience life, life itself is not something we can ever have a relationship with. A relationship is, by its very definition, reciprocal. It is a give-and-take. We can have many expectations or opinions about life, but life, on the other hand, has no thoughts about us. It doesn't feel anything about us, nor does it directly give or do anything to us at all. It is a neutral place where other relationships are allowed to happen.

Think about this for a moment. The way we talk about life—even in adages that might be funny, throwaway, or flippant—is very revealing, and says quite a lot about the way we truly feel about life. Take the proverbial saying, "When life gives you lemons, make lemonade!" It's a great one because most people see it as an encouragement to take a more positive outlook on life. Even if you get something sour, like a lemon, you can always choose to sweeten it up. That may be a nice thought, but when I started to really think about this expression, I discovered underlying messages I had never previously considered.

What we are actually expressing is our belief that life has the capacity to give us lemons, and that in all likelihood at some point it will probably do so. Now, whether you choose to see lemons as positive or negative, the bottom line is that we have subconsciously set ourselves up to view life through the lens of a relationship dynamic. Life will give us lemons, or so the saying goes. We internalize this message and expect it, whatever " lemons" represents to us.

In reality, life doesn't give anyone lemons, or hardships, or fruit, or anything at all. Life is neutral. It doesn't have that kind of give-and-take relationship with us, no matter what the belief. Take a moment to think about it. The belief that you are owed things *from* life, or being dumped on unfairly *by* life, whatever your take on that might be, will tell you so much more about yourself and your expectations than anything about life itself.

Life is not the one to give us lemons. When we see what others have and wish we could have the same, we need to acknowledge that it is not life that gives unequally to some and withholds from others. This is what people, not life, do to each other. Life is the realm within which all opportunities and possibilities are created and reside. It serves as the stage upon which we are called to take action, and the place where we come together to interact with each other. While it is a sacred space to be respected, life itself doesn't ever interact directly with us, and it isn't some force that causes us to feel bad or good. Instead, we are the ones who interact with each other, within the wide-open stage of possibility that life offers.

Our One-Sided Relationship

How did we get here? What has led us to create a relationship with something that cannot have a relationship with us? Why do we ascribe feelings, motives, and actions to life, something that cannot feel, think, or act upon us? In effect, this idea of a relationship we create is in itself a layer. We create it for the same reason that we create any other layer: to protect ourselves. If all layers are fundamentally about protection, what is it about this one-sided relationship that makes us feel protected?

The belief that life is hard, out to get us, a struggle, a trial, or simply the belief that we have a relationship with life at all—these disempowering thoughts—help us distance ourselves from having to be accountable, truthful with ourselves, and honest about what choices we have made to get us to where we are. When we say, "It's okay, life is hard," what we're really saying is, "It wasn't my fault," or "I'm not responsible." Or when we say, "Why is this happening to me? Why is life out to get me?" We are, in effect, saying that life has all the power, and we don't.

While relinquishing power may seem counterintuitive at first glance, in reality it is a form of protection. We are protecting ourselves from the responsibility that it may be us, rather than life, running the show. Remember, the brain dislikes change at all costs. It would be destabilizing and even upsetting to realize that we were in control this whole time, but did not know how to navigate—or worse, that we simply didn't choose what we actually needed and wanted when we could have. If this becomes a pattern, it will, over time, become a disempowering layer.

We often unknowingly coast along for a while with our layers taking the reins, feeling a quiet sort of discontent but pushing it away because we aren't ready to face it. It builds up until we wake up one day with the realization that we have no idea how we got here, and no idea how to change it. And yet, it remains easier to just believe that there is something wrong with life, rather than learn to stand in our own power.

We are so afraid of being empowered because with it comes complete responsibility for all of our choices. It means taking agency over all of our actions and inactions. Blaming things on life allows us to surrender our control and at least some accountability for our choices. "It's not my fault," we tell ourselves, passively accepting that life is just the way it is and there is nothing we can do about it. If we take the position that it isn't our fault, we are absolved of doing anything about it, but also powerless to direct it as we see fit.

What else could we do? We did our best. It seems easier to be passive than empowered. It doesn't feel good, but we endure the discomfort so long as we believe it is keeping us safe. So long as we are convinced we are safely doing all we can do, the layers we form guard us and prevent us from seeking the unknown and changing the status quo—from rocking the boat, so to speak.

In the previous chapter, we explored how looking back through the layers we have found so far in our journey can often reveal patterns, themes, or common elements that protect specific tender areas in our lives. This one-sided relationship we have created with life is often one of those areas.

What compels us to create this one-sided relationship? Relationships are the only way we know how to relate to anything inside and outside of us. As humans, we are wired for connection and therefore look to form close bonds with others. We are born helpless and, in our early years, are completely dependent on others for survival. It is also why we are born with features that endear us to our caregivers, and instincts that make them bond closely with us in return. As we grow, we learn both consciously and subconsciously that, as we depend on others, we must reciprocate and do what's expected of us in order to contribute to the collective health of our family, community, or social unit. All of these behaviors and instincts can be attributed to one important source: survival. The more we work together, the better relationships we develop and the more we ensure our survival.

When we have good relationships and connections with others, we have a better chance of surviving, and even thriving. The same is true for the internal connection, the relationship we have with ourselves. People with a stronger internal connection have a more optimistic and curious mindset, a more open and adventurous look on life, and are more resilient. They know themselves, which means they have done work to look inwardly and nurture that inner relationship. They are empowered and can confidently take action to go and do whatever they set out to do. It doesn't mean that they will not falter. It means they will stand in their own power no matter what. It means they know they are neither their successes nor their failures, and don't define themselves by them.

Subconsciously, we do know being connected to ourselves is empowering. Thus, even though we might fear connection, and fear the vulnerability that comes with it, we still seek it. As we are hardwired to seek out and form relationships with others, we end up inadvertently looking to life and relating to it, almost as we would to another person. When things don't turn out the way we think they should, we often have a tendency to connect them to life itself and point a blaming finger at it. It is a protective mechanism akin to layers.

How does this belief in a one-sided relationship with life turn into a layer? When we encounter difficulties in life, either because of the choices we have made or the actions that others have taken, our brains form opinions about them in an effort to simplify decision-making in the future. We learn about the way the world works, what we can and cannot count on from others, and the supposed "rules" of life. Just like with our other beliefs about ourselves and about others, our beliefs about life can turn into layers if we let them.

I want us to pause here for a moment. How is this landing for you? If you find this resonates with you, take some time to sit with it for a while and consider how your expectations and beliefs about life may be affecting you, and consequently how things play out for you. For example, are there things you have heard about life that are coming to mind now? Beliefs you may have internalized that no longer feel right and you now want to question?

An Empowered Life

It is so much easier to blame life when bad things happen. While the car accident and subsequent concussion happened to me, nothing about what happened was actually against me. Life didn't give me that accident. It didn't make the car crash into me, and it didn't give me a concussion. Life was simply the stage or context upon which these events unfolded.

If life isn't doing anything at all to us, then what does that mean? When we create this one-sided relationship with life in our minds, it makes us look at life with expectations. When we cling to these expectations about life—expecting that it will be good or bad, difficult or easy, fair or unjust—whatever we feel about what happens around us, we make it personal as if it's directed at us. We will form a layer around it, and that layer will be what guides us to live on autopilot, in a way to keep us safe, but all the while also limiting and confining us to our newfound belief.

We carry all these expectations around and subconsciously wait for things to happen at us, or to be given to us. When our experiences don't match our expectations, we feel disempowered, frustrated, or angry because life did not happen the way we expected it to. This kind of subconscious approach to life, and all the layers we don't even realize we have within us, shape our approach to life—and, by extension, every single relationship we have with others.

Remember, every layer we have is a way for our brain to take charge and help keep us safe in the best way it knows. But the more we are under the sway of these so-called safety precautions, these rules, expectations, and "truths" that aren't true at all and perhaps never were, the more we surrender our power.

The message of disempowerment we internalize from society, and our interactions with others, creates a whole story about life that we live out over and over. We are taught that disempowerment is safer, that pushing aside our own needs is what we need to do in order to be safe, loved, accepted, and to fit in with others. Ultimately, we are given the message that fitting in with others is often more important than fitting in with ourselves or living our truth. This defines our identity at a very deep level, but it also continues to disempower us. If we keep moving through life without the awareness of just how much our layers shape our perspective, we will never be fully empowered and able to choose the things that are in alignment with our higher self. We will keep living out the same story, having the same perspective about life, and feel as if it's acting upon us, rather than us being the captains of our own ships.

Empowering ourselves in life is the goal, and our misconceptions and layers don't help us in that regard. It is crucial for us to understand that life is not meant to give us anything specific. Life itself is a gift, an offering of neutral space full of limitless potential where we interact with both ourselves and others. It offers us the opportunity to create our own story and our own unique experience of it. While life is the realm of all opportunities and possibilities, it is not a living being, has no opinion about us, no relationship with us, and it always remains neutral toward us. It graciously allows us to go about our interactions in the ways we see fit.

Life as Our Playground

"Life is nothing more and nothing less than a magnificent playground, inviting us into it to do as we will."

It is safe to say that every person reading this book has been a child, and most likely has been to a playground. Some of you might run to the playground that is life, eager and excited to try everything, and some might go right for the swings, or the monkey bars, or the sand pit. As children, some of you might have fallen off a swing, or experienced a fearful time on the slide, and so you ran to something else—anything else, but not those things. Still others will stand on the side of the playground, fearful to engage in play due to a past fall or a bad interaction with children who bullied them. In every case, the playground remains the same. It is the constant. As humans, we stand on the edge of the playground and look in on it, and all the layers we have inside of us inform our perspective of that playground, how we feel about it, and what mindset we have each and every day. So, what does it actually mean to think of life as a playground? It means that rather than life being some force that gives us anything good or bad, life is the venue where the actions are meant to take place.

Like playgrounds, life itself, on its own, does not change. What changes is our experience of it. Everybody in life will have a different and unique experience. This is because we don't directly interact with life, we interact with ourselves and others while in life. If you run in front of someone on the swings, you may get knocked down. Sitting on one side of a seesaw while waiting for another person to come play, you might feel lonely and neglected. Nevertheless, it isn't the swings or the seesaw that do anything to you. We interact with other people within the context of the playground of life, but the playground—life itself—remains both neutral and constant.

This shift in awareness changes everything about how we engage with life, if we let it. It can be easier and might feel safer to blame the swings, the sand, or the seesaw because it takes the power and therefore the responsibility out of our hands. "See?" we exclaim, pointing at the swing set. "Life knocked me down!" But was it actually life? If we are honest with ourselves for a moment, was it life itself, your interaction with another person, or a pattern of choices in life that led to that? Sometimes it is others who hurt us, whether intentionally or unintentionally, while other times we do it to ourselves. When we surrender our power and blame life, when we adopt a disempowered perspective, we enter into a one-sided relationship with life, where we expect things that life cannot provide, or we anticipate things that set us up for failure before we have even begun. We might even start to believe life is against us.

When we become more aware of this one-sided relationship, we become more aware of the layers, judgments, and expectations we hold within ourselves, and that allows us to examine them objectively, rather than taking everything so personally.

Consider these questions:

- Who was it that told us life gives us lemons, or life is hard, or life is a struggle?

- When did we learn that was true?

- What would it be like if those things weren't true?

- What would it be like if we could truly relate to life as a neutral playing field, a playground where any experience and interaction was possible?

- And instead of believing life is in charge, what if it was up to us to navigate life?

Rachel's Story — When High Achievement Hits a Wall

One of my clients, Rachel, came to me with a recurring problem in her work life. She had recently reached a growth milestone in her business, but a few weeks into the expansion, she felt just as stuck, frustrated, and defeated as she had when she was first starting off. It wasn't about the added workload, or even the new team of employees she had to manage. By all accounts, her business was thriving, and the results she was able to produce were a success. Yet she didn't feel content nor deserving of what she had accomplished. The harder she worked, the better her results, and the worse she felt.

This experience was not new for her. Throughout her life, the more

Rachel pushed herself to achieve, the more externally successful she was, the more she felt as if life was a struggle and she was faking it. Rachel told me, "I just feel like life itself is closing in on me, no matter what I do. I think I must really be bad at life!"

Ironically, from the outside, Rachel not only appeared to be a very successful woman, but she also felt she had a generally positive outlook on life, if she could only get this issue around her business under control. However, by exploring her layers and the expectations she had about life, Rachel would soon discover that the issue she was experiencing ran much deeper than work and exhibited itself in every pillar of her life experience.

Many times, the issue people are struggling with isn't the issue that truly holds them back. Because of their layers, however, they have these blind spots, places where the autopilot part of their brain does not really want them to go. In past chapters, we looked at how internal layers can be a tainted or blurred lens through which we view the world. Being able to identify the members of our internal committee who cause us to view things through such a lens brings about a new awareness and an ability to question: "Is this really what I believe about myself? Is this really true? What would it be like if this wasn't accurate?" And, most importantly, "Is this actually my choice?"

The same is true for our view of life, too.

We are often completely unaware of the ideas we hold to be true about life, or the relationship we create with it, let alone all our expectations of life that cannot possibly be met. Once we realize that we have surrendered our power to something that is in fact the stage upon which we are meant to act, the playground on which we are invited to play in any way we choose, then we can choose differently. We become empowered to be active participants in our own lives, rather than passive, disempowered, or reactive, and begin to make choices that bring us into alignment with what our higher self is seeking.

Sometimes layers around life are the hardest ones to change because they are the most difficult to see. As you become aware of them, you can begin to ask questions, such as:

- Is this really what I believe about life?
- Is it actually true?
- What would it be like if I saw life as neutral?
- What would it change about what I believe I can do?
- What am I capable of?
- What do I want my life experience to be?
- What's holding me back?

Ultimately, your life experience is based on your own expectations. If you want to have different feelings about your life experience, change your expectations. If you don't enjoy your experience on the playground, what are you willing to do about it? Would you consider consulting your inner committee and discovering what comes up?

In Rachel's case, she believed herself to be a positive person who was doing her best, despite what life kept constantly throwing at her. Once she could see how her layers were disempowering her, a monumental shift took place. She understood that each time she approached life with an expectation it could never provide, she was disempowering herself. Rachel saw that she was the one in control, and that she had more choices than she had ever given herself credit for. She was able to dissolve the layers around her view of life and take back control over her own choices and expectations. She dropped the path of struggle and courageously downsized her business, focused on the stream of revenue that made her most happy. Today she has a business partner, a sustainable business, and most importantly, she feels more capable of navigating life, working on making choices that keep her empowered.

Protection or Empowerment: You Can't Have Both

Our personal layers filter our view of ourselves, and the layers we have about life itself shape how we interact with life and what we hold as true. What we believe can deeply direct how we live.

- If we believe life is meaningless, we probably won't go looking for meaning. We will protect ourselves from the responsibility of defining our own path and avoid anything that could hold any true meaning.

- If we believe life is difficult, we will look to protect ourselves, aim low, and avoid challenges, good or bad, so as to avoid potential failures. We will not grow or learn from them how to become our higher selves.

- If we believe life is scary, we will choose a path that makes us the smallest, the least threatening, the least noticeable. We will protect ourselves from connecting with other people because deep down we don't believe we are worth being cared for, respected, or valued.

In Rachel's case, once she realized she had a specific belief around life itself, she was able to go deep and question some of the layers she had around life and change her view of it. Instead of believing that life was hard and was against her, she asked different questions. "If life was not meant to be hard, what would my experience of it look like?" Once Rachel started to ask the deeper questions, she gained awareness, clarity, and knew how to plan her next steps.

What would it mean for you if you could do the same? What would change?

What if the saying went: "If you want lemonade, go get lemons and make it for yourself."

This is such a shift from the known saying that it almost sounds funny. But in reality it means that rather than being reactive to what comes at you, what if you could be proactive? It would require a paradigm shift. A completely different, totally empowered, self-aware, and aligned mindset. One where you take agency over your own life. You own your experience. It may not be comfortable, but it is empowering.

We aren't meant to be comfortable all of the time. Often, staying in a place of comfort means we are fearful of change, relying on existing protective layers, and working with impossible, unhealthy expectations. Remember, our brain is great at defining and executing routines for us, but it is terrible at discernment. It gets overwhelmed and overly protective when it's in charge, and it is precisely then that questioning becomes so crucial. We need to question. It is our right and our responsibility to ask questions. It's what *No More Layers* is all about. Questioning leads to awareness, awareness leads to choice, and choice leads to alignment and freedom.

It is important to note that exercising choice is the goal. Getting the perfect result isn't. It is possible to make a choice and still not have the outcome you predicted or wanted. Choosing an action and carrying it out is entirely within our control. The end result is not and never was. The important thing is to get to a place where you allow yourself to truly choose, rather than allowing your layers to, by default, decide for you. Choosing implies you have consulted your inner committee, heard yourself fully, and found what best aligns with you in that moment. It allows you to retain agency over yourself and be accountable for your own actions, both of which lead to awareness and ultimately empowerment. Even as you practice choosing, old habits and triggers can sometimes pull you right back into a place of helplessness and powerlessness. When that happens, and it will, pause, catch it in the moment, and take it as an opportunity to check in with yourself, delve deeper into the triggered layer, gain more awareness around it, and consciously return to a place of choosing.

As you develop a neutral approach to life, you can choose to clear those old layers and even keep new ones from forming. Like stepping into the boardroom and taking your place at the head of the table, you gain the power and agency over your own life, your own identity. On the great playground of life, you become the free-spirited individual you were always meant to be, and it becomes up to you how you want to play each day. That's when the real fun begins.

The Laws of the Playground

Regardless of how our different life experiences play out, each of us has been afforded the opportunity to experience it. The same laws of life apply to all of us. What differs, however, is our unique experience of it, which stems from who we are, our internal blueprint, early childhood, interpersonal encounters, our purpose and perceptions. Someone born to a neglectful parent will have a very different early childhood experience when compared to someone born into a family that's supportive, just as someone born into poverty will have a different life experience in comparison to someone born into wealth. Someone who experienced trauma as a child, or who suffers from PTSD as a result, will undoubtedly have a different perception when compared to someone who did not. But they will all experience life.

While each of us will form different layers based on our unique life experiences, all of us will have layers nonetheless. Whether we construct a protective layer around poverty or one around our own beauty, once we define ourselves by something external to us, it can become a layer—one that will, over time, define us. Those layers become the funnel through which we interact in life, setting expectations in order to keep us safe, limiting us and preventing us from exploring and explaining ourselves further. But again, all of these are a result of human interactions and not life itself.

You may be tempted to look at someone who has family wealth as lucky and having an easy life. But how do we define "easy," and what do we actually know about that person and their challenges? They may have something that we want, but those external things cannot guarantee true happiness, inner peace, freedom, or even true self-awareness.

It is not life's doing whether you have a bad day or a good one. Life does not allow or disallow any specific thing. It remains constant no matter what occurs upon it. Take a simple example such as gravity. It is a law of nature and it is a constant: while it is necessary to keep us grounded to earth and essential to our daily lives, it is not helpful when attempting a high jump or wanting to fly. Yet gravity doesn't have it out for you, nor does it proactively interact with you. Its rules apply to everyone equally, as do the rules of life. Life is there for all of us, and it is neutral regardless of who you are or what you have.

As you continue on this journey through your layers, it becomes clearer that it's up to you, and only you, to do all of the inner work that prepares you to have the kind of experience you want to have in this life. But sometimes, what we experience can feel so overwhelming that we begin to believe there is nothing we can do to cope, and we may feel paralyzed, angry, or resentful about what comes at us in life.

After experiencing my concussion and the subsequent recovery period, I expected that a part of me would have wondered, "Why me? Why did this have to happen to me? I can't believe how life is." These questions, and these feelings, are very human. It is easy to feel gratitude when things turn out well or even better than we expect, but when things fall short and our expectations are not met, we perceive it as negative, often feeling a need to attribute blame. Blaming ourselves, blaming others, or even blaming life.

If you have ever experienced any kind of injustice, trauma, pain, struggle, or strife, even to the point of PTSD, I want you to know that life itself did not do that to you—your interactions with other people did. Continuing to blame life itself for the experiences you had robs you of your power to direct the course of your own life experience and how you choose to perceive it. Yes, those things happened, but they don't have the power to define you.

There is tremendous benefit in knowing the difference. It opens you up to the power to choose that which has been within you all this time, waiting beyond your layers. As you begin to examine your layers and clear them, there will likely be tender areas, newly exposed raw spots and uncertainties. You may falter and fail, and all of that's okay. Building resilience and an adventurous spirit means you can face whatever comes to you with curiosity and not fear. This doesn't mean that life will be easy, but it means you will know yourself better, whatever happens. And when you know yourself, you can also trust yourself. Trust that you can create a life experience that serves you best. Just like when you prepare for an important job interview, all you can do is prepare for it, study the company, present yourself the way you want others to see you. The choice to hire you is up to other people, but regardless of what happens, you know you have done your best, showed up for yourself fully, and unconditionally continue to respect your relationship with yourself regardless of the outcome. You become reliant on yourself as you interact with others in the playground that is life. If we let our past fears and layers define us, and if we surrender our control and our agency, we'll never feel like we truly know ourselves. We will always feel like we are being pulled from place to place, relationship to relationship, job to job, and that our happiness is outside of our control. This is not an ideal way to live, and we can change it by looking inward, considering our beliefs about life, beginning to clear existing ones, and choosing the ones we actually align with.

You would be surprised at how many of my clients had underlying beliefs about life that, once uncovered and questioned, were ones they didn't even truly agree with. And yet, until our work together, their actions and sense of wellbeing were governed by them.

Exercise — Shift Your Experience

In order to dive deeper into this idea of life as a playground, and to step into our own power as the changemakers in our own lives, I invite you to do some journaling on this idea using the prompts below.

Take some time to write down your current feelings about life. When you think, "Life is _____," what comes up for you? Write down whatever comes to mind. Some examples to get you started might be:

- Life is disappointing
- Life is meaningful
- Life is scary

Now, take those statements and rephrase them to be: "My experience of life is ..."

- My experience of life is disappointing
- My experience of life is meaningful
- My experience of life is scary

What is different for you in each of these two sets of statements? How does rephrasing change your perspective?

Keep in mind that since life is neutral, it doesn't change. What you can change, however, is your experience of it.

When you say, "Life is enjoyable or challenging," the onus is put on life and whatever you feel, good or bad, is about life itself. Life is causing you to feel a certain way, and you are subject to it. In one sentence, you've made yourself completely dependent on life and handed over all of your power to it.

Now whether you say, "My experience of life is enjoyable or challenging," life in this instance is recognized for what it is: neutral. What changes is your experience. It's no longer about life itself, but rather about you and how you experience life. It's *yours*. You create it, own it, and sustain it. It puts you in the driver's seat.

Once you're in control, it then becomes up to you. The power is all yours. You choose which experiences you have and want to continue, and which you want to change.

If you find this helpful, consider making two columns. In the first, include feelings and experiences you resonate with and want more of, and in the second, ones you want to shift for yourself.

What do you notice about your columns? Which column is longer? What are your columns filled with? How does each feel to you? What comes up for you?

Begin by choosing one thing from your second column. I would encourage you to get curious about any feelings of disempowerment and dissatisfaction that come up, and really take ownership of them. What are you doing, or not doing, that contributes to this feeling? What layers are at play? Ask yourself what you could do differently to shift your experience from one that belongs in your second column to one you would want to include in your first column.

Exercise — Find Your Power on the Playground

As you become more and more familiar with your layers, you can do this exercise daily. It will help shift you away from what no longer serves you. Consider recording or journaling your feelings and experiences, and start looking for patterns.

Before stepping out on to the playground of life, ask yourself:

- What is my feeling about life today, right here and right now? Is it the same as it was yesterday?
- If I could have a conversation with life, what would I want to say to it?
- What do I think its response might be?
- What challenges or obstacles should I address to have more fun and fulfillment on the playground of life?
- What layers are coming up for me?

Imagine you are standing on the edge of the playground of life.

- What does the playground look like to you?
- What activities or things to play with are there?
- Is the playground full or empty?
- Is the weather warm and sunny or rainy?
- What activity most excites you? What scares you?

CHAPTER NINE

Reflecting on Life

"The work we do within ourselves allows us to show up as open, interactive, and receptive human beings as we go out into the playground of life."

As we continue on this journey from the relationship with ourselves and toward the relationships we have with others, it is important to remember that this is a journey and not a destination point. You can't reach empowerment and then stay there for the rest of your life without ongoing awareness, thoughtful maintenance, and checking in. Therefore, it's important to have a way to check in and make sure you're still empowered. Your brain will continue to form layers, wanting to "help" out and keep you safe. But what the brain wants is often different from what may best serve your true self. How then can you make sure that you're still running your own show? Or that layers haven't snuck in without your knowledge and remain within you, without your approval?

Developing your relationship with yourself is essential—by now, you most likely have begun to see some changes that manifest in your life by going within and clearing out these old layers—but having a layer-free, empowered, and honest relationship with yourself isn't the end goal. Life is meant to be lived, and in order to live it to the fullest, you're meant to step outside yourself and interact with others. The reason we begin the work within ourselves is because the relationships we have with others can never be better than the relationship we have with ourselves. That's why relationship work can be so challenging; if you only focus externally but don't address the layers within, nothing will change. However, when you do the inner work, you grow, expand, become freer, and, in turn, everything around you changes as well.

Having just peeled away these old layers that held prior beliefs you had about yourself, you may now feel raw, fragile, or exposed. Or you may feel braver, bolder, and eager. Wherever you are in this process, the key thing to remember is that this is a lifelong journey, a method you can rely on to check in with yourself, a skill set you can develop and return to in order to keep yourself aware of what's ahead of you, and ready to face whatever comes.

Having the knowledge that life itself is a neutral playground on which we get to interact with others gives each of us the space and power to choose:

- What experience of life do I want to have today?
- What action do I want to take in order to bring me closer to that experience?
- How do I check to see if I'm still on the path of empowerment?
- And if I've gone off that path, what do I do to get back on track?

Throughout this chapter, we'll explore these subjects more deeply, and examine how our layers influence us, as well as what we can do about it so we can get the life we want.

Life is a Mirror

"Life serves as a stage for the relationships we have with others, but it also reflects back to us the relationship we have with ourselves."

When we're able to shift away from the idea that life itself is good or bad, we can instead consider that we are the ones who are responsible for navigating our own experience. This isn't necessarily about being accountable for the outcome or result. As we discussed in the last chapter, you can prepare all you want for an interview, put your best foot forward, and still not land the job for reasons that are totally outside of your control. But that should not keep you from choosing to put your best suit on and presenting yourself in a way that reflects who you are and how you want to be received. Your life experience is about showing up for yourself fully and unconditionally.

All of this work we do within ourselves—uncovering, observing, considering, and shedding our layers—serves us in becoming the best, most open, most interactive, and receptive human beings we can possibly be as we go out into the playground of life. When we do the internal work, we're better prepared to have not just a good experience on the playground, but the experience that we choose to have. We become active participants, rather than passive or reactive passengers.

No matter how much internal work we do, however, our life experiences can only occur within the context of life. You have to go to the playground, and that always involves other players. You're never at the playground alone. We're not meant to be a lone individual with no relationship to anyone else. Therefore, before you actually step out on to the playground, you'll want to check in with yourself. Are you ready for something that's outside of yourself?

This question is often more revealing than people first expect.

Just like the concept of the boardroom can serve as a way to be in conversation with the other internal aspects of yourself, listening and responding to each of the silenced, ignored, or diminished parts of yourself that show up around your table, so too can your feelings about that playground serve as a sort of mirror for you to check in with yourself before you step outside.

Life serves as a stage for the relationships you have with others, but it also reflects back to you the relationship you have with yourself. This process uses a similar process to the conversation you nurture with your internal committee but serves a slightly different purpose. When you're in your boardroom, you're seeking awareness within. When you're using life as a mirror, it's an external check-in to ensure you're showing up the way you intend to. Let me explain.

Imagine for a moment that you're getting ready for your day, doing what you usually do: styling your hair, choosing your shoes, or perhaps wearing your new, custom-tailored suit. You're getting ready to go out into the world and begin your day of interactions. Once you're ready to go, what do you do before you leave the house? You're most likely going to take a quick look in the mirror. In fact, if you were fixing your hair or shaving, you probably looked in the mirror as you were doing so as well.

We already check on our reflection while getting ready, so why do we look back again in the mirror just as we're leaving? We look to make sure that what we want to be presenting to the world is actually how we're showing up, and to make sure that we don't look messy, have on a mismatched outfit, or missed a spot shaving.

If we did look in the mirror and saw something we didn't expect, what would we do about it? In all likelihood we'd probably fix it and move on. We wouldn't get angry at the mirror because the mirror isn't responsible for messing up our look or choosing how we look in our clothes. We wouldn't yell at the mirror, blame the mirror, say, "Why me? Why does the mirror always make me look bad? The mirror is just so unfair!" That would be silly.

As silly as it sounds, if we did do that—and sometimes we might feel tempted to—it would indicate something about where we're at, not the mirror. The mirror is simply reflecting back what we're putting in front of it. A mirror provides information we have come to rely on every single day. What if the mirror showed us everything was perfect and in its place when it actually wasn't? What if it was untruthful and dishonest? Would it not lose its purpose? We would consider it unreliable, discard it, and learn to live without it blindly.

Life works the same way.

Before you step outside of yourself, it's important to make sure that what you think you look like—how you believe you're ready to show up, interact with the world, and put yourself out there—is really, truly where you are at. For example, if you never check yourself in the mirror, you will be unaware of any potential issues that might be as obvious as the disheveled hair on your head or the shaving cream on your face. But once you do check, and gain new insight and new information, then you have the power to choose what, if anything, you'll do about it.

So much of this process is about gaining awareness. What could be more powerful than taking stock of yourself in the biggest and clearest mirror there is: life itself.

Cecelia's Story — Coworker Conflicts

Cecelia came to me with a challenge she was facing at work: a recurring conflict she had with one specific coworker on her team. She and her coworker were each responsible for their own accounts and their own sphere of work, and not in opposition to each other, but it often felt as if this coworker was being unnecessarily competitive, and it grated on Cecelia and made her feel deeply uncomfortable.

"She isn't doing anything wrong," Cecelia told me of her coworker. "In fact, her work is great. She doesn't try to poach my clients, or step on my toes directly. She doesn't insult me or put me down, either. She hasn't done anything to me, it's just that when she constantly tries to get more attention from our boss, it makes me feel like I need to do the same thing. It makes me feel like I'm not doing enough."

Cecelia's feelings about this situation were complicated, and, as we began to discover, they ran much deeper than she first imagined.

When she first came to me, Cecelia explored some of her layers that had been formed in early childhood, layers that surrounded a particularly contentious, difficult relationship she had with her older sister. From a very young age, Cecelia had felt compared to her sister, who was high-achieving, bright and vivacious, attention-getting, and often the recipient of effusive praise by their parents and other family members. While Cecelia had her own gifts and talents, she never felt good enough or worthy enough of the same amount of attention and praise as her older sister. This naturally led to the kind of layers that ran deep within Cecelia, ones that led her to doubt her own self-worth and merit.

While we had worked through parts and sub-layers of that layer, and even seen some improvements in her own sense of self-worth, it was startling for Cecelia to realize that it was this very same layer that was resurging here in the context of her workplace.

She and the coworker weren't siblings, and it had never even occurred to her how much that old layer about her older sister and the surrounding family dynamic was still affecting her. The feelings Cecelia felt had nothing to do with the coworker, just as they had nothing to do with her sister. It had everything to do with the layer she had, the protective beliefs she'd formed at a very young age about her own worth, and what it could mean for her if she could allow herself to be the person she truly was. As we worked together through these deep emotions, and through this layer, Cecelia began to understand and reaffirm that, when it came to her work relationships, she didn't need to be like her attention-seeking coworker in order to feel that she was valuable and good at her job. She just needed to be more of herself.

When she was able to affirm that, and as she continued to check in with how she felt about life each day, everything changed. Instead of attributing her reaction toward her coworker as something that was a flaw in her coworker, she looked within and considered what those feelings meant about how she felt about herself. More specifically, she looked to identify the layers she held from the past that were still within her. It wasn't about the coworker; in fact, in our interactions with others, the things that happen at or around us very rarely, if ever, are truly about us. Knowing what she knew about this coworker's behavior, their way of being, what did Cecelia need to examine, understand, or change about herself in order to be content and empowered?

Cecelia realized that the way this coworker was showing up was the right path for them, but not the right path for her. She began to understand and accept that visibility and expression was their way of being, while her own quiet steadiness was really her strength. By focusing on her own path, Cecelia realized that her layer had been telling her that the only way to "win" at life was to compete with others, but the truth of it was that the only way for Cecelia to "win" was to stop trying to be like others, and instead be as much of herself as she could be. It was her responsibility to become the best version of herself, in her way, no matter what others were doing around her, or what ways they chose to live their lives.

Choices vs. Decisions

Cecelia's story highlights one very important concept that is key to the process of *No More Layers*, that of choosing. We might make a million decisions every day, but not all of them are choices.

So, what's the difference between a choice and a decision?

A decision may appear much easier in the short term. It's like going to the store and seeing a red shirt and a blue shirt and deciding between the two of them, even though you were looking for a green shirt all along. Since those are the options presented to you, you decide and pick one of them, sometimes almost arbitrarily, convincing yourself that somehow it will do, just to get it over with.

But a choice means sitting down, assessing, listening, addressing the underlying issue, and coming to a point of alignment within yourself. If you choose rather than decide, it is a whole other process and can lead you to a different result. A choice might mean that before you left for the store, you knew you would buy a green shirt, should you find one. And you also knew you didn't want a red or blue one. Neither of them would do, because what you need is a green one to go with your new suit. That's what you want and need, and so that's what you keep searching for. While this is a very simplistic example, how many times do we do something just to get it off our plate, only to regret it later, having succumbed to impatience, impulse, or some other layer?

We owe it to ourselves to do what it takes to turn our decisions into choices. Using our feelings about life as a mirror before we step out onto the playground and interact with others means that we can do a last-minute final check-in with ourselves and ask, "Am I as ready as I think? What is it that I feel? What is it that I want? What do I need to know? What am I not seeing? What's the mirror showing me today?" Bringing this conscious attention to our everyday interactions makes the difference between being led and pulled in all directions by life as it unfolds or leading yourself through all the unfolding of life.

This perceived lack of control over our own lives is a source of immense distress and discomfort for us, mostly because we all desire to be active participants in our own lives. In fact, we deserve to be in charge of our own lives, but many of us are not, and we don't even know it. This feeling of powerlessness creates all kinds of problems for us, even if we can't easily trace it to the source. We may feel disconnected, passionless, fearful, resentful, hopeless, or defeated.

This experience is immensely distressing because, for many of us, it recalls a time early on in our lives where we truly didn't have agency. In fact, many developmental ages that are known as being "difficult," such as the so-called "terrible twos," arise from this new awareness of limitation and lack of control. Their cries and tantrums tell us: "I see what it is that I want, but I can't get there, and I don't know the words to communicate what I feel. The world is so big, and I'm so small. I don't have any power, and I know it."

Children are often not given much of a choice about the things they're required to do. They're picked up and moved from place to place, told to be quiet, fed certain foods, or put down for a nap on someone else's schedule. From little infants, who might learn whether when they cry a parent comes to tend to them or not, to older children who wonder why they're required to sit in a classroom all day when the sun is shining outside, children become aware very early on that there is a huge disconnect between their ability to see an array of possibilities and their actual ability to choose from any of those possibilities.

Many of our deepest layers are formed during these vulnerable times in childhood. As children, we're like sponges. We pick up all sorts of information about the world, and we use that information to form our ideas about ourselves, about others, and about the world itself. Just because things were formed in childhood doesn't mean they should still stay with us as adults. In fact, more often than not they don't serve us as we get older, but we will never even know they're obstructing our path unless we check.

No matter our experience in life, there are basic laws of nature that apply to all of us, and in the same way. We are all born, and eventually our experience of life here on earth ends, and in between those two points we're given many opportunities to make choices. While there are some periods of our lives where we feel we may not really be in control, for the most part, we have much more agency than we give ourselves credit for. Whatever events in your past have brought you to this moment, it's important that you know that you do have a choice.

An empowered life isn't about making lemonade out of lemons, or just throwing your hands up in the air and saying, "Well, there's nothing I can do, life has just thrown me a curveball." It's about choosing what you want out of all the things that are available to you in life. When problems arise, you can choose how you define the problem in the first place. How you define it then determines which solutions you will find.

We have already explored the idea that life doesn't give us lemons at all, and it's up to us to go out and get them if we want. This means it's also up to us to choose whether we see the things that happen to us as lemons in the first place. We have more power than we realize and need not limit ourselves to perceiving a situation and defining it reactively, based on an autopilot, surface-level understanding of it. We have the power to consciously choose a different perspective, one that perhaps opens up more doors or allows for different options and possibilities that serve us better.

Choosing is different from *deciding*.

A decision entails picking one of an array of potential options before us, without questioning whether those options are the only options, let alone whether any of them align with us. Choosing, on the other hand, begins with determining what, if any, of the things available are actually desirable to us.

If the options available to you don't align with you, then in reality they don't constitute options at all. You don't need to decide on one of them just because they're there in front of you. Instead, go back to the situation, reevaluate it, and consider different options. Only choose from those you align with the most. And if the answer is "none of them," then you need to reevaluate your situation and find better, more aligned options. There is always another option, it's just a question of creatively rethinking, processing anew, and redefining what's before you, until you get to an option that aligns with you.

This concept is true for just about anything. In fact, it's a fundamental principle of how we're truly meant to interact. We are meant to make choices, not just decisions. We can choose when we become aware of how different options land for us. We gain that awareness when we take the time to check in with ourselves, make sure we have clarity, and see what it is that serves our higher self and not our layers.

So often we surrender our control to life, and then become angry that we didn't get to choose. We reluctantly buy the blue shirt, so to speak, and convince ourselves it's good enough. If it's not what you really want or need, and you know so because you have checked in with yourself, then it isn't good enough. If the options presented to you aren't a fit, you can create new ones.

Just as the glass of a mirror reflects your outward appearance back to you, your perspective on life at any given moment reflects your inner world and state of being. It helps provide inner insight and awareness that we may otherwise be completely blind to, and yet subconsciously controlled by. Seeking clarity within ourselves gives us insight and empowers us to make choices, not just decisions.

The Power to Question

"Questioning oneself is a gift as well as a responsibility. It is only by questioning that we can find the answers that lead us to awareness and our path to personal freedom of choice."

What's important about this process of checking in and using life as our mirror is asking *what* questions rather than *why* questions. Using *what* shifts us from fear and judgment to a mindset of curiosity and exploration.

Instead of saying, "Why don't I want to go to work today?" consider shifting it to "What would it be like if I felt excited about work today?" The shift gives our brain a puzzle to solve, a theoretical mystery to explore in the safety of our own imagination. Developing this mindset of curiosity and adventure means that we have no expectations about how life will unfold for us. It keeps us open to possibility, and encourages us to check in, remain aware, and look at what's being reflected back to us with clearer eyes. It is how we begin to understand how we can lead ourselves through life with the mindset of an adventurer, ever-curious, open, and empowered as we venture out into the playground of life.

Living with an adventure mindset means you don't know what will happen, or how life will unfold when you venture out and engage. With this mindset, you want to check in and ask yourself if you're ready. And if you're not ready, that's okay. When those feelings arise, you want to return to your boardroom and ask: "What do I need to work on, change, or dissolve to be ready?"

Keeping an adventure mindset, and using our feelings about life as a mirror, means we can create space between us and whatever we're confronting. In that space there are infinite possibilities to seek out other choices, other options, other avenues besides just the ones we perceive when we're right up close to it. When we are too close to a situation, we forget that, for example, there are other clothing stores besides just the one that's nearest to our residence. We forget that the things we believe to be foundational, set in stone, immutable, and totally inflexible aren't really as rigid as we think. There is more to play with when we question and get curious. The gap between our believed capacity and our actual capacity is monumental, and we're so much more capable than we believe we are if we give ourselves the chance to choose.

At times, we all grapple with a resistance to choosing and slip back into deciding. The reason why we disempower ourselves is that it feels easier than contending with the internal resistance we encounter from our layers to re-empower ourselves. When we're disempowered, we do one of two things: chase or avoid. We chase what we believe will make us feel good and avoid what could make us feel bad or uncomfortable. Yet feelings are temporary, brain-generated sensations that only last until they're replaced by the next feeling. Unfortunately, being busy with chasing and avoiding feelings causes us to miss out on knowing our true selves. In today's world, we spend so much of our time chasing things, whether shopping, mindless distraction on social media, material things, money, popularity, or professional status. While these can absolutely be enjoyable, what we are primarily in a constant search for are the feelings we believe obtaining those things will either give us or spare us from.

Deep down, we know that this isn't satisfying for long and that those feelings are fleeting. When they pass, as all feelings eventually do, we repeat the same cycles in the hopes of recreating them. Whether or not we're aware of our layers, we like to feel good, so that's what we chase. Imagine how powerful we could be if we were aware enough to choose, to align ourselves with the best for us, and feel positive and empowered, excited about the road ahead. We would be free of the cycle of chasing and avoiding, less fearful of feeling, and, instead, we would be busy truly living.

The power to choose and to question is a huge gift as well as a responsibility we have to ourselves. In life, it's always a question of the domino effect, but which way do you want the dominoes to fall? When you start to choose, the whole array of possibilities opens up for you, and while that's amazing, it may at times feel overwhelming.

This process may very well bring up some resistance for you, and that's okay. When you feel that resistance, uneasiness, or fear, remember that you can decide what you want to do with it. Have a conversation with yourself. Validate, listen, question, and remain curious. Once you identify it, it loosens its grip. With my clients, I liken this process to the experience of putting on a sweater. When you put on a sweater, you put your arms through, your head, your body, and you settle it down around you. Creating a layer follows a similar process. Removing a layer is like taking off that sweater; you became used to going about your day with it on, and now as you're about to remove it, you may experience temporary discomfort. You will feel its texture as it comes off of you, and you might feel cold, exposed, or vulnerable. All of this is okay. This is part of the process. Depending on how ingrained it is within you, removing a layer may feel uncomfortable or painful, making you feel that specific vulnerability, which it was created to protect you from in the first place. At times it may feel as if the layer is coming to life and being created all over again. If this is your experience, remember it's a temporary upheaval. The sensation and emotions you're experiencing are those of the layer "coming off" and being on its way out, for the sole purpose of freeing yourself of it.

Experiences come and go and are rarely the same. Remembering that life is simply a space to create what we wish for ourselves allows us to reframe an unpleasant encounter. Rather than feel defeated "by life," we can remain empowered and choose what to do about it.

Ready for Adventure

"Adventure, real adventure, is about being open
to whatever comes to you in life."

When you set aside the expectations you had for life, the whole world opens up. When you approach life as a mirror, it means you can use it as a tool to check in with yourself, to reflect back on yourself. Do you like what you see in the mirror? How does it make you feel about yourself? Do you feel an urge to change the mirror, blame the mirror, or hide from the mirror? Or can you look at the mirror of life with eyes wide open, seeking out new and better choices that are in alignment with your higher self? The power is, and always has been, in your own hands.

When you approach life as a playground, a stage, a neutral space where you can create anything you want through your own choices, you set yourself up to have deeper, more authentic relationships with everyone else you meet. There is a key reason why the process of *No More Layers* begins inward, with the layers you carry and how they affect the relationship you have with yourself. Before you go out and have a relationship with anyone else, you must first establish a positive relationship with yourself. Take your rightful place at the head of your boardroom table and listen to what your inner committee members are telling you. You need to be in conversation with them, taking gentle control over the parts of yourself that have been running on autopilot, the ones that deferred to your layers, and to the loudest, most demanding voices, for so long. And then, when you go out into the world, the way you approach life will change.

All of this prepares you for a life of adventure.

Now, when I say adventure, I don't mean that you'll be expected to explore unknown jungles, climb active volcanoes, go skydiving, wrestle with bears in the woods, or get into a high-stakes car chase across a busy metropolis. Adventure, real adventure, is about being open to whatever comes to us in life. Because there will always be things that come to us, things that happen at or around us, things that are caused by others or by our own choices or decisions. How well we can deal with them and remain true to our higher self is the journey of life. That's the adventure.

Having an adventure mindset can be scary. Our brains crave control, comfort, safety, and routine. Routine can be great; it gives us structure and guidance, but it can also become a safety net. Layers are a form of safety, too, and are the ultimate comfort zone for your brain. They keep things safe for us, black and white, good or bad, yes or no. They bypass all of the higher functions of discernment in our minds, our higher selves, in order to keep our view of ourselves, of the world, and of others as simple as possible. You can experience one bad relationship and your brain will define how you approach dating, what you expect of yourself, whether or not you're desirable, lovable, worthy of respect. You may have had a distant parent growing up and your brain will have very deeply established layers that will unconsciously affect many aspects of your life.

Both stability and creativity have a place in our lives, but our dependence on rigid structure and safety can prevent us from being who we're truly meant to be. We all have these embedded safety nets, but they aren't the end of our story. If the boundaries shift, then that's part of your adventure. It opens up new possibilities and new ways of thinking and being that you never thought possible. Our brains crave steadiness and stability, but there's no creativity in routine, no adventure. Part of the adventure mindset is being open to change.

Yes, it may be easier to never question these layers, to keep the cast on, so to speak, and just go with the flow. But as you begin this journey, you will find that, once you see yourself in the mirror, you can't unsee it. Once you ask yourself, "Do I really want to have the mirror hide this fact from me? Would I want to see the truth, so I can make an empowered choice about how I show up in the world?" You'll know the answer. As scary as it is, it's so much better to live a life coming from a place of awareness, rather than covering your eyes, hiding your mirror, and pretending like you're fine. Over time, the long-term effects of this kind of disempowerment can be devastating and will pop up in all kinds of ways in nearly every aspect of your life. Emotions are a form of propelled energy, and, like energy, they can neither be created nor destroyed. They can only flow or become a strong current, but they have to go somewhere—and wouldn't you rather direct where they go, considering you're the one that has to feel them?

It's true that, sometimes, being alone with your own thoughts can be a scary place. It's intensely vulnerable because, when the layers are all stripped away, all that's left is you. Do you like who you see in the mirror? Not everyone can say they do.

The experience of life is different for everyone. Two people can walk the same forest path and stand in total silence for ten minutes, and their experiences might be totally different. Some people will experience peace, while others will want to crawl out of their skin. Almost opposite reactions, though it's the same path and the same trees. What makes each person react so differently? We all have different experiences of life, and those experiences are based on who we are, what we expect, how we look at life, and the layers we've formed within us. When we live from a place of vulnerability, there are more unknowns, more risks, more fears of being embarrassed or judged. But the rewards that come from this vulnerability are tremendous: a life fully lived, a self fully realized, and deeper, more intimate relationships with the people around us.

How we show up as our best selves within the playground of life isn't about forcing ourselves to be positive all the time or putting on a happy face when we don't feel happy inside. Often, "Fake it till you make it" doesn't work. It doesn't feel aligned. Real positivity is about empowerment, and empowerment is about ownership of oneself. All of the positive affirmations, uplifting relationships, job promotions, wealth, status, and everything external won't mean much if there's chaos inside of you.

In the next chapters, we'll explore some of the specific relationships and daily interactions that we encounter in life, such as the relationship between child and parent, between peers and spouses, and between a boss and an employee. Each of these relationships could be explored in their own book, but rather than going deeply into specifics, it's my hope that by starting off this book with the internal work and then stepping back to consider your engagement within life itself, you will now be equipped to review these relationship chapters through the lens of everything you have learned and put into practice. I hope you'll return to these chapters and refresh, go deeper, and continue to explore all the potential that is within you, as you identify and clear layers, awaken your adventure mindset, and begin to live the life experiences you seek and were meant to have ... the ones you *choose* to have.

Exercise — Conversations in the Mirror

I invite you now to find a mirror to practice with. It could be any size mirror, in any location that feels safe and comfortable. Even a handheld mirror works, although you may want to find a place to set it down, so your body is completely free to move. You may want to find a private space where you can feel safe to express whatever comes up.

Mirror Reflection Exercise

Find a quiet space and stand in front of a mirror. Take a few deep breaths to center yourself.

Gaze and observe: Can you maintain your own gaze, or do you feel the urge to look away? Sit with this sensation, acknowledge any emotions that arise as you peer at your reflection. Allow your mind to settle and simply observe yourself. Notice any shifts in your feelings as you continue to look. Avoid analyzing or suppressing what you experience; simply be an observer. If your thoughts or eyes wander, don't be concerned. This is normal. Bring your focus back to the mirror without self-criticism.

When you're ready, ask yourself: What am I noticing about what I'm feeling when I look so intently at myself? What thoughts just crossed my mind? What, if any, discomfort comes up for me? What's surprising you about what comes up? Is it comfortable, difficult, calming, or something else?

When you're ready, continue asking yourself these questions to probe deeper into what you're feeling:

- What are my choices?
- How do I feel about myself right now?
- Do I feel safe?
- Do I feel ready?
- Am I free of expectations about my day, and about my life today?
- Did I miss something?

Whichever questions arise, feel free to answer them in your own time and in your own way. Some of my clients write in their journal, while others dance it out. Others talk it through or send themselves a voice memo. There's no right or wrong way, just the one that works for you, honors you, and leads you to knowing more of who you are.

CHAPTER TEN

Our Relationships with Others

"The relationships we have with other people is like a hall of mirrors, with reflections of one another bouncing back and forth, shaped, distorted, and transmuted in real time by all the layers at play, and all without anyone's knowledge or permission."

Relationships are how we thrive. While the internal world is all about exploration, discovery, and potential, the external world is where the action takes place. It's a world of opportunity, with complex dynamics to navigate, lessons to learn, and choices to be made. Without the foundation of real awareness, we exist as merely responsive and reactive creatures, categorizing our interactions as "good" or "bad," and never integrating the tools that are being offered to us. But when we approach the relationships we have with others with a sense of clarity, curiosity, awareness, and intention, we learn so much more about ourselves, as well as about each other. Let's explore further.

Let's say your coworker comes into your office with a scowl on their face, and immediately you imagine your day is ruined. Or your boss schedules a vague "we need to talk" meeting, and you're consumed by anxiety for the rest of the day. Maybe you and your spouse are having an important conversation about finances and spending habits, which leads to an emotionally charged interaction and perhaps even blame.

The moment you step outside of yourself and your inner world on to the playground of life, you encounter a variety of interactions and relationships with individuals who are just as complex as you are, each having their own layers, as you do.

These relationships are crucial to who we are as evolving human beings. So far, we've explored the most important relationship we'll ever have—the relationship we develop with ourselves—as well as our one-sided relationship with life (which, as we've explored, isn't really a relationship at all). But it's within the relationships and interactions we do have with close friends, family members, parents, spouses, acquaintances, managers, employees, and all of the other people we encounter that we can further discover our layers and experience them at play. It's where our best growth can happen.

These relationships can and do truly present some of the greatest challenges, and yet it's through these challenges that some profound insights about our own layers are revealed. Unless you plan on staying indoors for the duration of your time here on earth and never interacting with another human being, you'll have relationships in your life that challenge you, make you grow, and reflect back to you insights about your inner self that you would never otherwise see on your own.

What Are Relationships?

"The paradox of all relationships is that the ones that love us best can both hurt us the most and help us the most, because through our interactions with them we will grow the most."

As human beings we're part of an intricate interconnected web of energy, an exchange of give and take that exists between all living beings. A relationship with others is based not only on the connection as it stands but also on the quality of energy both parties put into it. It's a dynamic, ideally reciprocal flow, dependent on the level of shared trust, awareness, and communication. When we invest our energy, a relationship has a greater chance of flourishing; when we withdraw it, it may wither and fade away. But unlike the relationship we have with ourselves, where we're one hundred percent accountable for both the give and the take, in our relationships to others, we can only ever be responsible for our own share of it.

That dynamic flow must be balanced for a relationship to truly thrive. Pouring more and more of ourselves into a relationship, energetically, doesn't guarantee its success. If you've ever had a friend become untrustworthy, unkind, or detached, you know how difficult, and eventually impossible, it is to maintain that one-sided relationship. Energetically you might feel that the flow is no longer reciprocal and the relationship no longer balanced. If one's partner lets their attention and affection dwindle, the other partner will often feel that shift energetically before they may even know the facts. They may pull back, and the relationship—that delicate alchemy of shared energies—becomes altered. Many people know what it's like to lose a friendship, end a partnership, break apart from a work dynamic, or consciously withdraw from an intimate relationship that's no longer an energetic fit. We know what it's like to draw our energy out of the equation and step away.

On the other hand, we also know what it's like to begin a relationship. Meeting a new person and "clicking" with them instantly is a sign of an energetic match in some way. Going on a first date and feeling like we want the day to go on forever because there's just so much to talk about, share, and enjoy about this new, interesting person is another clear sign of matching energy, at least at that stage. Relationships ebb and flow, and throughout our lifetimes we'll gain new ones, grow out of or end others, all the while riding the waves of our vast and complex interconnectedness as we grow, mature, and—perhaps most importantly—become aware of our own layers.

While the dynamic we have with life itself acts as a one-sided mirror that reflects us back to ourselves and our readiness to engage with the world, relationships we have with others act as an amplified version of that mirror. Every person that we're connected to provides us real-time, instant feedback, and we do the same for them. Every interaction and every relationship, no matter how new or deeply intimate, consists of an exchange and a mirroring of sorts, creating its own unique flow. The layers we have within us impact both what we mirror to others as well as how we perceive what's being mirrored back to us.

In other words, the layers we have determine if and how we receive our reflection back from another person. Those layers—when and as they come up—distort the lens through which we receive what the other person is reflecting back to us. Our layers tint and distort how that lands for us, which, in turn, impacts what we say and do in response, and how we mirror back. All of it, on both sides of the exchange, is impacted by all these layered distortions. The relationship we have with the other person becomes like a hall of mirrors, with reflections of one another bouncing back and forth, flowing, evolving, being shaped, distorted, and transmuted in real time by all the layers at play, and all without anyone's knowledge or permission.

It's almost as if our layers are having the conversations without us.

Consider seemingly simple interactions in the workplace between a manager and their employee. When the manager comes to tell their employee, "I like the presentation you gave at the meeting, but it ran a little long. Next time, do you think you could keep it to fifteen minutes, so we don't run over the allotted time?"

The manager may intend this advice to be received exactly as it is meant: we have a set amount of time for a meeting, and we want to be respectful of other people's time. However, if the employee has a layer within them that tells them "I talk too much. Nobody really wants to hear what I have to say or they wouldn't have minded me going over my allotted time," they will interpret that message with that layer in place. They may subconsciously revert to their childlike state and the internal age they were when they learned that message about themselves, and, at that moment, that same message will once again hold true for them as if it were reality.

This layer has distorted the message and will most likely distort the next thing that employee says or does as well. While they may not be rude or confrontational to their manager, in the future they may not volunteer to do presentations or try to back out of them, all for fear of being cut short or feeling unappreciated, even if they're truly good at what they do. All to avoid that same feeling again.

With different layers in place, however, the interpretation of that very same exchange could be wildly different. A primary layer of unworthiness might make the employee receive that message as "I don't know why I ever thought I was good enough to give that presentation. I'm never going to volunteer to do it. I feel so stupid." In contrast, a primary layer of entitlement might make the employee believe that the manager was threatened by how well they presented and was really using that criticism to cut them down and make them feel inadequate. All of these distortions and interpretations arise as a result of layers.

Another example of this kind of distortion happens all the time between partners and spouses. There is a vast chasm of difference between two equally authentic individuals having a conversation about household chores and two people accusing each other, saying, "You *never* do the laundry!" "Well, you *never* load the dishwasher or help me out when I need you to!" People lash out like this because the layers within them have told them something else is going on, something deeper than household chores or even partnership. Whatever layer is triggered and reacting, whether it's a layer of self-worth, acceptance, not being seen, or a fear of not being enough, the exchange has long shifted from simple housekeeping tasks to something much more personal and visceral. Eventually, it turns into the belief that this is the only quality of relationship they can have with each other.

Thankfully, that's not the truth. But this mirroring dynamic can so quickly become distorted when layers are at play—and because it's not just you with you, but you with another person, you have your own layers and they have theirs, and both become part of every interaction.

We categorize our relationships instinctively, including acquaintances, friends, colleagues, best friends, boyfriend, girlfriend, spouse, partner. Intuitively, we understand that the closer we are to someone, the more the focus narrows and the energy becomes precise, almost like a laser. A compliment from a stranger is nice, but a compliment from someone who knows us best means so much more. Likewise, an insult from a stranger might sting, but an insult from someone close to us hurts at a much deeper level. The paradox of all relationships is that the ones that love us best can hurt us the most. The energetic exchange of a relationship becomes more focused, more intense, more rewarding, and, yes, "riskier"—the more intimate the relationship, the closer our mirrors are to one another.

But when it comes to those precious, close, and fulfilling relationships, the risk is definitely worth the ensuing reward. It's a growing pain of sorts, and a lesson in being comfortable with our own vulnerability.

Our Layered Relationships

"Being triggered in a relationship means that a layer is trying to let us know it's there, but we often mistake this call for a lack that exists in the other person."

It's important to understand that all relationships are affected by layers. This almost feels like it goes without saying because all of us are affected by our layers, but sometimes when it comes to how we show up for other people and relate to other people, we forget. And not only do we forget that we're affected by our own layers and filter our experience of the other person through those layers, the other person is doing it, too, in their own way. Someone might say or do something that, to them, is perfectly innocuous, but because of our own layers we get triggered by it. Like the example before about the manager and employee, if the employee is not aware of their own layers, he or she will accept the distorted view and take it at face value. This will actually serve to reinforce that layer, not heal it! A lack of awareness of our own layers only serves to deeply ingrain that layer within us even more.

Being triggered in a relationship means that a layer is trying to let us know it's there. It's asking us to get curious, take a look, and explore what's there—but we often mistake this call for a lack existing in the other person. While it's true that sometimes there are overt signals that a relationship isn't balanced, serving us, or an energetic match, we also have a duty to look inward and seek to understand ourselves based on what this trigger is alerting us to examine. If we don't, and if we never use this opportunity to self-reflect when we're in a triggered state, then we'll never have the ability to show up for any relationship with a fully authentic self. Without looking inwardly to consider whether this person has triggered a layer within us, we might keep accepting the distorted message without questioning it, and keep reacting every time it's triggered.

All of this work takes place within. It's not our work to clear someone else's layers for them, and in fact, it's not even possible for us to do so. But as we work through our own layers, and feel ourselves from the inside out, we show up more authentically in every relationship, affecting shifts in our social dynamics and becoming a less distorted, more authentic mirror. The people we interact with will naturally begin to show up differently to us, based on the new and improved mirror we are now capable of being.

Connecting in a Disconnected World

*"Putting some space between you and the distortion
is the first step to reconnection."*

Self-ownership is absolutely essential to a life lived to the fullest. And yet there's so much of our world, and our approach to relationships, that stifles, hides, and diminishes these abilities. Despite all of the advantages that our hyper-connected world offers, we still struggle with relationships and disconnection from others. As social animals, this causes a profound amount of subconscious discomfort for us. We yearn for connection and understanding, but don't know how and where to find it. And although we may try and try throughout our lives, the layers we have within us distort our view of every single relationship we have—unless we make the conscious choice to see our layers, shift them, and dissolve them.

We are meant to show up to every relationship as our most authentic self, because when we do, everything changes. When we approach others with openness, honesty, and self-awareness, we're able to accept their responses with perspective and understand that they, too, have layers that inevitably affect the way in which they receive ours.

The moment we can create even the smallest amount of distance and space within us, between ourselves and our layers, then the real healing can begin. Within that space, no matter how small or brief, we gain perspective. Just as we understand that we're not our brains, we can see that we're not our layers. We don't have to believe the distorted view of the situation, and instead we can choose to look at it with perspective.

When our employee heard the message about their meeting running too long, their layer may have told them, "Ah, of course; you're always overdoing and overstepping." Or, "You love talking endlessly and taking up space. You think you're better than everyone. Better be quiet and don't make waves." With a bit of distance, a place to pause, breathe, and consider, the employee can instead ask themselves some important questions:

- Is there something here that is making me feel threatened and uncertain?

- When did I learn that I was too talkative and should be quiet to make people happier?

- What's beneath that belief, and do I still need to hold on to that layer?

Within that safe energetic space, the employee may find a sense of calm wash over them as the real awareness arrives: Their manager never told them to be quieter. They have a layer and it's been triggered, and they don't want it affecting their view of the world or their relationships anymore. It's the employee's responsibility to do this work, just as it is for all of us in our own ways.

For the couple that argues about household chores, if only one of them could find that space, that distance, to go to their boardroom even briefly and check in with themselves, they may find that they have a layer affecting how receptive they are to their partner's message. This layer is distorting that message and, in turn, directly shaping how they feel, react, and respond to both their partner's message and their partner. With a bit of distance and a pause for breath, they can instead ask these important questions:

- Is this really about laundry or dishes, or is there something else going on within me?

- What in me is being triggered? Where am I feeling it? What is it trying to tell me about myself?

- Is this how I want to show up in this relationship? Is this in alignment with who I am?

There's no single right answer that can "fix" every single relationship, because every relationship is a unique alchemical combination of the energy of both people, meeting, interacting, and flowing in the space between them. It may be easy to say, "I'll just stop doing the dishes, then you'll see how hard it really is!" But reactive answers don't actually cause real progress or growth. Even seemingly innocuous answers don't cause real change if they're made without self-examination and remain out of alignment.

The key is curiosity, inquiry, and questioning. Layers reveal themselves and dissolve when they're questioned. But if they're never examined, never questioned, and never cleared away, they will continue to show up in every area of your life until you can choose to look within.

Erica's Story — Letting Go of the Past

Erica lived what most would call a dynamic, adventurous, successful life. She explored multiple careers, traveled the world, and had recently begun the process of proactively downsizing her life in order to travel full-time and pursue her passion. And yet, underneath it all, she lived with this deep uncertainty that what she thought she wanted wasn't really what she wanted. Although this hadn't been the initial reason she had sought me out, the recurring theme soon emerged when she looked back throughout her life.

"This keeps happening for me, and I can't understand why!" Erica said. "I want to follow my heart, and I want to live aligned, but as I work hard it always feels like it's slipping away. I don't know what I'm doing wrong!"

As Erica and I worked through some of the layers surrounding this idea and her various "passions" throughout the course of her life, an interesting pattern emerged. Erica would be brimming with ideas and inspiration, only to feel as if she were getting tugged away by some invisible force. She was incredibly hard on herself and kept pushing herself to find new passions, as if she had to find a purpose for her existence and keep proving it over and over again. Though she was accomplished, these pursuits never felt entirely good, which confused her even more. Erica realized that she had formed a pattern of never staying very long doing one thing and was highly critical of herself. She didn't allow herself to feel bad, tired, or sad. She barely allowed herself time to think. Where did all this come from? Was her passion real or was it acting as a distraction? And if so, from what?

The timing of this newfound awareness wasn't a coincidence. In the process of downsizing her home, Erica was saying goodbye to a lot of inherited family heirlooms that she'd been holding onto for a long time. Many things that were her mother's specifically triggered a strong emotional response, and at first, Erica couldn't discern why.

"I loved my mother," Erica told me. "She was firm, but she was always there for me."

But the love that Erica's mother gave her throughout her life was always tinted through a very specific lens. One that, as it turned out, had shaped a profound layer within Erica.

Erica's mother had been a successful businesswoman at a time when it was rare for women to achieve positions of power. She'd worked so hard to get to where she was, and then had fallen unexpectedly pregnant with Erica. While dealing with what now would likely be diagnosed as postpartum depression, Erica's mother struggled profoundly and eventually let go of her business. Unsupported, and likely without her knowing it, she was left to transfer all of those feelings of frustration to Erica.

At the heart of the issue was something Erica never would have guessed. A layer of shame had formed so deeply and solidly within her. She was shocked to bear witness to it as it emerged before her.

It wasn't Erica's fault that she had been born at that time, to those parents, in that specific circumstance. Of course, her parents didn't outwardly blame Erica, and she hadn't done anything to shame her father, spite her mother, or "ruin her life." Logically, Erica knew this, and yet her understanding of the messages she received from both of her parents formed a profound layer within her that filled her with shame and feelings of undue responsibility and guilt. She felt shame as she believed she was the cause of her father taking on a second job as a waiter after her birth, one he himself was ashamed of. She had feelings of guilt because her mother had effectively been forced to abandon her career to tend to her. Because neither of her parents had ever examined their own layers, they had passed all of this down to Erica, who absorbed it all, as all children do.

All this time, this buildup of shame had caused Erica to respond fearfully, always needing goals as a way to prove herself, almost having to justify her right to be alive and distract herself from her deeply rooted layers. Because she had no awareness of her own layers and took at face value whatever was reflected back at her, she'd never thought to question whether there was some pattern or recurring theme in all of these different, seemingly disconnected events throughout her life. But with awareness, she could suddenly understand that carrying her mother's frustration and her father's shame had resulted in her own layer of shame—a feeling that she'd never really chosen or cared to carry. In fact, she didn't even agree with the premise for this layer at all.

Once she could gain enough space to observe this layer—and it was a significant one, so it did take some time and gentle awareness—Erica gained a whole new awareness of herself. She didn't want to be burdened by shame, and she didn't want to allow that layer to make her respond and react fearfully. She was afraid, but not for the reason she thought; it wasn't because her dream this time was out of alignment, but rather that she didn't see herself clearly. Once she did, she transformed, and was able to declutter her life and begin her joyful travels. Her first destination was a quiet Caribbean Island, where she'd have less distractions and a chance to be with herself.

The Power of Inner Alignment

While it surprised Erica to discover her recurrent theme and patterns, once she uncovered the source and dealt with this primary protective layer, so many things began to fall into alignment for her. Instead of running away from things and distracting herself so she didn't have to ever confront those feelings of shame, Erica was able to resolve that layer through internal work and choose for herself what was based on her new inner alignment.

While some of you may see yourselves in Erica's story and relate to recurring shame or feelings of guilt, others might not. For each of you reading this, your own primary layer will be specific to you. The goal with all of this is for you to find your place of inner alignment, the place where you no longer need to distract yourself from who you would be if you didn't have that layer in place limiting you.

When a layer is in place, we find ourselves disempowered, making decisions rather than choices. Decisions are not based on internal alignment and therefore can result in feelings of resentment, dissatisfaction, distress, or discomfort. Until we know who we are, we cannot ever truly be satisfied and content.

I'd like to invite you to take a moment and pause to explore yourself after everything you've learned so far. In a journal, or in any exploration method that works for you, think about these questions:

- What do I do to distract myself from uncomfortable feelings and situations?

- What am I actually distracting myself from? Name it.

- What would it be like if I didn't distract myself this way?

- Who would I be if I didn't need to distract myself from these things?

Feel free to sit with these questions and take note of whatever arises. Do you notice any patterns?

Note any insights you receive from this questioning.

A Dynamic Mirror

"The mirror held up to us by others is dynamic and ever evolving, based on both our layers and those of the ones we interact with."

In Chapter Four, we first introduced the idea of primary layers of protection. While we have touched on it a few more times since then, I'd like to return to that idea and go a little deeper. As you begin to develop this inner alignment, this awareness of who you truly are, you can begin to make more empowered choices. When this shift happens, you will find that you begin to move through the world in a very different way. Your perspective changes. As it does, your attitude, actions, and capacity to show up in the external world will feel more aligned with how you truly want to experience life.

While there are paths to enlightenment and different forms of self-development that call for isolation as a way to get there, most of us need to maintain connection with others. We're wired that way. For all the great internal work we do, it means very little if we can't continue to be out in the world interacting with others, regardless of the layers they have.

This journey is an internal one. Our primary layers are deep and profound, most often created within us from a very young age. They inform the way in which the energies we receive from others will become distorted. The same question might trigger very different feelings within each of us, depending on the primary layer we have.

A boss approaches their employee asking: "Can we talk later?" This can provoke an inner dialogue such as:

- *Shame:* "I'm so embarrassed; my boss shouldn't have to correct me."

- *Trust:* "My boss definitely has it out for me, does not trust me to do a good job, and can't even just tell me what's going on here and now."

- *Worthiness:* "Am I even good at my job?"

- *Perfection:* "Is it possible I made a mistake? I must have done something so wrong they have to talk to me privately!"

- *Identity:* "Is this even the right job for me? Maybe I don't really belong here after all."

- *Agency:* "I knew I should not have taken on this project in the first place."

- ***Entitlement:*** "I can't believe my boss wants to speak to me. He didn't even say when, and he of all people knows how much work I have to do. I don't have time. It's so annoying."

Because of our layers, we quickly write up an entire narrative when we feel as if some element of our core self is under attack. But are we truly under attack? And what do those questions have to do with our core self? When we have a primary layer, a totally neutral comment will have an added interpretation. So, what do we do when this happens?

Every relationship we have is an opportunity to see ourselves in the mirror that others hold up to us. It gives us invaluable insight into ourselves, once we know how and where to look for it. The same is true for others; we serve as a mirror to them. When we allow our layers to take over, however, the insight is lost, and all incoming messages are filtered through those layers. Without awareness, the only messages we get are distorted ones.

The mirror of life is static; in itself, it never changes and simply reflects who we are at any given moment. But the mirror we see in others is dynamic and ever evolving, based on both our layers and those of the person mirroring us. Because of this complexity, this mirror, unlike life, isn't objective. It's informed by our respective layers and the interaction between them. As we explore, question, and gain awareness, we can learn how to create just enough space to recognize, navigate, and ultimately dissolve our layers, becoming proactive in our interactions and leaving reactivity behind.

The Work Begins

There are approaches that suggest giving up all earthly possessions, or surrendering completely to the universe, or changing some aspect of your external life as the only way to find peace. While these approaches may work for some, there are no hard-and-fast rules about how many of your relationships to cultivate or discard, how many items of clothing to own or donate, or what part of the world you must live in, to find that peace. But as you grow in awareness, you will come to realize that all of the work is first and foremost internal. You don't have to change a single thing externally, and yet everything will begin to shift as you do the internal work.

The moment you create space to gain awareness of your layers, you can find that alignment and see the world with the openness and eyes of an adventurer. Then, everything shifts. You show up differently in all of your relationships. You mirror back to others more authentically and, in turn, what they mirror back to you changes. You both begin to nurture authenticity in each other.

Occasionally, however, showing up as your authentic self is so challenging to others that they simply can't be around it, or you, anymore. If you encounter such a situation, I want you to understand it has nothing to do with you and isn't a personal rejection of your growth. One reason why, at times, people may be reluctant to embrace the results of your inner work and embark on their own is that things really do shift in this kind of work. A brain that craves stability and status quo isn't always prepared to loosen its grip and allow for these shifts, as positive as they are. What is known, even if it continues to make people unhappy or miserable, is always deemed safer by the brain. Going within, taking a look at layers, healing, and growing can engender fear as it is unknown territory and therefore potentially unsafe.

Playing it safe is the position of choice for the brain. If you encounter resistance from someone in response to your growth, know that this is what may be at play for them. The brain will do its utmost to keep them safe by keeping their layers in place and resisting any movement, even toward their own authenticity. In such a case, it's important to remember that all you are responsible for in each of your relationships is to do the work to become as authentic a mirror as you can be. It is no more, or less, than that, and you're definitely not responsible for clearing anyone else's layers. While the status quo might give the illusion of safety and control, the reality is that it lacks alignment, which is ultimately what all human beings crave to feel fulfilled.

Doing the internal work means you show up more as yourself, and when that happens, your relationships shift, seemingly on their own. You see, your relationships are dependent on you. They match up to how you show up, and then reflect back to you where you're at. As you continue to show up more authentically, your interactions can only reflect that authenticity and will match your energy.

The following chapters explore some of the relationship dynamics that you may experience throughout your life. These include peer-to-peer, employee to employer, partners and spouses, and child to parent. These chapters will not examine the complexities of these dynamics and aren't intended to be an in-depth look at any of these relationships, but rather the start of an exploration into your own layers and how they're expressed within the context of these relationships and dynamics. As you work through them, feel free to return to this chapter and the exercise below.

Exercise — The Web of Relationships

As we prepare to dive deeper into specific types of relationships each of us encounter throughout our lives, it can be helpful to get a visual overview of which relationships are affecting us—both from our past as well as in our present. There are two ways to go about this, and I suggest doing both.

Relationship Circles

The first way is by creating our circle of relationships.

- On a piece of paper, write your name down and place it in a small circle.

- Draw a slightly larger circle around this one, and within that circle, write the names of people who are close to you. This could be your spouse, your best friend, your children, or anyone close to you.

- Continue drawing larger and larger circles for connections and relationships, placing people closer in or further away, depending on your connection to them.

Once you've created your circle of relationships, sit with it and consider if everyone is where you want them to be. Are there relationships which feel far too distant and you wish you could bring them closer? Are there people who are very close to you energetically but from whom you might want some distance? Feel free to journal about this and whatever comes up. There's no right way to do this, and it's perfectly fine if those individuals society expects you'd be closer to just don't fit energetically within that space. Be honest with yourself and remember to accept your feelings without judgment or criticism.

Relationship Tree

Another way to consider relationships that are affecting you energetically is through a genogram. A genogram is functionally a family tree, but it also includes relational and psychological information, not just lineage, dates, and names. Some genograms use different shapes for different groups or genders. There are also symbols for the type of relationships couples, siblings, or family members have to each other.

If you feel called to do so, you can explore and begin to create your relationship tree, or genogram, by simply finding any family tree template and using it as your guide. Doing this on paper is often much more impactful, although there are numerous online software options. The important fact is not the aesthetics but the information.

Add what you know about the lives, struggles, and challenges each member faced, to the extent you know them. Or you can take an abstract route and use color to denote mood, feeling, or general emotion. A grandfather who was light, bubbly, and friendly may be circled in yellow, for example, while an uncle who struggled with depression could have a symbol beside his name to note that. You may want to include current and deceased people within your circles if you discover their messages within your own layers.

With your circles and your genogram in front of you, answer these questions:

- What messages did you absorb from them that you would welcome into your daily life?

- Are there other ones you have absorbed that you're now ready to dissolve?

- In what way do your current relationships serve you?

- What insights did you learn?

- Feel free to journal or draw whatever comes up for you.

Remember a genogram is a dynamic document. It can serve you in identifying patterns and trends within your own past. You can refer back to it and update it at any time.

CHAPTER ELEVEN

Uncovering Our Family Layers

"We don't get to choose our families, and we don't arrive with the full understanding that the parents we are born to are on their own path of healing, self-alignment, and working through their own layers."

There's so much that can be said about the layers we inherit from our family of origin—from our parents, our ancestors, and everyone in our immediate sphere when we arrive in this world. When it comes to exploring layers, and the formation of layers, there's more than enough to cover an entire book just on the topic of family. With that said, I want to open the first of these four relationship-specific chapters with a clear context for what they are, and what they aren't.

This chapter is intended to be an exploration of the types of layers that can originate in childhood, and how and why we should be aware of them as we go through our own internal journey. It is a high-level overview of this incredibly complex topic. While we don't get to choose our families, we also don't arrive with the full understanding that the parents we are born to are on their own path of healing, self-alignment, and working through their own layers. Instead, we're born without layers, ready to absorb and take in all of these early interactions and experiences in order to help us define the parameters for "how to be a human." It is during this process that layers start to form within us.

Once this happens and the deep layers formed within us during our childhood moments become fixed, it is up to us and no one else to turn our awareness to the vast and complex expanse of our inner world, and our layers. With this knowledge, we can learn, grow, and gain awareness. To do so, we have to let go of the idea that it's our job to tend to anyone before ourselves; and with family, this can get challenging.

With this in mind, the purpose of this chapter is not to completely and thoroughly address every single possible family dynamic, or a way to diagnose or treat our loved ones, or a way to weaponize our own experience against them. Many people with complex and challenging families believe their only options are to "deal with it" or cut their family off completely, but this chapter won't advise you to do either. Rather, the goal of this chapter is to gain a deeper awareness and understanding of the layers you may have formed early on, in order to create space to grow and heal within yourself.

Every single other human, including our parents, is just as complex and layered as we are, whether or not they're conscious of their layers or working through them. This chapter is not intended to be an excuse or justification for the way things may have happened in your life, but it can offer some clarity. Clarity that can lead to awareness, which, as you've seen throughout this book, is the first step toward creating space for self-discovery, wholeness, and freedom.

The Deep Roots of Our Family Layers

"While we can never truly undo our earliest familial impact, we can absolutely acknowledge and resolve it however we choose to."

To me, the phrase "family of origin" means both the family you originate from as well as the origin of some of the deepest layers you have.

Just as we don't get to choose the family we're born into, we often don't have any say at all over the surrounding environmental factors that shape our early concept of the world, and of ourselves. In fact, while some can pinpoint exactly what it is in their family, upbringing or environment that caused them to form a layer, others go for decades completely unaware of the factors that contributed to their layers, let alone to having any layers.

In Chapter Four, we began exploring the idea that some of our most profound, core layers—our primary layers of protection—are often formed in childhood as a result of interactions with our family of origin. Even once we've identified primary layers, the steps in addressing these deeply entrenched layers are often easier said than done. Unlike any other relationship we have, which we can walk away from if it's no longer healthy for us, we can never truly erase our earliest familial impact. We can create physical and emotional distance or closeness with family members, but the messages, lessons, and layers formed by our early childhood experiences are deeply rooted within us, asking to be acknowledged and eventually resolved.

By now you have likely had the chance to begin exploring some of your own layers. If you were able to identify a recurrent theme or pattern, or if you do have a sense of what your primary layer of protection might be, this chapter will help you gain more awareness of what role your family of origin may have played in the development of that layer, as well as what you can do with that new awareness moving forward.

This chapter will explore some of the common primary layers that can be formed from these early childhood stages. You'll see how those primary layers can be expressed later in life. Finally, with this understanding, you can empower yourself to move forward with confidence, awareness, and a clearer internal alignment, all of which will lead you to what your higher self yearns to achieve.

Diving Deep into Our Primary Layers

"Primary layers are the key lens and structural support through which all other layers are formed. Choosing to work through a primary layer releases all derivative layers that come with it."

Let's take a look at some of the most common primary layers that are installed within us, so to speak, from our earliest moments of life.

Our family and early childhood experiences play a significant role in the layers we subconsciously develop. These core layers function as the key lens and structural support through which all of our other derivative layers are formed. This is key, as working through a primary layer releases all derivative layers that come with it. Exploring these primary layers is therefore essential. It requires us to take a look back at the early childhood perceptions we had of our outer and inner worlds at the time. It also entails considering what forces may have been at play that contributed to the formation of those layers.

As with all layers, awareness is key. So, let's look more deeply into some of these primary layers and work through some lines of questioning that can help uncover them for you.

Primary Layer: Trust

A child's first lesson is one of trust. We're born so helpless and vulnerable, desperately needy and hopelessly noisy compared to every other newborn mammal on the planet. We have no choice but to rely on our caregivers for everything we need. And it's important to remember that young children don't want things until their brains develop a little further; they only know what they need. Furthermore, up until a certain age they don't see a distinction between themselves and their caregiver. Their whole experience is initially based on how their caregivers respond or don't respond to their needs.

We have a lot of moralizing beliefs around children and neediness in our culture, and this isn't new. The idea that crying babies should be quiet, laying there even if it means suppressing their own needs in favor of our adult ones, is as absurd as it is pervasive. Often, young children are perceived as annoying, whiny, and demanding, as if they're waking up each morning choosing to make their parents' lives miserable just for their own amusement. In reality, their world is very different from the adult world. It's simply not developmentally reasonable to expect a young child to have anywhere near the reasoning capacity, nor the foresight, intention, or discernment of an adult.

Rationally, we know this. In practice, and as tired, often exhausted parents will tell you, it's difficult to always remember. That said, these trust-based layers often arise within families where the adults who were supposed to be reliable caregivers were not present, dependable, or consistent. This need not be as a result of a profound trauma, or deep and terrible neglect, but merely a pattern of behavior over time, from which the child viscerally learns that their needs won't be met. They cannot meet them themselves and therefore they cannot trust to have them met. The input these children receive in early childhood from their world is that when they're hungry, tired, or when they crave attention or comfort (as all humans do), they cannot always depend on having those needs met. For some, it may result in more neediness, and for others, the beginning of the suppression of their needs. In either case, it's a temporary solution intended to help, but often results in the creation of a layer.

A primary layer can show up in adults in different, almost contradictory ways, which makes it a fascinating layer to explore. Just like an infant who stops crying for food but remains hungry, the need doesn't simply go away with inattention. The messaging around meeting that need is where the layer forms. When needs are not met, that reality becomes buried. Sometimes, adults with these trust-based layers become hyper-resilient, extremely independent, and overextended, often reluctant to ask for any help, pushing people away, avoiding deeper connections, and often having trouble in relationships. Or they become totally disempowered, stuck, feeling unheard, angry, chronically disappointed that the world seemingly doesn't consider them. They continue to search, often for any outward source to meet their needs, never fully realizing their own capacity and inner power to have their needs finally met by themselves. Of course, it's not bad to be independent and capable, but we're social creatures, and we need community not just for assistance but for emotional support. As we've previously explored, we're meant to interact with each other, grow from one another, and act as a mirror to each other as authentically as we can.

If you identify a primary layer surrounding trust within you, take the time now to journal on the following questions:

- Do I trust myself to meet my own needs?
- What would that feel like? What needs of mine aren't getting met?
- Which of my unmet needs could I meet on my own?
- What would be different for me if those needs were met?

Primary Layer: Shame

Shame-based layers often hold us back from expressing our true selves, and they show up in private spaces, the places where we're most vulnerable and feel most exposed. Shame is a deeply rooted feeling and belief that no matter what you do, or don't do, whatever action you take, you're intrinsically shameful. Shame is something you can't wash off, and a primary shame layer can deeply impact individuals throughout their lives.

Shame-based layers often arise within families that have a strict moral code that focuses on the intrinsic nature of humans as being shameful in some way. Because of this, children learn very quickly that normal human behaviors and even phases of development are dirty, shameful, and worthy of scorn. It isn't that they did the wrong thing, but the message often received is that they're fundamentally bad or the source of "the problem" simply for being. Someone with a shame-based layer may still feel a deep sense of anxiety and shame even when they're "doing everything right."

This primary shame layer leads to an adult life where one tries to escape their life, may be very self-critical or make themselves small, living way beneath their potential. No matter what they do or don't do, they're not good. This traps people in a no-win scenario; no matter their efforts or intrinsic values, and even if they follow all of the rules set before them, they will never be free from shame until they release the internal layer around it.

If you identify a primary layer surrounding shame within you, take the time now to journal on the following questions:

- What is the earliest experience of feeling shame I recall? What happened?

- What is it that I feel shameful about today?

- Do I believe the shame I feel to be true?

- What would I believe about myself if I stopped feeling this shame?

Primary Layer: Worthiness

Worthiness is fundamentally about the right to take up space in the world, and it's a complicated primary layer to detangle. Some individuals who discover this layer often appear to be very well-adjusted, easygoing, even successful. Yet inside, individuals with this layer never feel like they deserve the things they've earned. They may rationalize to themselves, "Oh, they only listen to me because I'm the boss and they have to put up with me." They don't feel as if they have any real merit, and they can justify all of their success based on any other reason besides their own worth.

Worthiness-based layers often arise as a result of children feeling diminished, or as if their very existence, voice, and needs were of lesser importance. When children feel as if they must prove themselves or fight for their place in their family, they either become smaller and smaller to fit the little space of worth that's created for them, or they act in ways that try to "prove" their worth, which can run them ragged and feeling inadequate despite all of their efforts.

If you identify a primary layer surrounding worthiness within you, take the time now to journal on the following questions:

- In what aspect of my life do I find myself trying to prove something?
- Do I believe that people only like me because of what I do, and not who I am?
- Do I allow people to see "the real me"? If not, why?
- What would happen if I did allow that?

Primary Layer: Perfection

Perfection is the primary layer I had, and I know it entirely too well. For years and years, my primary layer of perfection gave me guidelines to follow in order to constantly better myself. With perfection, however, it's impossible to be perfect enough. There's an incessant striving behind perfection-based layers. Individuals with a critical eye, who are knowledge-seekers, innovators, and constantly curious can often be perfectionists. They see room for improvement everywhere, ways to optimize, perfect, and refine themselves in everything they do. If they're not careful and aware, they can become consumed by it.

If you identify a primary layer surrounding perfection within you, take the time now to journal on the following questions:

- Do I actually want to be perfect?

- Does being in strive mode and overreach make me feel happy?
- Have I ever considered any other way?
- What would I do differently if I didn't feel the pull to be perfect?

Primary Layer: Identity

Identity-based layers may be formed a little later in childhood, as it's a more complex question that's primarily explored during developmental periods of individuation. In a sense, this primary layer is about suppressing some fundamental aspect of your true identity in order to come into alignment with someone else's expectations. Children form identity-based layers when they're raised within families with rigid views on core aspects of identity, status, profession, behavior, or sexuality. When children are raised in families where they cannot express some aspect of their core identity, they may form a layer around that.

This type of layer shows up similarly to shame, but the difference is that identity-based layers are more about safety and belonging than authenticity. These primary layers inform people that there's no safe way to truly be who they are without being rejected by their families or communities.

If you identify a primary layer surrounding identity within you, take the time now to journal on the following questions:

- Do I know who I really am, what I like and dislike, and what I want?
- Are there things about me and my intrinsic identity I'm scared to question?
- What would happen if I explored or questioned those things?
- What would it look like to live authentically?

Primary Layer: Agency

Agency is more than just a deficit in confidence or a lack of willpower, it's a primary layer that keeps us safe by telling us not to risk a sure thing by stretching out to reach our dreams. A primary layer around agency keeps us small and safe, as all layers do, by making us well aware of how ill-equipped we are to venture out into the world with all of its perceived risks and dangers.

Agency-based layers might develop from parents that are a little too cautious, a little too quick to solve problems and whisk a child away from their challenges. As a result, children learn that any challenge is a threat, and threat means danger. They never get the chance to be frustrated, to fail and learn from that failure, to become resilient and capable despite setbacks. When this primary layer forms, a person might become bitter and resentful toward themselves or others. They know, deep down, that they want more from themselves, and that they really are capable of more, but the layer keeps them afraid of the things they want. Until they can create space between themselves and that layer, they won't be able to challenge that idea.

If you identify a primary layer surrounding agency within you, take the time now to journal on the following questions:

- Do I feel like I have power to direct my own life?
- Do I feel like someone else or some other force is really in control?
- What would it take for me to gain control over my own life, my choices, and my future?
- What actions can I take to empower myself for the life experience I desire?

Primary Layer: Entitlement

Entitlement is about the real or perceived right to have, do, or be something. It's about the right to take up a certain amount of space, often more than what's rightfully ours, usually without much consideration for others. People with a layer around entitlement often appear to sit on a high-and-mighty perch, looking down upon the world as they wait on people to fetch them everything. In reality, layers of entitlement often stem from feelings of being less-than, such that they'll attempt to compensate for this diminished, underdeveloped sense of self by looking to others. Instead of turning inward and allowing space for challenge, growth, and expansion, layers surrounding entitlement train people from a very young age to expect less from themselves and more from others, whether it's to provide for them physically, financially, or emotionally. They're inadvertently given the message that they're not only owed by others, but also that they may not be capable enough to do it themselves. Deep down they never learned to believe and trust that they're powerful, resilient, and capable enough to meet their needs for themselves. They weren't shown, nor did they experience the sense of fulfillment that comes with fully being in the driver's seat and directing their own life experience in a more authentic way.

Conversely, layers around entitlement can even arise when a child is exposed to an environment that lacks true kindness, compassion, and empathy. They learn they cannot count on their caregivers or the world around them to meet their emotional needs and provide them with a sense of safety. They learn they must fend for themselves and, since as young children they cannot yet do so, they feel disempowered. When disempowerment is repeatedly experienced, it creates a sense of helplessness and inadequacy. Over time, as the child becomes an adult, it can develop into a reactive, protective false inner sense that "the world and others owe me."

The underdeveloped sense of self causes protective layers to form and, as all layers do, they block you from your true, authentic, empowered self. If you identify a primary layer of entitlement within you, take the time now to journal on the following questions:

- Do I feel the need to take up a lot of space for fear of not having enough?

- Do I feel bad or belittled when I have to fend for myself?

- What would I have to shift about my belief in myself to feel empowered in life situations?

- Do I truly hold myself responsible for my actions?

A Word about Guilt and its Relationship to Shame

Guilt becomes familiar to most if not all of us at one point or another in our lives. It can be such a strong emotion and motivator, yet as you may have noticed, it is not explored in this book as a stand-alone primary layer.

While guilt and shame are often interconnected, can be mistaken for each other, and over time repeated feelings of guilt can even feed our shame, they are not the same. In this book we will be exploring shame as the primary layer rather than guilt, though at times you may see references to shame and guilt together.

The distinction is that guilt is about an undue feeling of responsibility for a given behavior, while shame runs deeper. Where guilt is a response to an action or inaction, shame is deeply seeded and a state of being.

Guilt is also often perceived as imposed upon us by someone else, and so, in this regard, guilt is externally driven. You'll often hear yourself or someone say: "I feel so guilty because I disappointed her," or "He expected me to help him out all day and I couldn't, and now he's trying to make me feel guilty."

In other instances, however, guilt is simply an uncomfortable message that we could have done better or perhaps we allowed something else to stand in our way of doing better. In such cases, guilt in healthy doses can serve as a catalyst and motivator to take ownership of one's actions, make amends, and do better.

In and of itself guilt is most always reactive, whereas shame is existential, takes us over, defines how we see ourselves, and impacts what we believe we are. In that sense shame becomes a primary layer. On the other hand, guilt, or rather the susceptibility and propensity we have for feeling guilt, is most often an indication and the expression of an existing foundational primary layer such as perfection, worthiness, or, you guessed it, shame.

The Mirror Doesn't Matter

"It's up to us to direct our own lives, heal, and consciously choose the future we desire."

As we've reviewed each of the primary layers, one or more may have resonated with you. This is certainly not a comprehensive list of all layers, and each of us is a complex system with unique layers and a unique view of the world. The most important thing to understand about this part of the process is that, when it comes to layers which are formed by our early childhood experiences, the mirror doesn't matter.

What does this mean?

We've spoken before about how relationships can be mirrors for us, and how the things others do or say often serve to reflect back the things we think and feel about ourselves. When we look in the mirror and see that we have a hair out of place, we don't get mad at the mirror for showing us something about ourselves. We gain awareness of what our hair looks like, and we can then choose if and what we do about it. The choice is ours. But at no point was the mirror itself the thing that needed to change, nor do we truly have any agency or responsibility to change the mirror either. Our only duty is to ourselves.

In the same way, we have no duty, responsibility, or even power to change how others have behaved, are behaving, or will behave in the future. It's completely out of our hands. Isn't that a relief? Much as we may want to change how other people treat us, we can't, and it's not our role to do so. This means that instead of directing all our frustrations at the people around us—the mirrors that are reflecting back some inner truth that only we can change—it's up to us to direct our own lives, heal, and consciously choose the life experience we desire.

What this looks like, in practice, is a perspective shift from external to internal. Your mother may not have had the tools, interest, or capacity to be there for you the way you needed and deserved her to be. Your father may have been overbearing and demanding, pushing you to achieve because he saw you as an extension of his own self. Your sibling may have rejected the role they played in the family and taken out their frustrations on you. All of these things, and so many more, can be absolutely true, as your very real, lived experience. These experiences may have likely formed layers within you that affect you even to this very moment. While all this is true, ask yourself the following question: is that what I still want?

Take a moment to truly consider that question. Do you want those layers to stay where they are, holding you in place, keeping you "safe," and preventing you from living the authentic life your higher self could otherwise choose? It sounds deceptively simple, but that's the question that sits at the heart of the matter. Is this what you still want?

People aren't static mirrors, it's true. People do and say all kinds of active, hurtful, toxic, damaging things to us. Sometimes they might even be the people who raised us and helped install our earliest layers. While they might continue their hurtful patterns, we have a profound emotional connection with these "mirrors" in our lives. Since everyone around us functions like a mirror, we can explore what's being reflected back to us at any given moment with curiosity and awareness. We can bravely dive deep into those reflected feelings and trace them back to the source: ourselves.

Our jobs are not to change the other person so that we feel better around them. Our responsibility is simply to grow and evolve ourselves so we can become a version where our interactions with other people are in alignment with who we are.

No matter your experience in childhood, healing is absolutely possible. You can always take steps to understand and acknowledge your starting point, and gain awareness in order to grow and heal. Whatever happened that caused you to form these layers wasn't your fault, nor was it the fault of those around you. They can be explored, worked through, and dissolved as you see fit with who you are today. Your past and your layers have brought you to this moment. Your present is meant to be lived and your future is yet to be written, and you have the right to write it in full alignment with who you are.

As you become aware, grow, and evolve, the dynamic with others evolves as well, almost organically. This is true in every relationship you have, and especially true in your family of origin and with your parents. As you focus on yourself and your own layers, the change you create within will subconsciously inspire others to change, without you having to do a single thing. This is why I say that the mirror doesn't matter. That person, or parent, may never have the capacity to search inside themselves, gain insight, remove layers, resolve their own past traumas, reach out with an apology, or do any single thing, but you're still in charge of you. There's no confrontation, no severing of ties, no diagnosing of others, nothing but the powerful internal work that you do as you curiously and bravely seek out your own layers, and achieve a sense of alignment, purpose, and self-knowing. From there, everything outside of you naturally shifts too, most often to match your newfound inner alignment.

There's Always a Solution
(and it's Usually You)

*"The answer is always within you and will be the one
that's truly in alignment with your higher self."*

As you continue your journey through this book, and through this process, you've undoubtedly begun to identify not only your own layers but also gained insight into what might be going on within other people in your circle. In one sense, it's easier to see something like this from an external perspective, but on the other, nobody truly knows what's going on inside someone's mind except the person themselves. Therefore, it's important at this stage to avoid rushing to any judgments, either of yourself or anyone else. We can theorize all we want, but the real work is within.

Families are complex, interconnected organisms. When you begin your own healing journey to resolve the layers formed within you during childhood, how do you continue to interact with other family members who can't or won't do the same? Families come in all shapes and sizes, from outright abuse to more subtle diminishment, from families that lack boundaries to ones that are threatened by depth and change. If you grew up in a family where the message surrounding uncomfortable feelings was, "We don't go there, and you can't either," or "Stay positive, cheer up, move on," being the person who starts to feel out of alignment with this philosophy will certainly make people react to your new energy. So, what do you do then?

Have you ever had a coworker or friend return from a long trip with their family and noticed changes in them? Maybe their way of speaking shifted slightly, they used words or expressions you haven't heard them say in a very long time, or their reactions seemed different, unusually more energetic or more subdued. Whether they're aware of this or not, it's always fascinating to see someone become a slightly different version of themselves after spending a concentrated amount of time with their family, away from their daily influences and context.

Maybe you've experienced this, too, or had someone point it out to you. Either way, it's one clear sign that, for many of us, family has a way of reactivating parts inside of us that have become dormant, suppressed, or expanded over time. Some of us may experience family reunions as limiting or constricting, where the landscape of the family dynamic doesn't allow for our expanded self to have its space, thus making us revert back to dependent childhood behaviors that we've otherwise long outgrown in our adult lives.

Spending even a little bit of time around a family member who triggers a layer can become an intensely destabilizing event, no matter how much inner work we've done. Because our primary protective layers are so linked to our family, spending even a small amount of time around family can pull us right back into position, as if with the push of a button on a time machine—no matter how old we are, or where we are at in our lives.

So, what can we do? As with all our other layers, the first step begins with awareness. We can heal those family layers by going within, getting a better sense of our inner landscape and triggers, and choosing what is in alignment with our higher selves. We can begin to heal if we can remain present, intentional, and consciously avoid reverting back to that autopilot, layered version of ourselves that perhaps once existed within that family dynamic but no longer has to.

When we let go of the mistaken idea that we can make someone else change if we just try hard enough, we stop feeling victimized, and instead become empowered to place our attention and intention on our own growth. Freeing ourselves from the idea that we must have control over another human being in order to reclaim any of our own power means we can actually reclaim all of our power to help ourselves. The people in our lives—even foundational family members—need not change for us to experience growth and healing. We're no longer dependent on anyone but ourselves. This realization came as a relief to many of my clients.

It's important to remember that by giving yourself the responsibility to heal, you're not assigning blame to yourself or anyone else. It's not even a question of fault, but rather one of agency. You're in charge of you: your layers, your awareness, and your authentic alignment.

When Family Layers Get Triggered

"The fascinating thing about the process of exploring primary layers is that you can change your entire family dynamic without ever having to address it with your family."

Even after becoming aware of a primary layer, the times when you're triggered by your family of origin can still be intensely challenging, upsetting, and complex. Not only that, but it can be incredibly difficult to depersonalize the actions other people take—to remember that the things they do aren't ever really about us.

Because the relationships we have with others act as mirrors, giving us a glimpse into ourselves by offering up a view of how other people's actions make us feel, we can understand that we can either react through a clear mirror, or through a layered one. Our layers—especially our core layers—tint our mirrors, so to speak. The fewer layers we have, the clearer and less distorted that mirroring will be. The mirroring back is really a reflection of how we understand things and how we interpret them through the filters of our own layers. This could be a pink-tinted veil that's very sheer, or a thick, dark, dense fog that obscures nearly everything. Regardless, when these layers are in place, we react to the filter and not the truth.

But the beauty of this mirroring is that it calls you to attention. Awareness is often found at a crossroads and in the moments of pause that you intentionally make space for. What you do with that awareness is always your choice. There is tremendous power in that space.

A trigger is the expression of a layer. It's not uncommon for clients that I've worked with to resolve many of their layers, see profound change in many areas of their lives, and still get triggered by the things their family members say or do—or the things they should do, but don't. It's astonishing how disempowering that dynamic can be, and how deeply rooted core layers are. The good news is that change is always possible.

- You are an empowered being.
- You are the source of your own freedom.
- You can control you, and that's more than enough.
- You matter, you have always mattered, and you
  will always matter.

You don't have to remain in a place of disempowerment and you don't have to give any of your power away. In fact, I need my power and you need yours. The freer you are of your layers, the more you'll interact in an empowered and neutral way. That means you don't attribute negative or positive connotations or any judgment on what's being reflected back—you just are, and it just is.

This means that, whether you're being given a compliment or a criticism, you're neutral to the information you receive. Essentially, you don't depend on it and don't have to take any of it personally. Instead of giving away your energy and trying to either please others or change them, you focus inward and explore your own layers. Once you free yourself of them, you become aligned with yourself, and, in turn, you can then be aligned with others.

People are capable of changing entire family dynamics without even saying a word to family members as they undergo the process of exploring their layers. I've seen this happen with clients and their adult siblings, as well as clients and their parents. When the internal changes, the external shifts as well, without any need for conversation and certainly without a confrontation. The way you show up to others will ultimately impact the way others show up to you. As you evolve and shift, everything else around you will shift and realign itself too. The key here is awareness, choice, and showing up authentically for yourself, no matter what.

When you get triggered, put some conscious space between you and the distortion, and follow that same pathway:

- *Be the Witness:* Something is triggering me. What is the feeling here? Where is this emotion coming from?

- *Call a Board Meeting:* What do I want to do with this information? Do I want to let it affect me? Do I prefer to just accept it and bring it along with me in my day, or in my life? Do I want to call a boardroom meeting? Am I ready to hear what this trigger is about?

- *Choose:* I don't want to carry the weight of this trigger. Right now, I'm choosing to acknowledge it. I get triggered whenever this happens, but it's okay. It's not going to ruin anything or upset me. I can accept it and be in flow with the rest of the day.

Remember that primary layers are deeply anchored and can be tricky to navigate. The goal is to keep the flow of questions happening so you can gain as much awareness around the layer as you're ready to receive. Remember to check in with yourself and act from a place of alignment.

Whenever we are triggered, we're quick to attribute it to the mirror, when in reality it's simply reflecting back what we're putting out: "I love this person because they make me feel good," or "I don't like this person because they make me look bad." But if everyone around us functions like a mirror, then the feelings they reflect back toward us are actually about ourselves, and we can explore them with curiosity and awareness. We can bravely dive deep into those reflected feelings and trace them back to the source: our layers.

The following are some questions to open with:

- What is this layer trying to tell me? Where is it asking me to place my attention?

- What aspect of this is most uncomfortable? Where in my body do I feel it?

- What purpose does this layer serve for me? In what way was it useful to me until now?

- Can I face it and let go of it? Do I wish to dissolve it at this time?

Wherever you land in this process, chances are you'll gain awareness. As you continue to question, your awareness will grow and the layer will weaken, things will begin to land differently for you, your perspective will change, and so will your actions and the way you show up.

As we take a step back from this deep and impactful topic of family-influenced core layers, a broader picture of the overall goal can once again be seen: all of us have layers, and it's our awareness of these layers that leads to a shift toward alignment with what truly resonates with our higher self. When we're not aware of our layers, we continue to be influenced by them, until something makes us stop and take notice. When we're aware of them, choose not to remove them, we're also actively choosing to have our lives be directed by those layers. But when we take the time to delve within ourselves, honestly and openly look at our layers, and receive them without judgment, we can check to see whether or not those layers are in alignment with our higher self. We can take back the reins and consciously choose what to do next.

Exercise — Questions for Self-Inquiry

It may be helpful to return to the genogram you created in the previous chapter, update, review, or amend it with any new insights you've gained. Feel free to draw in any symbols, colors, or shapes that represent origins for your own layers, or even draw a new version of it to reflect your new understanding. Use this genogram to guide you as you journal on the following questions:

- Was there anything specific that came up for me in this chapter?
- Why was this significant?
- What memories are connected to the emotions I'm feeling?
- What does my inner committee have to offer about this insight?
- Which committee members showed up to my boardroom? Why are they there?
- As I sit with this message, what happens?
- Is there a layer that comes up?
- What would it be like if I didn't have that layer?
- What might show up instead?

CHAPTER TWELVE

Layers of Friendship

""When we discern how and when our layers are being expressed in our friendships, we empower ourselves to be the friend we want to be."

Aafter our families of origin, our friendships represent some of our closest opportunities to form relationships—and as such, they are also an opportunity for layers to express themselves. From the very first friendships we make as children to the ones that come into our adult lives, friendships with peers can be a multi-faceted yet rewarding social landscape.

Humans are social animals. We have an innate draw to form alliances and friendship bonds, just as we do to partner off and engage in more intimate relationships. But unlike intimate partnerships, which speak to our instincts for companionship as well as continuation of our species, our understanding of friendship reflects our desire to be part of the collective, the tribe, the community. This is, ultimately, a survival instinct: we feel we're vulnerable when we're alone. With the collective around us, we feel safer, better able to weather the complex storms and seasons of our lives.

Like layers, which are hardwired subconscious systems of belief, the "community inclusion-equals-survival instinct" is, in some ways, a holdover from long ago, when inclusion into the community really did mean life and exclusion really could mean death. And yet now, despite the fact that the greatest consequence of being rejected by our friends and social groups is, at worst, only a social death, it surprisingly elicits a sense of real, existential threat within us. Because our brain wants us to remain alive at all costs, and protect us at all costs, the risk of social death engenders the same instinctive fear responses within us as would the real risk of physical death. It draws us to certain behaviors in order to remain safe and to keep those bonds strong. It results in the need to ensure we're a part of a group and belong somewhere, and to something. Put simply: for better or for worse, social risk means possible rejection, and rejection means eventual death.

So how do we learn to balance hardwired instincts, fears, and challenges with the additional ones brought on by our layers? We bring our layers to the playground when we interact with others, from our acquaintances to the friendships we form. We test the things we've learned and established, against other people's experiences and behaviors. We mirror back and forth, learning, shaping, and forming layers as we discover our place amongst our peers. And as these relationships deepen from superficial encounters to a more trusting give-and-take, we continue to form new layers and be influenced by them. The key is to become aware of this process, and to choose what we want to keep, and what no longer serves us.

This chapter's purpose is to help you understand some of the common layers that can affect different peer-to-peer relationships, from the everyday encounters you experience to the deeper friendships you cherish and intentionally maintain. By understanding the role layers play within you, and how every single one of your relationships can trigger your layers, you can look at life through a whole new perspective. The overall goal is to help you discern how and when your layers are being expressed in your friendships. It is also to empower you to be the best friend you can be and intentionally attract the kind of friendships which are in alignment with your higher self.

Pathways to Understanding

"Choosing how to write your story, no matter what anyone else does, is essential. Everything else is a decision or a reaction, but not a choice."

Do you find yourself at times easily annoyed, short-tempered, or feeling defeated, like you can just snap at people at any time for even the smallest thing? Not only is it okay to feel your feelings, but it's also important to feel them and express them. It's all a matter of knowing when your emotional responses are your choice and when they take you over, or are misdirected. We all have those days where we feel more irritable and react too quickly. Why is that? In regular, everyday interactions with people, even ones you barely know or don't know at all, your thoughts and outbursts can mean a layer is being triggered. The understanding and awareness of this is the birthplace of choosing something different for yourself, something better and more aligned.

We interact with strangers and acquaintances every day: our children's teachers, the doctor, a customer, our neighbor. These interactions aren't usually that important, and so not much thought goes into them while we're engaging. We just go about our day with whomever presents themselves and in whatever situations they show up before us. Most of the time, we don't realize that we're both mirroring someone else and being mirrored in the moment of the interaction, even if it's merely greeting somebody that you just see down the street.

But there will be times when we are caught off guard by an unexpected emotional charge. All of a sudden, seemingly out of nowhere, we can overreact or take something personally. What causes this to happen?

It's important to understand that, in every interaction, the human brain excels at following a certain pathway, often leading to a specific predetermined conclusion, even if the factual evidence for that conclusion isn't always fully supported in a particular situation. In other words, we respond to what our brain interprets as being a threat in a given moment, regardless of whether a real threat exists. It's part of our brain's wiring, fear response programming, and conditioning. As we become aware of it, however, we can shift our brain's reactivity and create a different pathway that serves us better.

As an example, let's use a seemingly innocuous exchange with a neighbor.

You're starting your day and it's not going according to plan. Your shower ran out of hot water while rinsing the shampoo out of your hair, you're running late, and you didn't have time to grab your coffee. Heading out the door, you're already not in the best frame of mind. It's garbage day and, while you roll the garbage bin up the driveway, you notice your neighbor across the street and wave hello. He doesn't say hi back. You think he saw you. In fact, you're pretty sure he heard you and now you believe you've been ignored.

Something got triggered and your brain decided to take it personally. Your brain followed its default pathway, drew a conclusion, and made up a whole story substantiating its conclusion. In that moment, your brain took over and decided to build upon and continue the rough start to your day. In the same way that your layers are created automatically, it's almost as if your brain automatically stepped in front of the facts to say: "Hold on a second, I need to continue on the same path and trajectory my person is already on, that of being annoyed, upset, making efforts, and having a day where things aren't going their way."

The brain doesn't like change. So, whatever your initial mindset was that morning, that's the one your brain will attempt to have you keep and believe. It will filter and interpret your day through the lens of that very mindset, all on your behalf and without your conscious knowledge. Consistency and continuation have a much stronger pull and influence than a mindset shift. The former simply takes up much less brain power and energy. Unless something external with more pull shows up to change it—or you step in with your conscious, empowered self—your brain will take one interaction and snowball it into a whole entire narrative to validate and maintain how you felt going into the interaction.

In effect, your brain triggers an inner dialogue that goes something like this: "It's been a rough morning, and now this person is ignoring me, and now I'm annoyed. In fact, my feelings are hurt. I should have never bothered saying hello. Isn't anyone nice anymore? I try so hard, but nothing ever goes right for me." This barrage of incoming thoughts becomes an attempt to confirm an already existing limiting belief, all because your mind decided to put pen to paper and imagine a whole story.

This is a layer. This is your layer, and it's being reflected back to you.

Even though you might think to yourself: "I have the worst luck," or "Nobody likes me, even my neighbor can't be bothered with me," or "Bad things come in threes, so what next?" All of this is coming from the distortion caused by a layer. And it is through this layer that your brain is writing a whole story that might not even be true, and one you would in all likelihood not agree with were you aware of it.

Whatever really happened, your brain made it all about you, without any verification of fact, and decided that this statement would dictate all interpretations of future interactions with others. From that point forward, you process, perceive, and understand everything through the lens of that layer, and that layer gets written somewhere in your subconscious and repeatedly reinforced. It becomes the truth, even though it's just a story.

Imagine the same scene, only this time you wake up after a great night's sleep, take an invigorating shower, and prepare yourself a delicious cup of coffee. You bring your garbage out to the curb and wave hello to your neighbor, who doesn't wave back. You barely notice and assume he didn't see you as he was rushing out of his driveway. The scene is the same from an external point of view, but internally, as you were in a more positive mindset and safe space to begin with, you showed up to the world from a more aligned space. Since you didn't take it personally, it landed differently for you. Now imagine cultivating this mindset within you, rewiring the pathway your mind automatically takes. It leads you to completely different places, ones that are much more aligned with how you want to experience life.

Finally, imagine a third take on this scenario, where you wake up feeling aligned and present, and it wouldn't matter if your morning routine went according to plan or not. It didn't matter whether or not your neighbor said hi back, and you didn't think twice about it because you recognize that you're the author of your own story. Your brain will always tell you a story because that's what it's built to do. But this shift in perspective allows you to be the author. If you don't like the story that's being written before you, from your brain, you can press pause. You can take a few seconds to put it on hold, return to your inner boardroom, examine the script before you choose to rewrite the story, so it aligns with your perspective.

Identifying Our Emotional Charges

"We are the author of our whole life story, and we can either create it with awareness or without it. How we write it is entirely up to us."

Though the above was an example of a casual, low-stakes interaction, the process is the same whether it's with a neighbor, a closer acquaintance, or a best friend. If you don't agree with something you're thinking or feeling, chances are it's not you. It's not about your essence, self-worth, or your right to exist or even be happy. It's most likely a layer that's been triggered. Perhaps it's an insecurity, a feeling of undue pressure, or shame, but whatever it is, some layer is trying to get your attention.

Look at it as a string of lights that you're plugging into it. The string is the emotional charge during a current event, and it's tied to lights that are turned on by some past events that ignite that response or feeling. The reaction you're having is strong because you're reacting to more than what's happening now; you're getting a charge from a series of past events. It's what happens when a layer is triggered, and all the more so when it's a primary one. So, when the neighbor didn't acknowledge you, it triggered an emotional charge from a longstanding layer.

We can have emotional charges with various people and at various levels of intensity. Sometimes lower-intensity emotional charges are harder to identify because they're often just little pokes at a layer. But high-intensity emotional charges can occur as reactions to any kind of peer-to-peer interaction. We can receive little pokes at a layer from a very close friend, and yet get higher intensity triggers from a total stranger.

No matter what the strength of the reaction is, it's in your best interest to become a witness to it, not to follow the pathway down and let your layers plot the course for you. Your awareness lives in the space, that moment of pause—if you can catch it—that lies between any given external event and the internal reaction you have to it. Look at what's been written in front of you and pause to consider it, witness it, and examine it before you act on it.

With this mindset shift, you can take charge of your own story. You no longer have to take things personally if you don't want to. If the neighbor didn't wave back or greet you, note how it landed for you. What is causing you to have the reaction you're experiencing? What can you learn about yourself from the reaction? Can you identify the layer at play? Answering these questions helps create space and more perspective. From there, you can choose how your internal story plays out, no matter what anyone else does. That choice is essential. Everything else is within the realm of a decision or a reaction, but not necessarily a choice.

The goal here is not to avoid ever having your layers triggered, it's about developing awareness of any given layer, and choosing what to do next. The more space you create between the stimulus and your reaction to it, the more you allow yourself to choose your thoughts, feelings, and actions. The more you can choose to turn off your autopilot setting, the more you become conscious, self-aware, and intentional. Once you're aware, you can redirect the writing of the story. You can't change anything about what the other person did, but you can change what your mind tells you about it—and you can do this by returning to your boardroom and creating a space of awareness to witness your layer. Once discovered, you can take back your rightful place at the writer's desk.

When things are triggered within you in any kind of social interaction, here are some lines of questioning you can bring to your boardroom:

- What emotion am I feeling right now?
- What story am I writing about this interaction?
- What am I really angry/sad/disappointed about?
- What layer could that triggering emotion be pointing to?
- Can I name that layer? Identify it for what it is?
- Without that layer, would this story be the same?
- Do I agree with what the layer is telling me? Do I agree with this story?
- Why do I have an emotional charge about something that's so neutral?
- Is this actually me? Is it who I truly want to be?

When you check in, remember that your essence will rarely, if ever, align with your layers. This practice will allow you to regain your power and choose what you do in whatever interaction you encounter.

Choosing an Adventure Mindset

"Becoming the conscious observer of our thoughts and feelings leads us on a path of awareness and questioning, one that takes us beyond our fears and back home to ourselves."

Living with an open, adventure mindset means there's always space between you and what's happening in your life. Through this process of self-inquiry and witnessing, you have the power to make your life an adventure, to write your own story, and to live from an empowered mindset rather than a triggered one. In every single interaction, we have a choice. Not only can we choose how the interaction will play out in our mind, but we can also minimize the negative effect it might have on us.

It's important to explore this aspect of layers because further awareness always means a better shot at authentically choosing how you show up to any given interaction and dynamic. As your interactions shift from day-to-day acquaintances to persons closer to you, the stakes get higher. You might be triggered by a casual interaction, but ultimately that stranger doesn't know the real you, so their words or actions might not cause any lasting impact (although that's still entirely possible!). When you're triggered by the things your friends say and do, it often cuts much deeper. You'll tend to take it personally, and your reaction may be emotionally charged. When that happens, remember it's almost always as a result of a layer. Notice your reaction, pause, and create enough space to question that layer, rather than simply accepting its narrative.

When it comes to friendships, not only do layers show up and impact our interactions with our friends, but they can also actually determine the types and quality of friendships we have, and the people we choose to become our friends. So, with that in mind, let's take a look at some common patterns that might come up surrounding friendships, in order to gain more insight into the layers at play.

Primary Layer: Trust

Children who step out onto the playground of life with a primary layer around trust often carry this layer with them into their friendships as well. As infants, we're entirely dependent upon our caregivers, but with our friendships, the exchange is more reciprocal. When a trust layer comes into play, every interaction can become tinted by the message of that layer. Consequently, a person with a primary layer around trust will subconsciously believe that, regardless of what their friends say or even do, their needs will never really be met. This layer can even cause them to pull back from their friendships in order to keep themselves from being hurt, taken advantage of, or disappointed.

If you've identified a primary layer surrounding trust within you, or if you resonate with it in any way, take the time now to journal on the following questions:

- Do I trust myself to know and express my own needs to my friends?
- Do I trust that they can receive that information and reciprocate?
- Do I listen to their needs and give back to them?
- Are my friendships balanced or imbalanced?
- What would it be like to create balanced, trustworthy friendships?

Primary Layer: Shame

Shame-based layers interact with friendships in two very polarizing ways: either they cause people to withdraw, conceal, and hide their true selves, or they overcompensate by being as shameless as possible in order to draw out criticism head-on, on their own terms.

In the former example, the shameful behavior is an attempt at seeking confirmation that they really are as shameful as they imagine themselves to be. Therefore, the behavior is a subconscious expression of predetermined expectations of oneself. "I truly am shameful, so I can and will only behave as such." The behavior will come to repeatedly confirm the underlying limiting belief.

In the latter, the brain preemptively creates shameful situations in an attempt to protect itself. The limiting belief around shame is still there. The reaction to it is what differs: "I can't truly be shameful at my core. I am, after all, the one deliberately acting this way, and I could choose to act differently. It's about control and protection of my core self. I'm intentionally acting this way, so people can be critical of my behavior, but that's okay, because they're not critical of me. I'm still safe. They don't see my true shamefulness."

In either case, the brain, in a most misguided way, is trying to protect them from these deep feelings of shame.

Regardless of how it's expressed, the core nature of a shame layer is the same: the deep inner belief that you at your core are shameful, down to your very being.

If you've identified a primary layer surrounding shame within you, or if you resonate with it in any way, take the time to journal on the following questions:

- Am I forthcoming with my friends?
- Do my friends share more than I do?
- What part of me am I most uncomfortable sharing with my friends?
- Do I embrace all of who I am? Could I?

Primary Layer: Worthiness

Worthiness is a layer that usually shows up in friendships as people pleasing. It makes us focused outwardly on others, rather than inwardly and in alignment with ourselves. The underlying layer is rooted in a sense of not feeling worthy enough to be accepted for who we are, and having to go that extra mile simply to gain acceptance.

Once again, this layer is a result of the brain trying its best to ensure that we're not ostracized from the group. If we belong somewhere, and if we seem to be accepted, that gives us a better shot at survival. A worthiness layer can also be expressed as needing ongoing confirmation and validation, and any action on the part of a friend who puts their own needs first or sets boundaries may be perceived, because of that layer, as confirmation of unworthiness.

Friendships impacted by worthiness layers are constantly being evaluated through that lens: "I should be grateful for the friends I have. Their lives are so much more interesting than mine. I shouldn't voice my true thoughts or feelings. I'm probably wrong anyway." And alternatively: "I mustn't be that worthy. If I was, I wouldn't have to work so hard to keep my friends."

If you've identified a primary layer surrounding worthiness within you, or if you resonate with it in any way, take the time now to journal on the following questions:

- What is my main motivator in doing things for my friends?
- How does it feel to say no? Where do I feel it? Can I do so with ease?
- Do I choose friends who are attuned to my needs? If not, what stands in my way?

Primary Layer: Perfection

The primary layer of perfection shows up as always seeking to be better, never giving themselves a break or sufficiently recognizing what they've achieved. They are also usually the ones who keep doing for others and show up as the best version of a friend they can be, often giving much more than they receive.

There is also another less common but important expression of a layer of perfection when it comes to interactions with others, including friendships. A perfection layer can show up as a highly controlling and critical personality. That person will judge you, not tolerate your shortcomings, tell you what to do and expect you'll follow their way, believing they are unequivocally right. That expression of a perfection layer will get triggered when it encounters any blatant lack of striving or imperfection.

If you've identified a primary layer surrounding perfection within you, or if you resonate with it in any way, take the time now to journal on the following questions:

- Would I feel relief if I didn't have to be a "perfect" friend?
- Do I find myself being critical of my friends who don't meet my (un)spoken standards? If so, do I perceive their behavior as a threat to me or my "need" for perfection?
- Do I feel that my friends hold me to a standard that's not realistic to achieve?
- Do I allow myself to be vulnerable with my friends?
- Do I ask for help or support when I need it?
- Do they make it safe for me to be vulnerable and authentic?

Primary Layer: Identity

A primary layer around identity fundamentally shows up as a lack of a stable sense of self, and can influence what a person thinks about themselves, who they feel or believe they are, the opinions and values they hold, and even the hobbies and interests they enjoy. Friendships can become too close, too fast, and the friend may want to be like you in order to be liked by you. They may begin to dress like you, adopt your mannerisms, buy the same car you have, and so forth. This identity layer causes one to fall in and out of opinions, careers, and friendships rapidly, and can be very disorienting and, ultimately, inauthentic.

If you've identified a primary layer surrounding identity within you, or if you resonate with it in any way, take the time now to journal on the following questions:

- Do I have personal boundaries in my friendships?
- Do I respect the boundaries my friends have?
- Do I feel safe enough to express my dissenting opinion?
- Am I easily swayed by my friends?
- Do I make sure to balance time spent alone, pursuing my own interests, and time spent with friends?

Primary Layer: Agency

When it comes to friendships, a primary layer of agency can often show up in times of transitions. When we begin to move from one phase of our life to the next, we may realize we've outgrown a friendship, simply grown apart, or for whatever reason we want to experience the friendship in a different way, one that better reflects where we're at. If we have a strong sense of agency, we can go to our inner boardroom, explore, question, and navigate this transition authentically. Without agency, however, we can become easily disempowered.

An example of this would be the shift in a friendship dynamic that takes place as a group of single friends begin to pair off and get married, or when one friend becomes a first-time parent and the other chooses not to. Self-aware, empowered adults can navigate that transition, continue to be upfront about their choices, makes plans without spouses at times, or provide a balance of activities that a new parent can engage in, acknowledging evolving life expectations and responsibilities. Friendships where one or more friends has a layer around agency means there is a lack of ownership of oneself, little to no taking of accountability, and often these dynamics can cause much resentment.

If you've identified a primary layer surrounding agency within you, or if you resonate with it in any way, take the time now to journal on the following questions:

- Do my friendships authentically reflect where I am now in my life, who I am, and what I want?
- Do I feel resentment toward my friends?
- Is there space for me in my friendships?

Primary Layer: Entitlement

A primary layer of entitlement is about our own perceived limited capacity and expectations of others. It is a layer that's quite visible to others, but one we're often unaware of having. If we feel entitled, expecting too much from our friends can leave them feeling put-upon, taken advantage of, and used.

Entitlement also shows up in the friendship dynamic we cultivate. For example, if we expect our friends to be better friends to us than we are to them, always excusing our own behavior away, it may be an indication of a layer of entitlement at play. Such a layer creates disconnection in friendships and prevents any genuine authentic exchange. Someone with a layer around entitlement will consistently put their needs and wants first, and they will find it challenging to be a good friend or see things from another's perspective. We all crave deep, genuine connection. It is therefore important to look within and see if there are areas in our lives where layers around entitlement are at play.

If you identified a primary layer surrounding entitlement within you, or if you resonate with this feeling, take the time now to journal on the following questions:

- What expectations do I have of my friends?
- Could any of these expectations be an expression of a layer?

- Do I typically count on my friends more than they can count on me?

- In what way do my friends challenge me?

- Do I respect my friends for what they stand for?

***

Overall, whatever type of interaction you have, from those with strangers to your close-knit friendships, if conflict arises, you always have the opportunity to examine it more closely. By giving yourself the tools to go to your inner boardroom and get curious before you react, you can create space to see whether that reaction emanates from your layers. And if so, get curious and discover what layer is at play. Reaction from layers is different from authentic choice, and if you don't like your reactions, it's up to you to explore why that is and seek out a different narrative. When people don't feel good about their reactions, it's usually an indication that a layer is actively triggered. It's the perfect opportunity to turn inward and work through it, rather than trying to change the other person. Not only is it impossible to change others, but it isn't necessary. When you work through your own layers, things will naturally change for you from the inside out.

Every one of us deserves to be empowered. Step outside of a situation or impulse, make some space to become a witness to your reaction, and call your awareness into it. This is where the seat of your power resides and what will bring you to ultimately live a life of choice. One where you can choose whatever you want. From a place of deeper awareness, you may even discover choices you didn't even know you had, before you went into your inner boardroom. If you encounter a trigger, or some misalignment, own it fully. That ownership is what will give you the power to work through it and change it.

Creating the life you want, and the friendships that match your truest, most authentic self, is an exciting adventure, even if it can feel scary at times. It's how you unlearn patterns and conditioning that no longer serve you, and how you can remove layers that have been holding you in place. The more you go inside and gain awareness, the more you can show up in the world from a kinder, gentler, safer, and more loving place. You start to love and accept yourself more, and the more you do, the better you show up to the world. It's beautiful and heart-opening, and it will enhance your experience of life.

Exercise — Questions for Self-Inquiry

The dance of friendships is one you will encounter throughout your life, and it serves as an opportunity for self-reflection and growth in awareness.

Use these questions to prompt further insight as you continue to return to your own boardroom and check in with yourself:

- How do I view my friendships?
- What kind of friend do I consider myself to be?
- Am I aligned in my friendships?
- What thoughts and emotions do I feel when I think of each of my friendships?
- Where in my body do I feel those emotions?
- When I check in with my inner committee, which members show up to my boardroom? Why are they there?

- What does my inner committee have to offer?

- What layers show up for me in my friendship dynamics? Are any recurrent?

- What would be different in my friendships if I didn't have those layers?

CHAPTER THIRTEEN

Layers at Work

*"Our layers come with us wherever we go, and
the workplace is no exception."*

D o you remember your first job? Maybe you were a bright-eyed, eager young mailroom clerk, an office worker just learning the ropes, or a server in a restaurant. Even though it was probably some time ago, you may still remember the mixed feelings of stepping into the role of an employee for the very first time: uncertainty, trepidation, wanting to please, excited to learn.

The employee-employer relationship is one of the only adult peer-to-peer relationships that can inherently trigger layers around authority. For some it resembles the relationship of a parent to a child, or teacher to student. While the employee-employer relationship appears to be unequal and imbalanced, it really isn't. Our perception of it as a dynamic of authority, however, not only brings up old layers but can also often grow and reinforce them.

In this chapter, we'll explore some of the common ways in which layers can insidiously show up in the workplace and impact work relationships, whether as an employee, manager, boss, or owner. Exploring these layers will help to better manage work situations as they arise.

A Transactional Playground

*"Due to the transactional and hierarchical nature
of workplace environments, this playground can
surprisingly be one of the most triggering."*

Of all of the emotions that arise when you step into your first job, one of the most exciting was likely the anticipation of getting your first paycheck. Entering the workforce comes with responsibilities and lessons, but it also allows you to gain some newfound independence. Whether you spent your first paycheck, saved it, or somewhere in-between, it's important to remember that the workplace is a transactional playground.

Your interactions with others take place on the playground of life itself, and work is no exception. And yet, unlike any other dynamic on the playground of life, work is inherently transactional. You enter into an agreement to trade your time, effort, and skills in exchange for pay. In short: regardless of growth, mastery, and contribution, working to get paid and getting paid to work inherently resides at the core of any work dynamic. Because it is easy to forget this transactional nature, it can also be easy to slip into all kinds of underlying feelings that trigger deeply rooted layers around perceived authority, regardless of your position at work. For example:

- You may begin to feel resentful, unworthy, or perhaps even unloved if you don't feel like you're receiving the compensation you believe you are due, triggering a layer around value, money, and self-worth.

- You may begin to feel hurt if you want to be friends with your employer, but they don't feel the same way, triggering a layer around friendships or even echoing family layers.

- You may begin to feel controlled or unfairly put-upon when given tasks and expectations by your direct supervisor, triggering a layer around independence or entitlement.

- You may begin to feel ignored and disrespected when the individual you just hired doesn't perform as you expected, triggering a layer around your own power, agency, and worthiness.

All of these arise as a result of this unique, transactional dynamic, and the expectations you may have about it. It's the one place where the intentional peer-to-peer dynamic is complicated by the appearance of authority. Workplaces are often structured on the appearance of a hierarchy, one based upon the assumption of power, worthiness, and value. Wherever you are on this hierarchy, this money-for-time dynamic is still, at its heart, an energetic exchange, one in which no one is in control of the other. You give or receive instructions, carry out tasks, and are compensated for it. That doesn't actually place one person above another.

The workplace is a very specific playground that exists in a very specific place for a very defined purpose. Looking at it this way—like an energetic exchange, rather than a place that defines you—you can ask yourself key questions that can help you show up to the playground from an authentic, empowered, intentional frame of mind, such as:

- Am I bringing the best version of myself to the workplace? Which layers have I brought along with me?

- How will I choose to play here? How is this workplace different from any of my other playground interactions?

- What do I need to be aware of? What can I take back to my inner boardroom to help improve my interactions?

Feel free to sit with these questions, or any others that come up for you, before reading through this chapter.

Leading Without Layers

"True leaders inspire and empower others, acknowledging their own layers and leading with authenticity."

Being in a leadership, employer, or managerial position—guiding and directing other people in a workplace setting—can bring up different layers around leadership. Chances are that the way in which you were parented will impact the way you lead. While you may not have been aware of these connections, you'll gain more awareness as you delve deeper.

As an employer, layers can show up at work in many ways. The following is a simple example: if you had stern, authoritarian parents under the guise of teaching self-discipline and hard work, you might default to being a very demanding boss, holding your employees to a high standard, akin to what you perceived you were held to, regardless of whether or not it's justified, helpful, or yields positive results. You may show less understanding, compassion, or patience, and set high expectations—just as your parents modeled.

Conversely, you might swing in the complete opposite direction and become lenient, passive, or perhaps too permissive. Growing up with rules that were too soft or too rigid may influence your boundaries to be more, or less, firm than what would naturally be required to create a productive, stable work environment.

Despite the outward appearance of the employee-employer relationship, nobody can ever truly be the boss of anyone else. It's important to acknowledge that the relationship is fundamentally transactional. Employees give of their time—the most precious resource there is—using their intellect and making efforts in exchange for a paycheck and livelihood. There is no ownership of another, and no adult human being inherently sits in a position of authority over any other.

Employers, managers, and bosses are not directly responsible for the change, growth, or performance of another, but they are responsible for how they show up. Leadership is different from managing, employing, or bossing around.

Take some time to jot down whatever comes up to complete the following statement:

- A boss is ...

Now, replace the word "boss" with "leader" and see if those statements change.

- A leader is ...

Where does that land for you? What does it bring up? Take some time to reflect on this difference. What kind of a leader do you want to be? Is that different from being a boss, a manager, an employer?

As adults, we never stop trying to master life. We no longer struggle with the lack of agency in childhood, the hormonal shifts of our teenage years, and we've become more capable at navigating ourselves in our day-to-day life experiences. We have at least some social skills, basic life skills, and the competencies to venture out on our own and, for the most part, have become the decision-makers of our own lives. And yet, the employee-employer relationship can really shake us up.

Because this dynamic so strongly calls to mind the parent-child dynamic of our earliest years, it often causes us to feel the same vulnerabilities we felt in childhood. When that happens, it can feel as if a switch gets flipped and we shift right back into a dynamic from a very different time—even if we're in the "parent" role and sitting in the leader's seat. Layers can provoke feelings of inadequacy, or alternatively, entitlement. They can make us feel dependent upon other people's approval in the workplace, or resentful of the apparent lack of autonomy or agency over our time. It's fascinating to think about it. Even though we're adults and have a professional demeanor in our external behavior, a triggered layer can create havoc from within. Suddenly, we're on a roller coaster of emotions, leading us to all sorts of thoughts and feelings, and landing in places within us we believed were long healed and gone.

We carry layers with us wherever we go on the playground of life, and the workplace is certainly no exception. Unlike the relationships we have with friends and peers, layers at work are complex because of this illusion of authority. As always, through the process of inner work done with openness and curiosity, we can become aware of our layers and the effect they may be having on us in this context, and then authentically choose how to proceed. Remember, first and foremost we're here to strive to be the leaders of ourselves. Power struggles happen because something has knocked us out of that self-leadership space. It's important to explore our layers because, invited or not, they come with us wherever we go, including work.

Each and every person in a company is equally important to the overall dynamic. A positive landscape allows for all to play well in it and feel fulfilled. In such a dynamic, everyone in their respective roles contributes to this landscape and impacts the quality of that environment. It doesn't exist on its own. It's created, which means we have control over it and therefore we can choose it. So, the question then becomes: Can we inspire others in what we do? Can we thrive in this job? In what way can we do the inner work required to co-create this positive environment and get the best from each other? If we understand this dynamic, then nobody can take our self-worth or our abilities away, regardless of our role or rung on the corporate ladder. Returning to the inner boardroom, layers that get triggered in a workplace remind us that, just like life, the workplace is actually a playground, meaning it's neutral.

If your role is that of business owner and your employees are chronically dissatisfied, then it does mean you've brought some of your own layers to work with you. If you want some insight into what those layers might be, take a closer look at the environment you've created. What types of power struggles, conflicts, and challenges arise? Can you identify a common theme or pattern? Viewed through that lens, you'll begin to see beyond the daily conflicts and uncover the layers at play at the source of it all. Once you do, you can choose to release the layers and integrate new creative ways to approach day-to-day occurrences. When people approach work and the workplace dynamic from their authentic selves, struggle rarely occurs. Remember, true growth and change happens from the inside out. When you free yourself from layers, you shift internally, the way you show up naturally changes, and it causes others to show up to you differently as well. Because you mirror others differently, how you show up will be reflected back to you differently as well. The whole dynamic shifts to adapt to your inner shift. This is when you can help create an environment where people can show up as their best selves.

Remaining Your Best at Work

"Just as a boss isn't inherently a superior being, no employee is beneath any manager or employer, not in terms of human worth, dignity, or respect."

We spend so much of our lives at work that it would be worth our while to invest some time and mind space into figuring out how to make that time more enjoyable, more fulfilling, and more of a match for us on a vibrational level. And yet, so many of us feel we just can't seem to get around to it. Our layers get triggered, and we often find ourselves sitting with them for so much longer than necessary, and we do this for all kinds of reasons that feel very rational and reasonable in the moment.

Work will bring up the same kind of layers as any other triggering situation: rejection, disapproval, criticism, feeling accused, a sense of entitlement, a sense of arrogance, helplessness, or loss of control. When a layer is triggered, it can spark negative emotions, provoke irrational responses, and cause a person to panic, feel overwhelmed, withdraw, or react defensively. This is true for those in a leadership role, and it's also true for employees.

When an employee perceives their boss as someone who has power over them, or imagines themselves being in some form of disempowering work scenario, they can start self-sabotaging or resort to passive aggressive behavior, such as showing up late, making it difficult for their boss, or not giving their all. They may start acting out like a child. They don't necessarily do this on purpose, but their triggered layers start showing up and pulling the employee's "behavioral age" down, as if they were ten years old again and rebelling against their parents' rules. Except, they're not ten, they're adults now, having an interaction with another adult, another peer. A layer that was created out of a family dynamic can present itself at work in a way that can become incredibly toxic.

Just as a boss isn't a superior being, no employee is beneath any manager or employer, not in terms of human worth, dignity, or respect. If you look at your employee as a peer, it's going to be really difficult to be their boss but incredibly fulfilling to be their leader. Likewise, if you look at your employer as someone who is above you and better than you, it's going to be very hard for you to remain autonomous and independent and really put your best foot forward. You may find yourself reverting to childlike feelings of disempowerment or behaviors that you would never otherwise engage in. By looking at your employer or manager as a peer, you'll create the space for yourself to reframe your feelings and experiences. Instead of feeling hurt, antagonized, taken advantage of, or judged, you can ask yourself:

- What layer is coming up for me right now, and can I give myself more clarity around it?
- How would the same situation land for me if I weren't experiencing it through the lens of that layer?

- What am I being asked to internalize or improve?
- But for this layer, would I feel less hurt, vulnerable, annoyed, or disempowered?
- What can I learn from this situation?

Different people in the workplace may have different skills, experience, and levels of responsibility. They may have more or less knowledge in a certain area or have taken more or less financial risk. A person who chooses to step into a self-leadership role will rarely if ever feel inferior or less than another human being. Instead, they look at maintaining an open mindset, owning their actions, and growing from their experiences. They therefore see the "figure of authority" not as a superior but as a peer, and for whom they can work toward a common goal. A person's position in their place of work, regardless of what it is, does not define nor instruct their inherent value, worth, potential for self-awareness, or who they truly are.

Finding Common Ground

"There is no other true boss 'over' you. You may have many leaders, coaches, or mentors, and all can enrich you, but none are meant to have, nor should they be given, the space to disempower you."

Roles are assigned by the identifications and labels that the workplace gives us. Some will be CEOs, managers, or accountants. Others might be interns, employees, or assistants. We play these roles, but at the simplest level, we're all human beings, and we all have needs, innate inner power, and the choice to show up as ourselves. We can enter every interaction, every meeting, every job interview, and team building exercise reminding ourselves that we're much more alike than different. This reminder helps us keep our layers in check in an environment where we can, at times, easily become lost in heightened reactions when triggered. Employees could have meltdowns they would never have anywhere else, or managers could overreact in a way that is completely inappropriate. All of this happens because of the unique ways in which layers are triggered and show up in the workplace.

We need both leaders and employees; otherwise, the leader cannot lead and the one in need of guidance receives none. Some people are inherently better at following instructions, excel when supervised, and prefer it. Others are better at leading, cannot take direction, and would make for lousy employees. Some people are coachable, while others prefer to coach. Nobody is better than the other. Each is different and all are necessary.

There are many different interpretations of the hierarchy in the workplace. Each one is unique to the individuals and the culture within any given work environment. A boss is only a boss within a very carved-out, specific landscape that he or she created, within a specific area of the playground of life. Therein lies the challenge inherent to the workplace dynamic. Outside of it, there's no other true boss "over" you. You are your own boss. You have agency. You are the one to sit at the head of your boardroom table. The power is always inside you. You may have many leaders, coaches, or mentors, and all can enrich you, but none are meant to have, nor should they be given, the space to disempower you.

Whenever conflicts at work arise, it's an opportunity to pause and look inward to consider if and how you might have disempowered yourself. If you relinquish any internal authority, you can most certainly go to your inner boardroom to regain it. You can gather your inner committee and ask:

- Has a layer taken over in this moment?
- When did I relinquish my autonomy, and why?
- Why am I not present?
- What made me give up pieces of my self?
- What in this dynamic is making me feel disempowered?

All of the inner work you've done throughout this whole process can be used to empower yourself in every area of your life. The real challenge is to witness your layers and not judge them, so that you can consider them and choose to either keep or remove them. If you have a layer that keeps coming up in a workplace context, then it's worth exploring. It comes down to the right and responsibility you have to know yourself, own who you are, be the champion of your inner world, and empower yourself to choose the path that serves your higher, best self, rather than let your layers lead.

Exercise — Questions for Self-Inquiry

It takes a lot of openness to be a good leader, just as it takes a lot of confidence to be a fulfilled employee. Your inner boardroom (not the physical workplace) can become your best resource for exploring any layers that might be affecting you at work. By accessing your own inner committee, you can evaluate the situation you may be facing and take an open, honest look at what comes up.

Use the following employer inquiry questions to reflect on:

- How do I want to lead?
- Do I know what my inner core values are (beyond the layers)?
- Is there anything that might be masking or distorting any core value?
- What feels authentic to me as a leader?

- What do I stand for as a leader?

- What leadership style aligns with me?

- Am I as open and receptive as I expect my employees to be?

***

Remember that all relationships function as a mirror and an opportunity for self-reflection and growth, and this holds true at work, too. An employer and employee can bring out the best in each other, or the worst. Ask yourself: what kind of mirror are you to each other? Every problematic interaction is a reflection of a primary layer of protection. To resolve it requires us to avoid reverting to parent-child behavior, and instead choose to remain open, receptive, and confident while retaining autonomy and agency over ourselves.

CHAPTER FOURTEEN

Layers in Love

"Layers can show up in our most intimate partnerships
and trigger us in a way nothing else does."

We have been exploring how profoundly our childhood layers can affect us all throughout our lives, and our relationships and interactions with others are certainly no exception to this. Marriage and life partnerships can bring up layers that were first established in our families of origin, even if they likely show up differently. Chances are that what we see in childhood modeled by the adults around us will inform our perspective on partnership, and the way in which we show up to one. Layers around vulnerability, authenticity, and intimacy, and layers around gender roles, expectations, and power dynamics can arise even when we're certain we've left our childhood well behind us.

Just like the other relationships we've explored so far in these chapters, it's important to understand what a partnership is and what it isn't. Unlike the relationship mirroring that exists between a parent and child, we usually enter into a spousal or life partner relationship with a person of our choice, and without having the overall responsibility for that person's wellbeing the way we would as a parent for a child. Unlike the close relationships we may have with friends, an intimate partnership is about more than just two individuals who are enjoying the give-and-take of each other's friendship. And unlike our work relationships, no partner or spouse is meant to be the designated boss, leader, or subordinate of the other. The intimate relationship is not transactional, but rather deeply collaborative.

Looking at these partnerships or marriages through this new lens allows us to approach them, and ourselves, with a new perspective. Spousal or life partner relationships are the most intimate peer-to-peer relationships and are unlike any of the other types of relationships we have. In a partnership, this mirroring is chosen, consensual, and beyond equals. It is deep, intentional, and represents a purposeful co-creation of a shared story. Intimate partnerships can trigger each other in a way nothing else can. So, how do we navigate these complex, up-close, and personal relationships when they often become so effective at triggering our layers?

It takes a lot of confidence, awareness, self-ownership, and presence to be a good partner. Partnership is one of the most sacred relationships you can ever experience, one that allows space and possibility for some of the deepest, multi-dimensional mirroring between two peers. Depending on the primary layers that you and your partner have, you can bring out the best or the worst in the other through this dynamic mirroring process. You can consciously choose to contribute to each other's growth by working through your own layers. You can make the daily choice to be the most authentic mirror possible to your partner and, while understanding that they're doing the same for you, you can choose to receive their mirroring in the most authentic way you can at any given moment.

This isn't about achieving any degree of perfection whatsoever. This is about showing up as best as you can with intentionality, presence, and a clear vision of what partnership truly is for you. It's about showing up as authentically as possible and committing to be another person's most intimate mirror. It's also about receiving the same commitment from your partner and, in return, accepting, embracing, and receiving what they are mirroring back to you in the most authentic way possible. At any time, if a layer gets triggered within you—and it will—remember to revisit your inner boardroom, examine that layer, and choose from there.

Like the relationships we have with our families, layers in love could very well be the subject of a book all by itself. Instead of attempting to cover the entire topic, this chapter offers an overview of what role our layers play within our romantic relationships, and what is important to understand about ourselves and the purpose of partnership, so as not to bring our layers to the partner we choose to walk with in this lifetime.

Won't You Be My Mirror?

"The goal in a marriage or partnership is to become as authentic a mirror as possible to your partner, while being as authentically receptive to what is mirrored back to you."

Romantic relationships are distinct from any other type of relationship in two key ways. First, they are partnerships, which implies a joint life path, and second, they are a conscious choice. Each individual writes their own story, as is the case with our families, our friendships, and our work relationships. But with a partnership, it's more than just each person's individual story. There is a third, shared story being co-authored by both partners together. It's the one being written as they walk their joint path. Intimate partnerships are always about choice. While the purpose of all relationships is to interact, to mirror one another, and to grow, this partnership is also about growing together, which is what makes it distinct and unique. In effect, entering into such an intimate partnership is saying: I am your mirror, and you are mine.

That being said, most people entering into a romantic relationship don't go about it with the opening line: "Hi, do you want to be my mirror?" As human beings we engage in a complex dance of attraction and negotiation, using both verbal and nonverbal signals to first show our interest, then conversation, and it builds from there. This whole process is about vulnerability, about discovering the other to see if they're a good partner for us. It happens in conscious, obvious ways as well as deeply unconscious ones, which are often informed by our layers. We may not have much control over whom we're initially drawn to (usually by a chemical process and reaction we call attraction), but we can have control over ourselves and how we show up as we seek out others.

While we might not lead on the first date with "Do you want to be my mirror," we certainly can ask ourselves: "What do I want in a partner? To whom can I best be a mirror? What feels authentic to me and aligns with who I am?" We can bring these questions, and others, to our inner boardroom and search within. The responsibility we have to ourselves, and to our partner, is authenticity. Imagine looking at these relationships from this perspective: I am a mirror to that person, and they are a mirror to me.

Once we're able to search within and identify the layers that affect our ability to be authentically reflective and receptive to our intimate partners, we can effect shifts from the inside out. But in order to do this, we need to explore further and consider what role layers can and often do play within our romantic relationships, so we can dissolve them and clear our way to authenticity.

We owe it to ourselves, not to mention the partners we choose, to work on our own layers so we can show up openly and authentically, not only to offer the authentic truth but also be prepared to receive it—without allowing the layers formed by our past to take over and direct us without our knowledge or our permission.

When Our Past Still Instructs Our Future

"When a primary layer is triggered, the messages we internalized
in our childhood come right back to the surface."

As adults, we've hopefully reached the point in our lives where we're more capable of navigating ourselves through our day-to-day experiences. We're no longer fumbling around like children with a first crush, or teenagers with hormones running wild and free. We have begun to master living life, and our challenge now within our partnerships is to co-create the experiences we want and navigate them together. In a partnership, we're no longer the only decision-maker. We're choosing to create new ground together, to write this new story together, and that can shake up a lot of layers. We can want things and intellectually understand them, but never look inward and truly address the layers that affect us without our knowledge or permission.

Layers from our past affect us in relationships in so many ways, including:

- Our openness to learn and grow with and from another.
- Our feelings of independence and dependence, and even autonomy and agency.
- Our experiences surrounding inadequacy and maturity.
- Our feelings of entitlement, worthiness, and people pleasing behaviors.

When a primary layer is triggered, the messages you internalized in childhood come right back to the surface. Exposing your layers to your partner is a tremendous exercise in trust and vulnerability, allowing yourself to be seen and facing your fears of opening up. If you have layers in place around any of these things, they can directly impede your ability to be an authentic mirror and develop a rich and lasting partnership, regardless of how much you want it.

While this is the most intimate form of mirroring, all of the work required is internal, and therefore dependent only on you. That is both the sacredness and the power of this process, and of this shift in perspective. It's not dependent on any other person, event, circumstance, or thing. It's entirely within your control, ownership, and agency. It is there for you to explore, become aware of, choose, and grow.

Ultimately, uncovering your layers, getting to know yourself better, fully hearing yourself out, and allowing yourself to exercise your freedom of choice is the highest form of self-empowerment.

Mirror, Mirror On the Wall

"Mirroring and being mirrored is truly a labor
of sacred love, giving, and receiving."

Being an authentic mirror is easier said than done. When we explored the idea of life as a mirror, it was with the understanding that life is neutral, just like a mirror. It simply reflects back to us what we offer it, how we show up to it, and then it's up to us to take what we've seen and received, bring it to our boardroom, discuss it with our inner committee, and make authentic choices from that place of understanding.

Dynamic mirroring—the kind of give-and-take that happens between any relationship, whether it's a friendship, a family member, at work, or with a spouse—is always shifting. It's a flow, an exchange, and it's always shaped by what's going on within both people: the layers, feelings, emotions, conscious and unconscious thoughts, and even just what kind of a mood we're in at that moment.

Imagine looking in the mirror and seeing your hair in total disarray. Now, imagine that the mirror had a thought or opinion about it and judged you for it. Not only would it reflect back your disheveled hair but also its disdain and disappointment, and perhaps even get angry at you about it! If your mirror had emotions, thoughts, or feelings about you, you would find it much more challenging to even look at it and get ready in the morning. It would also be challenging for you to trust it. Thank goodness mirrors are neutral and never judge! On the other hand, imagine if you judged the mirror for reflecting your disheveled hair back to you. What purpose would that serve? A mirror is just that. It simply provides reflection and information, and what you do with it is entirely up to you.

Now imagine your partner as that mirror, returning your reflection in real time back to you, constantly and with every interaction. Can you refrain from being judgmental? Sometimes you might be able to, but often you will find you're struggling. There are different reasons you may find it challenging. Below are some common patterns you may encounter. You may find one or more resonates with you, depending on a specific scenario.

- You might assume what the other person is thinking or feeling, then, without further verification, pre-plan your response to it, thereby creating a self-fulfilling interaction that isn't based on authenticity.

- You arrive with expectations, and when they aren't met you feel as if your partner has disappointed or even betrayed you, even though the expectations were only ever in your own mind, and ones you never clearly communicated to your partner.

- You get complacent and choose shortcuts, unknowingly reverting to autopilot and preset patterns that lead inevitably to the same result.

Becoming the best mirror to your partner is an ongoing process, one that's dynamic and ever evolving. It's not a destination. It's a path of awareness, growth, and connection, and it's as much a discovery of self as it is a discovery of your partner. That's the beauty of intimate mirroring. You get to know both you and your partner simultaneously in ways that only this dynamic can allow. In order to do this, you have to commit to checking in with yourself, truly knowing yourself, surveying your internal landscape, and being aware of your layers, curious about them rather than judgmental, and making a conscious choice to keep or remove them in order to remain in alignment with your higher self. It's about showing up as fully as possible, which allows you to not only receive the clearest, unfiltered messages from your partner, but also to reflect back clearly and authentically as well.

From that position of authenticity, alignment, and choice, all relationship interactions shift. There's no other way. They can't remain the same if the underlying approach has changed. If you've ever been in an argument with someone who changes their approach mid-argument, you have most likely felt that dynamic shift, whether for good or not. When someone refuses to participate in an argument, the escalation dwindles and eventually the argument dies out. This doesn't mean the best way to end an argument with your spouse is to stonewall them, give them the silent treatment, or tune out their concerns, but it does mean there's a huge difference between shifting to check in with yourself to assess whether what you're doing is in alignment with yourself, versus continuing to engage in the fight because your layers are triggered and creating a spiral effect.

If your partner is reflecting something back to you that doesn't make sense, feel good, or something that provokes an unwanted response in you, what can you learn from it? If you react more strongly than you'd like to what a person is doing or saying, one of your layers has just been triggered. Can you identify it? What do you feel at that moment? Where are you feeling it?

When you react to how someone else is "making you feel," you are effectively reacting to how the triggered layers make you feel—which, because of your layers, is radically different from being authentically aligned with your choices. It's up to you to check in with your boardroom, hear out your internal committee, and identify and dissolve the layers so that you can be a more authentic mirror—not just for your partner's sake, but for your own as well.

To continue the example above, layers can drastically affect how people show up in a time of conflict and argument. A debate over the proper method of loading the dishwasher, the pile of unfolded laundry that grows on one side of the room or the planning of weekly meals might be the spark to the argument, but they're rarely, if ever, the deeper reason why tempers flare, emotions run high, and conflict arises. There's something else going on, otherwise the issue could be resolved for what it is. While it's usually not merely about the dishwasher, it can be about the feeling of being overworked, unappreciated, disrespected, ignored, needing to be in control, or feeling unsupported ... all of which are also expressions of underlying layers.

Consulting your inner committee will help you connect with yourself and uncover the layers that may be masking or distorting the mirror you want to be. To assist in this process, check in and ask yourself these questions during your visits to the boardroom:

- What layers are being expressed and affecting how I initially show up as a partner?

- Which layers are part of defining my partnership?

- Am I committed to being as authentic a mirror as I can be in this moment?

- What is coming up for me? Where in my body am I sensing it?

- If I could imagine anything distorting my mirror, what would that be?

- If I could imagine anything distorting my ability to mirror, what would that be?

- What is coming up for me? What is being triggered? A certain vulnerability? A fear?

- How can I show up to myself to help strengthen and heal it?

- How are my layers expressed by me in how I initially show up as a partner? And in my partnership?

At times, this process of self-exploration may feel like a winding road, with its ups and downs and growing pains, and you might want to quit. Don't. Remember that it's a road well worth taking. You owe it to yourself to know who you are, learn to trust yourself, choose your path, and walk in alignment.

Trusting the Mirror

"Trusting the mirror and what's being reflected back to you is challenging. It takes courage and curiosity to go within, know yourself at a deeper level and uncover the layers at their root."

While mirroring is a whole journey in authenticity, trusting the mirror and what's being reflected back to you by your partner is equally challenging. While being an authentic mirror to your partner may feel like you're more in control, being mirrored can feel at times a little too close for comfort. You may not always like what's being mirrored back to you. You may not always be ready to see it, face it, address it, and agree with it, and will often instead resort to denying it, demanding it be different, or resenting it.

A commitment to partnership involves both mirroring and accepting what's mirrored back to you, gaining awareness, insight, and using the mirror dynamic as a catalyst for your own inner growth. Acceptance, in this context, doesn't mean that you accept what your partner is mirroring to you as the objective truth. Learning and growing doesn't mean denying your inner truth from your boardroom in favor of your partner's view of things. What it means is that you're able to receive it, just like you receive what a physical, static mirror is showing you. You can check what you see and observe with your inner committee and see if it resonated with you. You can easily rely on a physical mirror to show you as accurate a representation of your disheveled hair or smudged mascara as possible—you have no reason to doubt its accuracy. But with your partner acting as a mirror, there are times when what you receive doesn't fit with what you understand or expect to be true of yourself or your partner.

Receiving the information and message and trusting the source are two different but important components of this intimate mirroring process. If you receive something that brings up a feeling or an emotion, first receive it for what it is, then assess what that emotion might be about, rather than turning on the mirror, invalidating it, or directing your emotions on to your partner. Being mirrored takes courage and curiosity to go within, to know yourself at a deeper level and uncover the layers at their root. Examining what's being mirrored and checking in with your inner committee doesn't mean you don't trust the mirror. It means you're looking to better understand what part of you is being reflected back to you, where it's landing for you, and what you can do about it. When you bring these feelings to your inner committee, you can check and see how you feel about the information you've received from your chosen mirror with questions such as:

- Where am I feeling the trigger?
- What am I feeling?
- What unmet need is this bringing up for me?
- What's the message in the trigger?
- What role, if any, does my partner have in it, right here and right now?

- Can I identify the primary layer coming up for me?

- Can I trust myself to dive a little deeper?

Relying on feelings and being triggered means there's something you perceive as a need, in that moment, that feels as if it's being threatened or unmet. Something you need or believe you need that you're not getting from the other. It's fascinating when you think about it. Even in adulthood, once a layer is triggered, it can create internal havoc, especially because of the proximity and intensity of the mirror. Becoming the best mirror to your partner entails first becoming the best partner to yourself. In that sense, the partner relationship dynamic calls for a unique type of delicate balance. One where each partner commits to both working to become whole within themselves and to mirroring each other as authentically as they can.

You Are Your Everything

"We must meet our own needs first and foremost, in order to be the best possible mirror for our partner."

In a committed, intentional, intimate partnership, it's important to remember that it's not about being your person's "everything." Likewise, he or she is not your "everything" either. The ultimate goal of a spouse is to be your closest mirror, but not your everything—and if you put this expectation on them, it will trigger layers, often both yours and your partner's.

But what does "everything" mean in this context? Remember that your primary relationship will always be the one you have with yourself. Therefore, only you truly own you. All throughout this process, you've seen the idea that your primary responsibility is to yourself: to know yourself, to explore and honor yourself, to tend to your own layers, and to fulfill your own emotional needs in a way that nobody else has the capacity to, no matter how much they try.

All of this begins inside us with the work we do on our own layers. We must take care of ourselves, show up for ourselves, and meet our own needs in order to be the best possible mirror for our partner. If we confuse what love is with what love isn't, or if we find ourselves expecting that our partner will or should do what falls within our responsibility and agency to do, it's time to revisit our boardroom, further explore our layers, and consider what might be going on under the surface. When we're willing to be open, curious, and take the time to truly examine these layers, we'll experience freedom from limiting beliefs, deeply rooted protective mechanisms, and fear. The truest form of freedom allows us to show up more authentically to ourselves and to our relationships.

Here are some questions you can bring to your boardroom to check in with yourself about this idea:

- What do I need from myself to feel whole?
- To what extent am I meeting those needs?
- How can I think differently, and what can I do differently to better meet my own needs?
- What are my expectations of my partner in meeting my own needs?
- Would I agree for my partner to have the same expectations of me?
- Are there ways I am placing unrealistic expectations on my partner?

Like life itself, people often have preconceived ideas about the concept of love. Love, it's said, "makes us crazy." If life supposedly gives us lemons, then love makes the world go round. Just like the layers that develop as a result of our one-sided relationship to life, the layers we have within us around love can affect how we show up in our romantic partnerships and intimate relationships. The majority of the things we so often ascribe to love—craziness, head-over-heels attraction, wanting time and attention, desire, all-consuming need—aren't really love at all.

Love is both a state of being and is action based. It's about doing and interacting through that lens. It's not an emotion or a sensation. Emotions are chemical byproducts, but they're fleeting. They're not sustainable in the long term, although they can be wonderful in the moment. They're not something to truly build a relationship on. To truly love somebody is about connection and expression, about seeing them for who they truly are, trusting that you, too, are being seen for precisely who you are, and engaging in this up-close mirroring back and forth. This requires intentionality. Love like this, as a state of being, is also a state of living, one intended to last, grow, and evolve, even as fleeting emotions come and go.

Taking steps to build an intentional partnership—or at the very least to commit to the responsibility of meeting our own needs, dealing with our own layers, and becoming the most authentic mirror to our partner that we can be—is an ongoing process, and one that takes being present, curious, aware, committed, and aligned. It's truly a labor of intimate love, giving and receiving, mirroring and being mirrored. It's the closest relationship we can ever choose to be a part of, and it offers the most opportunity for awareness and growth. Therefore, it's no surprise that it's also the one that presents the most opportunity for triggering layers, often at a very deep level. Once triggered, layers are a call to attention, asking us to take a closer look, work through them, dissolve them, and grow our capacity for authentic living and interacting.

Exercise — Questions for Self-Inquiry

More than any other encounter with other human beings, our intimate relationships tend to be the greatest mirror at reflecting our layers back to us. This is an opportunity to go deeper into the exploration of your layers. Take the time to prepare:

Create a Safe, Reflective Space

- Find a quiet and comfortable place, somewhere without distractions.

- Take some deep breaths to center yourself.
- Close your eyes and bring yourself into the boardroom in your body.
- Allow every voice and perspective that comes forward to emerge.

Choose a Recent Interaction to Address

- Bring to your attention the interaction you chose to explore. Maybe it's something your partner said that didn't sit well with you. Maybe it's something they did or didn't do that upset you. Perhaps it's something you said or did you don't feel good about. Notice what arises. See if you can identify what comes up for you.
- What are the emotions around it? Where are you feeling them?
- What is it about this situation that makes you feel this way?
- Can you identify the underlying layer?

Sit with What Comes Up, then Follow Through with a Deeper Inquiry

- In what way is this layer affecting your communication and dynamic with your partner?
- In what way would the interaction have played out differently without this layer?
- Allow in any committee members that wish to show up.
- What does each committee member have to say? What insight is each bringing to your consciousness?
- Continue to explore within yourself any beliefs or assumptions tied to this interaction.

With every interaction that unsettles you, continue this practice and this search. Each serves as a profound opportunity to explore your layers and find the deepest you beyond them.

Exercise — General Check-In

It's always good to check in with yourself from time to time. Feel free to use these questions to prompt further insight as you continue to return to your own inner boardroom, release your layers, and gain clarity about yourself in your relationship:

- What are my expectations in this relationship?
- Are there any patterns in my past or present relationship that I can now see?
- What does my inner committee have to offer about this insight?
- What memories are connected to these patterns?
- What emotions am I feeling?
- What layer could be connected to these emotions?
- What would I feel without this layer?
- What relationship would I choose to have without this layer?
- Is there something I am afraid of? If so, can I name the fear?
- Am I ready to release the layer?
- In what way will I choose to move forward and show up in my relationship?

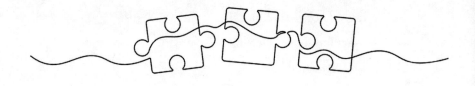

Part III

ALIGNMENT

CHAPTER FIFTEEN

No More Layers (The Three Pillars)

"Layers, no matter how deeply settled within you, can always be accessed, witnessed, and removed. Your layers are never who you are."

A s you know, writing this book began with the idea of sharing what I discovered during my post-concussive recovery. As I began writing, telling my story, and providing the downloads of universal wisdom I now had access to, I wanted to make this journey as accessible and tangible as possible. How could I help each of you walk through it? What if I could create some sort of framework to help with questioning and clarity?

To provide some structure meant creating a framework that would authentically translate the journey I had embarked on when my brain was incapacitated and had unintentionally cleared the path for me to go inward. I must say, putting down on paper how to do this work has been the most challenging part of writing this book, because it's so specific and customized to every individual at different points and times in their life. It's ongoing and evolving sacred work in real time.

As I sat with the process I had gone through, I found it could be broken down into three key components or pillars; markers along the journey that are intrinsic to it. I call them the "Three As": Adventure, Awareness, and Alignment. These are meant to help support you through this process and will be discussed in more depth in this chapter. Here's a little preview.

- *Adventure:* Develop the mindset of adventure that allows you to go within and discover your authentic self.
- *Awareness:* Live your life with the awareness of who you are, what your layers are, and what it is that's happening within and around you.
- *Alignment:* Grow the discernment that allows you to know whether or not a thought or action is in alignment with your higher self.

The Three Pillars are helpful in getting you ready to explore your layers and, once there, in directing your line of questioning. At each point, you can check in and ask yourself:

- Am I ready for Adventure?
- Am I Aware of myself, and of my layers? Can I tell the difference between the two?
- Am I in Alignment? Am I making a choice or settling for a decision?

The First Step Inward

This entire process—whether we are exploring our own primary layers, considering how they might be affecting us in the workplace or with our friend groups, or even reflecting back on the family dynamic that shaped the layers in the first place—is fundamentally about a mindset shift.

We know that mindset is the tone that sets you up for everything else. The starting point of living a life with *No More Layers* is a mindset shift from being fixed, controlled, negative, or disillusioned to conceiving that there may be other possibilities, some other way of doing and being that you can explore. It's what I call an adventure mindset. When we are willing to try something new with discernment, assessment, and without judgment, we expand our field of vision and other possibilities open up to us.

So, why is it that the brain keeps getting in the way of such awesomeness? The brain establishes neural pathways based on the patterns and experiences that we repeat. It is hardwired to keep us doing what we have always done, so as to keep us safe and alive. No change, no risk. This is why it is so hard to break a habit. It isn't a lack of willpower, it's programming. It is also why it's so hard to effect any internal change. The brain is programmed to view changes as threats and, although it's acting in good faith, this misguided preset programming is very good at keeping us stuck in a loop.

While I succeeded in getting out of this loop as a result of my journey into my concussed brain, you shouldn't have to experience a traumatic event to gain any sort of positive shift. You can access awareness at any moment. It is already all within you. Once you see your programming, you can reprogram it, be it excessive mind chatter, anxiety, fear, or self-doubt. When you begin to integrate your own self-discovery, insights, and tools, you can catch yourself worrying too much about the past or becoming overly anxious about the future. You can do this! Over time, practicing awareness will interrupt the overthinking, overprotective brain in its tracks, help you get ahead of it, and shift your mindset to what serves you best. Once that shift begins to take place, it becomes a way of life, something to strive toward, not just a static place. A mindset shift is dynamic, flexible, adaptable, constantly curious, and ever evolving. When you reprogram your brain to have an open, adventure mindset instead of a protective mindset, you will show up to your day more open and ready for what comes your way.

Throughout this book, and specifically within this chapter, I offer tools and perspectives as you walk your journey so you can check in with yourself and start living from a more intuitively aligned place from within you. Over time, and with practice, this check-in process will become second nature to you, and you will grow more and more confident about your own inward journey.

Beginning your Adventure

An adventure mindset does not mean that you need to put this book down right now and go skydiving. It isn't about actively seeking danger, threat, or risk for the sake of it. It simply means you remain open. You trust that you are ready for what comes your way, and you know that whatever happens you will still be you when you face it.

When you go on real physical adventures, you gain more awareness about the world, nature, different cultures, and new experiences, and it's all very enriching. When exploring your inner world, you gain awareness about your own self and how you function internally. This awareness directs your attention to the unexamined parts of yourself: exploring, discovering, hanging out there, seeking, searching, gaining, getting to know the core that's you. You can spend as much or as little time as you choose and go in as often as you like.

If you stay on the adventure, or you leave and come back to learn more, you keep gaining new awareness. You get to know what energizes you and what depletes you. What gives you meaning and what doesn't. What is your true voice and what matters to you. What aligns with you and what feels off. As you focus inward, the awareness becomes richer and deeper. You gain it by taking the risk of the adventure, relying on your strengths, and meeting your layers. You also meet yourself and begin to intimately experience who you are, your essence. And know this: you are an entire whole being, one that can only experience this depth of being-ness by venturing inward into your awareness.

Adventure is about seeking opportunities and possibilities despite the fearful, cautious, or limiting messages your brain or even layers may be telling you. It is the attitude of openness in the face of uncertainty. As you continually seek to understand yourself and your inner world, curiosity will lead you to frame your experiences through a different mindset. This trip inward is all about boldly going where you may have possibly never ventured to go before.

My own venture inward didn't happen because I was so gung-ho and adventurous. On the contrary, at the time I was concussed and stumbled upon an "open, adventure mindset" simply by virtue of the fact that I didn't really have a mindset at all. My brain wasn't in the way because it wasn't working the way it always had been. This led me on an adventure of a lifetime, one that allowed me to eventually regain my brain, rewire it, and show up to life with an open mindset that serves me best.

Remember, having an adventure mindset is not something that happens overnight, nor is it self-sustained; it's an ongoing conscious choice to courageously embrace stepping into the unknown, challenge yourself, and grow. With practice and dedication, you'll cultivate a mindset that thrives on adventure, and it will allow you to choose how you show up to it.

In Joseph's story back in Chapter Six, we explored the idea of how a lack of self-trust was preventing Joseph from being open enough to go within, explore his sadness and unhappiness, and create a better life experience for himself. The idea of facing that part of himself frightened him. It caused him distress and feelings of powerlessness.

Through our work together, he began to see that limiting beliefs he had around his personal power and life had been preventing him from connecting with himself, and indeed, from being open to his true self. Once he was able to clear those initial layers of fear, he created a safer, more accessible internal landscape that he was comfortable to explore with curiosity rather than fear.

The way we show up to life's playground reflects the depths to which we have explored ourselves, and the intentional choices we make based on what is presented to us. It is a step on the path, one that calls for boldness, openness, and discernment. If you get stuck at any point, the following are some prompts to help you gain clarity when you start to feel disempowered, disconnected, or fearful to go within.

First, take a few deep breaths in and out. It will help quiet the mind chatter and allow you to be fully present. Next, close your eyes for a few minutes and, as you breathe, feel your body. Focus on where in your body you feel the inhales and exhales, and the sensations they evoke. Allow your mind to quiet down further. Then you can begin questioning. You may prefer to do this with your eyes open, but getting more comfortable closing your eyes while you question will allow you to go deeper and get more clarity. You can use this mindset exercise every time you go within, no matter the layer you are addressing:

- Do I feel ready to go within?
- What can I reframe to help me go within?
- What in this moment am I trying to control?
- What layer or fear within me might be offering resistance?
- Is there a layer here that is shaping how I am interpreting and understanding what I think I might find if I go inward?
- Can I instead tap into my curiosity?

Cultivating your Awareness

Living with awareness means that you can name and identify what is going on when a moment of friction, tension, or discord occurs within you or in a relationship with another person. Awareness is like walking around a room in full daylight and being able to see all the furniture that's there, so you can avoid bumping into anything. When you see what's there, you can modify your course of action and choose a different path.

On the other hand, lacking awareness is like walking into a pitch-dark room, feeling your way around, with nothing to help you stay away from any obstacles. You cannot avoid what you are not aware of. If you are walking around in that dark room, you may very well bump into a piece of furniture or stub your toe. Think of your layers as those obstacles. When they are triggered, it's as if you've bumped up against them. They dictate your feelings and reactions, and confine you to limiting beliefs and subconscious patterns. It's painful. But in that moment you have a choice. Just like you do when stepping into a dark room. Will you give in to the darkness or will you courageously go looking for the light switch?

The moment you reach the point where you become fed up with being in the dark is when the quest for something better gets ignited within you. This is the seed of your awareness, the beginning of the journey to leading yourself back to the true aspects of your authenticity that have been buried beneath your layers.

There are different levels of awareness, from total darkness to the full light of day. While perhaps not yet in full awareness, even shadows indicate some presence of nearby light and can help point you in the direction of that clarity. Awareness grows over time and, as it does, you'll get to know your layers, decide on their shelf life, and choose which to work through and dismantle. Awareness puts you in charge, and it gives you the power to choose what to do next. From that point forward you begin to have options. The important thing at any stage of awareness is to be gentle with yourself, and to give yourself grace and gratitude for the understanding you have achieved.

Understanding that layers are, for all intents and purposes, well-established, subconscious fight-or-flight triggers, what happens when you realize that it is you actually keeping yourself in the dark and your layers blocking you from your own light?

In Chapter Seven, George gained a new level of awareness of a deeply entrenched layer around worthiness and intelligence that had been within him since he had been very young. Even though he was no longer that child anymore and had no reason to doubt his potential and capabilities, this layer had continued to haunt him. He had been unaware of how much control it had exerted over his whole life. By learning to face it, name it, and work through it, George chose to release his layer and regained authority over his life.

The awareness we bring to ourselves can only help to illuminate the path we walk. There is always an opportunity to seek just enough space within us to start becoming aware of our layers. Working from a place of curiosity and inquiry, we can learn so much about ourselves through this work about the relationship we have with ourselves and subsequently with others.

In any given situation, you can take a moment to check in with yourself and go into your boardroom. It is all yours. It is where all the members of your inner committee provide you with the information, knowledge, and wisdom you seek. This is where your power is. Your power resides in the space that is created when you choose to pause and check in. Some questions you might want to lead with:

- Is there something here I'm not seeing?
- Am I in control of myself?
- If not, what layer is running my show?
- Can I identify it?
- Can I take a closer look at it?
- What if I didn't have this layer? How would that change my experience?
- How would showing up without this layer feel for me?

Write whatever clarity and answers that come to you. And once you're ready, ask yourself the following:

- Now that I know about this layer, what will I choose to do?
- Am I ready to release it?

Finding your Alignment

Living in alignment means that you can use your awareness to know when things are for you, and when they are not. If you feel a thrill of excitement, joy, and eager anticipation at the thought of skydiving, then your higher self is saying, "Yes! That's for me!" But if you don't feel that joy, it might be worth examining why that is. It is important to understand that something can be a perfectly wonderful choice for someone else, but that doesn't mean it is for you. How can you tell the difference?

It may be easy to discern from these examples whether or not something like skydiving is what we want to do. But within ourselves and our relationships, it isn't always so simple. Answers to our existential questions are not found in the external world. Rather they can be explored in our boardroom, through the wisdom of our inner committee. Entering a marriage, leaving a relationship, evolving from a business partner, none of those things happen in a vacuum. There is a reason why people stay in relationships when they know (or energetically feel) that the relationship has run its course. Or why others are reluctant to get too close. Making those choices, even when we base them on awareness and alignment, can still be incredibly difficult. The adventure mindset is there to support us through any changes and transitions, and the awareness helps us navigate through pain, the unknown, and any layers we encounter along the way.

In the client story in Chapter Five, Sam dealt with a deep and surprising amount of anger surrounding the choices he had made. He was angry at his anger, and he berated himself for his supposed failures and the way he kept self-sabotaging through his behaviors that ran contrary to what he had believed he wanted. Sam was open, curious, and even aware of some of the limiting beliefs that were in place, but what he needed to do was go into his boardroom and listen, truly listen.

As soon as Sam felt safe, and that all of the members of his inner committee could be heard, the alignment was clear as daylight. Discovering shame surprised him, but questioning it without judgment allowed him to listen to that shame, and even learn from it. As soon as he could sit in this internal conversation, he gained so much wisdom that had been waiting there, concealed behind layers the whole time. He could finally begin to live in alignment, no longer self-sabotaging and living out old patterns that no longer served him.

Like Sam, you too have the power to make informed choices about how you will navigate various situations in your life. With a deeper understanding of what's happening within you, you can consciously choose the approach, attitude, and actions that will best serve you in each circumstance. Remember, you are the author of your own story, and by leveraging this newfound understanding, you get to shape a more aligned, fulfilling, and purposeful life.

Being in alignment is an incredibly powerful state from which to experience life. With it comes the ability to discern, choose, and move forward with a sense of purpose and action. Without it, we continue to be led by our layers, which are limiting and reactive by nature, and unexpectedly come to life whenever triggered.

When faced with a choice that you're not aligned with, you can always call an inner boardroom meeting and present any questions to your committee for review. Consider some of the following:

- What is asking me to move forward under these circumstances?
- What is the loudest voice around my boardroom table?
- What am I feeling about this option?
- Am I experiencing fear or impatience? Where am I feeling it? What is it telling me?
- What is driving my need to select a particular option?
- What would I feel if I didn't make this particular choice?

Whenever we go into our boardroom, we give ourselves the opportunity to change our self-talk, challenge our beliefs, and choose better for ourselves. When we go there, we get to face our fears around our vulnerability, humanity, and all that's unknown but matters the most to us. We get to explore, question, and dissolve what no longer serves us. We finally allow ourselves to reconnect with our truth. We begin to live with awareness and choose our thoughts and actions from a place of intentionality, core values, and consciousness.

My Encounter with the Three Pillars

I never thought of myself as athletic. I still don't. When I was younger, I remember being one of the first ones always to run out of breath when we would do laps around the gym at school. And even though I played on the high school basketball team, did figure skating, and later began exercising, my belief remained unchanged.

We define ourselves by our thoughts, our life experiences, what we're good at and what we're not. I have always been intellectual, spiritual, and emotionally strong, but have never had great physical strength or endurance.

It's who I knew myself to be and what I believed. My cardiovascular capacity is not very strong, and neither are my bones. And yet back in February of 2022, I would choose to do something I had never done before. I would run a half-marathon. That's 22.1km. The most I had ever power walked was 5km. I had no time to train for it and no idea how I would do it; I just knew I felt pulled to do it. It was a very important cause to me. My friend Kelley had recently passed away from cancer and the marathon was also a fundraiser for cancer. She had always been the athletic one and I could do it in her name. As if that weren't enough, the timing of it all felt like a strong message from the universe—of all possible dates, the marathon fell on her birthday.

Yet I had doubts. Could I do it? Was it even safe for me to do?

I went through the Three Pillars. Adventure. Awareness. Alignment. First step, I checked in with my adventure mindset. Was I worried about what would come up for me? Did I feel ready to see it, face it, and name it? The answer was yes. My mind was ready, and I really wanted to know.

Next, I called a board meeting and went within myself. I needed more awareness. I consulted with my inner committee. I found beliefs and doubts around my physical capacities. I questioned them. Were they actual limitations or simply beliefs to keep me safe? I knew my brain would not be the one to be able to give me an answer, as it had created these beliefs in the first place. I decided to tap into the wisdom of my body and into my intuition. Could I actually physically do it?

I stayed with that question as I waited for guidance and intuition to lead me to my place of alignment. I held space for as long as it took and allowed my true self to emerge. Did my body believe it could do it? What was I feeling aligned with? I got my answer and knew what to do next. My choice was clear. I was whole with it.

I chose to be all in, with choice being the key. From that moment on, I had no more doubts, no more fears, and I just knew I would do it. That morning I woke up at 4:30 a.m. I was psyched and already felt like an athlete. And that was the key. It was about embodying and feeling the vibration of what it is that I wanted to be. Become it before you do it. When you wholly embody something, you let your body, mind, and emotions know that it's possible. You make it familiar in advance and bring that forth with you in everything that you do. It's like an energetic warm-up, so to speak. You don't start doing something with cold muscles, you warm them up and then you move into the actual action. It's the same with your mindset and energy.

I kept imagining myself getting to that finish line and embraced that feeling, the one you get just moments before you cross it. That exquisite space of freedom from limitation. At first my brain was in charge, and it was monitoring my pace. If I was going to make it through these 22.1km, I had to get out of my head completely. It was my choice. Suddenly, as if my brain had simply deferred to my body, it took over and seemed to know exactly what to do. It knew when to slow down and when to speed up, maintaining a certain pace so that my muscles could manage and not cramp up from the lactic acid so I could keep going.

As you can imagine, the last 5km were the toughest. It is when your muscles start letting you know that you're at your max. And yet I kept plowing through. I put energizing music in my ears. I had some energy balls that I ate, and I kept drinking. As I was drinking, I felt my body simply absorbing the water almost instantly and directing it to exactly where my cells needed it. My body had never been in charge in this way before and I was fully aware of it. It was absolutely incredible. It knew exactly what to do. It knew how to run, how to power walk, what pace to adopt, when to switch it up, how much to drink, so that I could accomplish what I had set out to do that day. I was in awe. My body was pushing itself and doing all this just for me. We were working as one, in a way I had never known possible. That day I experienced the magnificence that is our body and the universal wisdom that resides in each of us if we just let it. I had fully landed in my body, and I inhabited every part of it. I embraced it and became one with it. I had never experienced being in my body in that way. My body was wholeheartedly working for me, and all it had needed from me was that partnership and oneness I had accomplished by pushing myself beyond the limitations that were constructed years ago by my brain in an attempt to keep me safe. I was breaking through those barriers, fully trusting my body and following its lead. My brain did not know what to do, but my body did. I crossed the finish line that day and it was one of the highlights of my life. It showed me that we have the capacity to break through beliefs we don't even know are limiting, and to do whatever we choose and are aligned with. We have the capacity to transform and the right to be authentically ourselves.

Integrating the Principles
of No More Layers

In effect, the guided process you learned in this book is a navigation tool—like coordinates on your GPS meant to take you to your new starting point, the one from which you can begin to live authentically. It's an exploration, a connect-the-dots exercise into parts unknown beneath your layers. It's an approach, a perspective, an attitude, a mindset. What it's not is a destination. In your first experience with this process, you might feel apprehensive or scared because it's new and unfamiliar, but once you see a layer and dissolve it, you will feel expanded, empowered, and in alignment with yourself. There's so much that can be experienced.

Because life is dynamic and not static, as you embark upon the journey back to yourself, there will be bumps along the way, new challenges, and interactions that trigger layers. This is a part of living life. Know that, at any time, you can return to that place of awareness, go into your boardroom, question, hear what your inner committee has to say, and gain clarity. Once you experience that feeling of self-ownership, not only can you get to it again and again, but you will also want to.

To be clear, there's no end to the process of self-exploration and self-development, and in that process you'll encounter moments of difficulty as you learn, grow, and live your life. When you find a blockage or a moment of difficulty, you're going to have to contend with your brain and identify where you are being blocked. The Three Pillars will help you identify which type of blockage you're encountering and what to do about it. When something triggers your brain into protective mode, the pillars will help you understand the type of trigger and how to pinpoint it. You will know to place your attention right on it, go to your inner boardroom, and question.

The following are some pointers to help guide you:

- A blockage in mindset prevents you from approaching the process with an adventure mindset and being open to what arises.

- A blockage in awareness prevents you from truly seeing the layers for what they are, even though you may be open to them or trying your hardest to be.

- A blockage in alignment may mean that, although you felt open to what came up and could see and perceive it, a layer is still standing between you and your choice to be truly in alignment.

If you experience any of these blockages at any time, allow yourself the space to take a moment and be mindful of what's going on in your thoughts and bring your awareness into your body. Let yourself get quiet, journal, meditate, and give yourself the space to do what works best for you in this process of self-discovery. Seeing yourself from within is a profound life change. It allows you to gain deep awareness and choose your responses and actions, free from your layers. It is by letting go of those layers that no longer serve you that you'll become free and regain the power that's always been within you. It is when you begin to feel that every aspect of life is exactly how you aspire it to be: aligned with who you are.

***

These tools together will allow you to live through that lens. Imagine working through your layers as climbing to the top of a mountain. While you see things from a new, distinct, and high-level viewpoint, you aren't meant to stay on that mountaintop forever. You're meant to integrate the experience and live through this new viewpoint and perspective as you interact with others, learn, grow, and continue to evolve throughout your entire life. Here, too, the ultimate goal is to navigate your life from this new perspective, become a better version of yourself, develop the best relationship with yourself, and be empowered, aware, and as aligned as you can be. Your relationship with yourself will grow within you, and as it does, that growth will continue to empower you to choose what truly aligns.

It is my sincere hope that this process will help further guide you on your path back to you. That it will lead you to experience the authentic, real joy and freedom of dissolving your layers, meeting your truest self, and finally experiencing your essence.

CHAPTER SIXTEEN

The Integrated Brain

"Once we shift our thinking, regain control over our brain, and tap into the calling of our higher self, we can once again feel connected to the wholeness that is our soul, and to where our purpose lies."

Our journey here on earth begins the moment we come into human existence. It begins long before any specific threshold moment, and I believe all of us have the same opportunity to experience that powerful shift and find our own individual path back toward empowerment and self-ownership.

Looking back on everything that's happened in my life, I am so grateful to bear witness to all of the empowerment and growth that I experienced, both within myself and in my work with my clients.

The shift I personally experienced set me on a pathway that brought together my logical, curious brain with my sensitive, spiritual soul. But in all truthfulness, my journey didn't simply start with my concussion, and it didn't end after healing my brain, either. It is an ongoing process toward discovery, awareness, and choice.

Even after years of giving private sessions, leading discussion groups, and speaking, the dread of putting myself out there still creeps in. It's usually about five minutes before I go on where the question pops up for me: "Why did I agree to do this again?" I allow it to be, pass through me, and dissolve, and then I get into another zone. But it still happens every time, even if but for a moment. A while back, with my adventure mindset in place, my curiosity took over and I chose to explore it further.

It seems that one of the biggest fears that people commonly have today is of public speaking. It was found that this fear comes from evolution. In the past, when humans were threatened by large predators, it certainly meant death. Thousands of years ago, living as a group was a basic survival necessity and ostracism or separation of any kind meant the potential for death. If you would speak up, or say something that was not accepted, or speak out of turn, you could be shamed, separated, or ostracized from your community. If that happened, you wouldn't have shelter or food, without which you could eventually die. Public speaking also elicits feelings of exposure and vulnerability. Our brain associates it with yet another visceral trigger, that of being watched. Predators would watch their prey before pouncing on it. Hence our brain's reaction to what it perceives as us being hunted as prey. While our lives and circumstances have evolved, our brain has not. We won't die of public speaking, but the brain-based fear of shame, separation, ostracism, or being live prey remains to this day. It's an existential fear that was hardwired within us thousands of years ago, and our brain has not evolved from that visceral trigger. Today this same fear finds its expression as a fear of public speaking, or not enough likes for a video post or reel, because on a deeper level people still feel terrified that their audience will shame them, reject them, or worse.

I found this journey into the brain fascinating, and, though it is clearly not as well equipped and often misguided for today's world and lifestyles, it showed me how much of what we do is run by our brain. More often than not, our brain shows up in hyper-protective mode, much more so than what the reality of a situation warrants, such as speaking to a crowd that came to hear you share ideas.

So now, for those few minutes I feel that dread before I speak, I simply bear witness to it, lean into it, hear my brain's message, and let it know, "Thank you for your concern. I can take it from here." I then channel my attention and intention toward my audience, and I'm ready to go. My awareness takes the lead.

Remember, fear thrives in darkness, but flees in light. Layers, no matter how deeply they are settled within you, or how profoundly they have woven their way into your life, can always be accessed, witnessed, and removed. Your layers are not who you are.

All the discontent, distress, fear, shame, and dissatisfaction we experience as individuals is a result of subconscious routines, protective mechanisms, and layers that disempower us. We walk throughout our precious lives as souls living a human experience without taking the time to consider what that actually means. We attach ourselves to our layers, identify with them until we believe we are them, and then we suffer the results of surrendering this power. What was put in place to keep us safe now holds us back. But as we have seen, this doesn't have to be true any longer.

As my clients transform through this work, it ripples outward from each person who begins this process of renewing their relationship with themselves, stepping into their inner boardroom, and opening up to possibility. It's my hope that by sharing my own journey with you, I can show you that this kind of deep and profound shift to awareness is possible. More than just possible, it's essential. It is necessary to walk this inner path, to bear witness to our own layers, and to make the conscious choice to shape the future we desire for ourselves, both inwardly and outwardly.

It is never too late to begin removing the barriers between you and your individual soul pathway and purpose. You have the tools to do it. This is where the ongoing work begins—the joyous work of a lifetime toward living authentically, intentionally, and profoundly, empowered by the relationship you nurture with yourself.

Our Brain on Overwhelm

*"We have strayed from our true nature, and our job
is to find our way back home to ourselves."*

I believe that at the root of humanity is, amongst other things, the need for belonging, and without the safety net of community within the societal, educational, financial, and political structures, we have lost our way a bit. Today there exists the real peril of breakdown, either familial, social, financial, emotional, or spiritual. We have grown further apart, disconnected from one another, and worse, even from our own selves. This dysfunction is causing a gaping hole in people. There is the endlessness of long working hours, personal commitments and obligations, a whole host of daily stressors, and digital communication and virtual socializing.

While we may believe we are in the pursuit of true joy and happiness, as a society we pursue material ease, comfort, and popularity, hoping that it will bring us just that. We value external symbols of health, wealth, and happiness more than we do the comforts and stability of inner peace, contentment, and freedom. In a way we have strayed from our true nature, and our job is to find our way back home to ourselves. The age of technology gave us aspirations for life to be better, richer, and fuller for everyone, with opportunity for each according to ability or achievement, and that became the focus. Ambitions, cultural expectations, and social norms turn the focus on to outward pursuits, and that is what has become important. When our value system shifts in this way, it is no longer a natural value system. It becomes skewed to the point where the status of a person becomes more important and impressive than their inner qualities, the number of followers they gain more than their positive contributions, and the noise and distraction they provide more than the values they embody. This is when we begin to lose our innate sense of self.

However, with all the noise and distractions that surround us, we might not even realize that we're losing ourselves to it all. Have you noticed how increasingly difficult it has become to find any quiet to go within? Our brains are overwhelmed in the fast-paced way we live today. While we think we are equipped for it, our brain isn't. We pride ourselves on doing more, being faster, and sleeping less, and yet we aren't built for constant chaos and stimulation. It's not sustainable. Instead, it's conducive to the prevalence of stress and anxiety. With social anxiety and anxiety in general, all sorts of things come up: chronic illness, discontentment, sadness, pain, and general lack of ease. If stress and anxiety are becoming mainstream, we are clearly missing the point.

Think about the care and devotion that was inherent in the structure of how small communities and villages functioned. Think of the village life, where one family would lean on another if ever there was a need or a void. Think of the times when people lived in multi-generational homes and weren't alone to fend for themselves. Or simpler times, where front doors were left unlocked for kids to come in and out to play on the street. This was a time when community and contentment meant everything.

In times before ours, people were dealing daily with existential threats and issues to resolve. No one wondered what the neighbors were thinking or worried if someone didn't answer a text right away. The brain wasn't being asked to decipher if this was a real threat or another socially anxious provocation. In today's infrastructure—our concrete jungles of industrialized, urban cities and the suburban outskirts—it is extremely unlikely for someone to be eaten by a lion or a tiger. Instead, things pop up these days that never challenged the brain before. On its own, our brain cannot discern the difference between real and imagined threats. It treats any interpretation or semblance of threats in today's terms as real threats.

Do you remember the panic with the COVID-19 lockdowns?

Very intelligent, successful, otherwise totally functional individuals were rushing to purchase all the water, toilet paper, and flour they could get their hands on. People were stocking up on everything they considered the essentials in the 2020s. There's reasonable fear, worry, or anxiousness, which is healthy in realistic doses, but when our nerves are frayed and the anxiousness spikes, it can become debilitating. This is one example of the autopilot reaction that we are still, thousands of years later, wired for.

You don't have to blindly believe your brain when it is signaling that you're in danger. The fear of being rejected, judged, or criticized in social situations can become excessive and take over your life to the point where you're not in charge anymore. When anxiety takes over, it is a signal to pause, slow down, and take some time for stillness. You can then choose to reprogram your brain to discern and set the parameters for real danger.

We are meant for simpler living. It is often the reason we feel the need to take off and disconnect at times, often going back to nature. We seek to once again feel and experience who we are. We climb mountains, hike through the rainforest, visit a farm, swim underwater to witness ocean life. There is a special kind of stillness we find when we leave the chaos of our daily lives and go back to nature. It is often the place where people look to find themselves.

When we take pause and quieten our environment around us, we are able to slow down and relax our brain. We can tap into who we are, once again feeling connected to the wholeness that is our soul, and to where our purpose lies. That is where meaning is found and where love exists. It's all there, inside of us. It has always been there, waiting to be rediscovered. We can shift out of our autopilot thinking and processing, and into awareness, presence, and alignment.

Living Aware and Aligned:
A Mindset Choice

"Living with an adventure mindset means you trust you
are ready for what comes your way, and you know that,
whatever happens, you will still be you when you face it."

In the previous chapter, you were introduced to the Three Pillars: Adventure, Awareness, and Alignment. These pillars tap into the essence of a life lived authentically, one with *No More Layers*. The starting point always comes back to mindset. The way in which you approach *No More Layers* is the way in which you can approach and live just about every aspect of your life. Let's take a closer look together.

Even as you get better at this process, at times you may still experience initial foundational fear, nervousness, or resistance that doesn't allow you to freely approach a situation or an interaction with the attitude you wish to have. When that happens, and it will, it's okay. Notice it as it arises, then take a few seconds or minutes to reset it so you can approach the situation with a re-opened mind. This pause and reset will allow you to stay in the question mark and enter every new thing with curiosity, even wonder. With the mindset of an "adventurer," your fear quietens and you can continue to explore the unknown territory of your internal landscape, without your brain constantly going into fight or flight.

Your layers and foundational landscape were formed when you were very young. By virtue of that alone, they can only become restrictive over time. When you discover a layer, you can always choose to remove or keep it. It really is up to you. You can do this with every layer you meet, whatever feels right to you in that moment. But as you're undergoing that process, you're already beginning to free yourself. Simply by taking the first step, you're giving yourself permission to go within and to rearrange your landscape into one that's more reflective of who you are in that moment and what you aspire to be. Just as you can look in the mirror and change your hairstyle, for example, so too can you go inward and reconfigure your inner landscape, clean up layers that no longer serve you, and bring more of your true self to the forefront. You have the choice; in fact, you own that choice, as well as the capacity to make it.

With this mindful approach and awareness, you can go into everything unfamiliar with the curiosity of a beginner. Without the avoidance that fear triggers, you can become proactive, regain control, and reclaim your empowered self. This is the source of your empowerment, and it is the pathway to living a life with *No More Layers*. It's how you come to know yourself, free yourself, and ultimately be yourself.

This process can serve you in everything you do. It is the way to reprogram your brain into aligned thinking. Consciously choose what mindset you wake up with in the morning, because your mindset will dictate the rest of your day. It defines your attitude and approach to life. You can choose it anew at any point in your daily life, before entering into any conversation, meeting, activity, or taking any action. Choosing the mindset you go in with, and through which you filter your experiences, can offset the many thoughts and conclusions that your brain draws when on autopilot, below your conscious level and awareness. It keeps you aware and aligned.

Having the mindset of an adventurer allows you to go within, call boardroom meetings, and listen to what comes up. It's there that you gain the awareness needed to make aligned choices.

Unaware, you won't even know that there are choices. If there is something not sitting well with you, if you're jumping to conclusions, or making rash decisions to get something "off your plate", awareness will help you pause, create some space, and present you with ideas, perspectives, and choices you wouldn't formulate or have seen before. Without awareness, you never really know if you're doing the right thing for yourself. You may only know it after the fact, in retrospect. Have you ever caught yourself saying something or sending a message and then kicking yourself, wishing you hadn't and wishing you could have a do-over? Rather than letting all these subconscious tracks lead to outcomes you don't want, bringing yourself into the awareness pillar will help you to consciously create options and choose what you want.

While freedom of choice is part of your blueprint and our DNA, it has become less intuitive. As you dive deeper into this work, you will continue to nurture your inner relationship, raise your consciousness, and become more aware and present in real time. You will become more attuned to yourself, your needs, and how to feel whole, complete, and content. In time, you will no longer be governed and controlled by fears, limiting beliefs, and reactions. The process of truly choosing will start to become second nature and you will do more of what you do with conscious awareness. It is in making choices in alignment with who you are that allows you to know yourself better, and, as you do, you will become more authentically you.

The Global Vision

"While we cannot single-handedly change the entire world, we can absolutely change our world by changing how we show up to it."

As more people around the world walk the path of awareness and expansion, together we form a chain of energetic connection that stretches across the globe. As we dissolve our layers, each of us is creating the space for more love, compassion, and understanding. No matter how seemingly small it may seem, together we are raising the vibration of the collective consciousness.

Seeing life as an adventure is a first step on to that path. It entails being open to uncertainty, which can be frightening and uncomfortable because we like to control. However, the more we recognize this illusion of control for what it is, the more we will become open rather than fearful, inclusive rather than exclusive, and the more we will be able to change not just what is within us, but everything around us. As we each contribute more positively to the collective consciousness, our collective existence becomes more enlightened and harmonious. The dissatisfaction, discontent, aggression, and divisiveness we see in the world can begin to dissipate, as more and more people gain awareness and begin to heal themselves from the inside out.

While we cannot single-handedly change the entire world, we can absolutely change our world by changing how we show up to it. And when we do, those around us shift how they respond and interact with us. Just as every one of my clients experienced shifts in their individual relationships, I believe that the more people take this journey, the more we can change the world together. The world is, after all, a reflection of our collective energies. The truth is that, if we could all live with awareness, we would not have to change the world. Living from a place of awareness allows us to make choices from a place of authenticity. Where there is authenticity, conflict cannot thrive, as there is no place for it in that realm of existence. Instead, we become open to positive shift, growth, and global betterment. The power to do so lies within each of us.

As we grow and evolve, the outside world, or at least our outer world, changes and adapts to us. If we can each change our own sliver of the world, then together we can change the world. Each individual who makes the choice to journey inward, witness their layers, and even simply consider that there could be some other way of living, being, and feeling helps effect global change.

My sincere hope for this process is to help as many individuals as possible come into alignment, and to see the effects of this individual mindset shift in the world at large. It is my personal vision for this work as it continues to evolve. I believe that collectively we have the capacity to make this happen. I see it with each of my clients and in everyone who embarks upon their inner journey.

When overall awareness rises on a collective level, we can experience the kind of changes that our world so desperately needs. We can use our inner growth to foster openness and a higher level of awareness—creating a more authentic world where we are aligned, soul and body, and no longer disconnected. As we each contribute our light, the world can finally be illuminated, and as we show up more expanded, soul-driven human beings, what we can accomplish here on earth becomes limitless. The choice is ours.

Postscript

Writing this book has been about inspiring each and every one of you to recognize the power you have, and to understand that, as a human being, it is your birthright to know yourself, understand yourself, and get to that place of freedom within you. It is your absolute right to exercise your true freedom of choice and experience the essence of who you are. My book is your written invitation to do so.

MARTINE COHEN

THE PATH TO YOUR INNER POWER STARTS HERE!

Welcome to the No More Layers community and to a transformative journey toward your true self.

This is an invitation to create your best life from the inside out. To help you along your journey, I've created helpful bonuses for you that you will find on my website at
www.MartineCohen.com/nmlbookbonus
(Or point your phone camera to the QR code image below)

On the website, you'll also find exclusive invitations to the No More Layers book club, challenges, and live events designed to help you break free from limiting beliefs and embrace your true self.

Be sure to join our community on Facebook at
www.facebook.com/groups/wmartinecohen
and connect with me on my other social channels (below).

 @martinecohenml

 @martinecohen_

GET YOUR BOOK BONUSES HERE!

Exercises Index

Illustration Credits

- Illustrations on pages 6, 58, 81, 104, 126, 146, 166, 185, 210, 227, 239, 255: Olga Rai via AdobeStock

- Page 28 (Brain): nikvector via AdobeStock

- Page 42 (Two Brains): Yuliia via AdobeStock

- Page 76 (Boardroom): Modified from an illustration by samuii via AdobeStock

- Page 128 (Swing): Modified from an illustration by Simple Line via AdobeStock

- Page 168 (Sitting Group): GarkushaArt via AdobeStock

- Page 252 (Relationship Mirror): Kaitlin Kelly

- Page 258 (puzzle pieces): Віталій Баріда via AdobeStock

Acknowledgments

"I am grateful for the inspiration, access to universal wisdom, and the gift that is life."

This has been such a deep and creative journey. And, as is true in most journeys, there are always people and wonderful souls who show up to help you along the way. I feel blessed to have had the right people show up for me in the right time.

Writing this book has truly been a process—one of vulnerability, openness, courage, and growth. It truly does take a village—a village of love, support, family, friends, and professionals in the field.

First and foremost, I want to thank my parents, my brother, my children to whom this book is dedicated, and my family for being my biggest fans, for believing in this sacred work, and for allowing me the space to simply be me. And to my son and my mom, who somewhere along the way happily took on the role of beta readers for the manuscript.

To Bryna Haynes, my editor whose help has been invaluable throughout this process, and to her team, Marie Schnoor, Paul Baillie-Lane, and my cover designer, Mila.

To my local editor Shari Reinhart, who witnessed my downloads, showed up fully for me, and knew just the right questions to ask along the way.

To Suzanne Lawlor, who has witnessed my expansion and continues to be there for me as I walk this path.

To Dahna Weber, for always being ready to help, and for encouraging me to see the bigger vision.

To Lisa McKenzie, for always pushing me outside my comfort zone, and to my marketing team who have learned to work with me when and how the inspiration hits and still choose to work with me.

To Kelley, for our special friendship, though you were taken too soon, and the ongoing inspiration. Somehow, I feel you watching from above.

To Miriam, my oldest friend in the world, for cheering me on, sharing in each other's journeys, giving me her take on all things graphic, and introducing me to some of my book helpers.

To my cousin Celyne, for all the special moments we share, for the meaningful memories we intentionally continue to create together, and for filling each other's cup.

To my extended family and my friends, who have shown me unconditional love, supported me throughout this process, and with whom I continue to share many laughs and create special moments.

To my clients, who saw me writing this book before I did, and from whom I have learned so much.

Finally, to you, reader, for whom this book was written, for showing up for yourself and accepting this invitation to go within.

I am forever grateful for you all.

About the Author

Martine Cohen grew up in Montreal, and attended McGill University, earning degrees in civil law and common law. She has been an attorney for over 25 years, and has a love for everything strategy. She spent the first few years of her career in litigation, before entering the corporate world, advising and consulting for growth companies.

Back in 2016, Martine's world came crashing down after a car accident that left her with a severe concussion. It was a pivotal turning point in her life that catapulted her onto an extraordinary journey of profound awareness, self-discovery, and freedom. In the process, she gained a deep and unique understanding of the intricacies of the brain, its fears, and protective layers, which ultimately led her to successfully heal herself energetically—from the inside out.

As the founder of No More Layers, Martine draws on her strategic acumen and transformative approach to guide her clients to become the leaders of their own lives and experience success from the inside out. She works privately with individuals, entrepreneurs, and professionals as an executive leadership consultant, life strategies coach, and mentor.

She is also an inspirational speaker on the topics of conscious communication, mindset shifts, and life strategies. Martine holds a teaching diploma, a life coach certification, and has training in various healing and energy modalities.

When she is not writing or speaking, you'll find Martine spending time with loved ones, being in nature, volunteering, practicing yoga, meditating, and enjoying cappuccinos from around the word. She currently lives with her family and pet poodle in Montreal.

For more information, visit www.martinecohen.com

About the Publisher

Founded in 2021 by Bryna Haynes, WorldChangers Media is a boutique publishing company focused on "Ideas for Impact." We know that great books change lives, topple outdated paradigms, and build movements. Our commitment is to deliver superior-quality transformational nonfiction by, and for, the next generation of thought leaders.

Ready to write and publish your thought leadership book? Learn more at www.WorldChangers.Media.

Made in United States
North Haven, CT
30 January 2025

65137518R00188